Letters to Father

Di V. S. Molto Ill.

Firenze

Al molto Ill. Sg Padre

Il Sg. Galileo Galilei.

Letters to Father

Suor Maria Celeste
to
Galileo
[1623–1633]

Translated and annotated by
Dava Sobel

PENGUIN
VIKING

VIKING
Published by the Penguin Group
Penguin Books Canada Ltd, 10 Alcorn Avenue, Toronto, Ontario, Canada M4V 3B2
Penguin Books Ltd, 80 Strand, London WC2R 0RL, England
Penguin Putnam Inc., 375 Hudson Street, New York, New York 10014, U.S.A.
Penguin Books Australia Ltd, Ringwood, Victoria, Australia
Penguin Books (NZ) Ltd, cnr Rosedale and Airborne Roads, Albany, Auckland 1310, New Zealand

Penguin Books Ltd. Registered Offices: Harmondsworth, Middlesex, England

First published in 2001

10 9 8 7 6 5 4 3 2 1

Book design and composition by Mspace*ny*/Maura Fadden Rosenthal

Printed and bound in the United States of America on acid free paper

National Library of Canada Cataloguing in Publication Data

Galilei, Maria, Celeste, 1600–1634
Letters to father: suor Maria Celeste to Galileo, 1623–1633

Letters in Italian, with English translation. Introduction and annotations in English.
ISBN 0-670-04306-0

1. Galilei, Galileo, 1564–1642–Correspondence. 2. Galilei, Maria Celeste, 1600–1634–Correspondence. 3. Astronomers–Italy–Biography. I. Sobel, Dava. II. Title.
QB36.G2A4 2001a 520'.92 C2001-901741-3

Visit Penguin Canada's website at **www.penguin.ca**

For Mother Mary Francis, P.C.C.,

Beloved Abbess of the Poor Clare Monastery of

Our Lady of Guadalupe in Roswell, New Mexico,

and her 18,000 sisters worldwide,

who carry on Suor Maria Celeste's tradition of cloistered prayer.

Introduction

The young woman who wrote these letters led a cloistered life in a gilded age. Virginia Galilei, or Suor Maria Celeste as she signs herself here, entered a convent near Florence at the age of thirteen and spent the rest of her days within its walls. Although she devoted most of her time to prayer, she served as the convent's apothecary, tended the sick nuns in the infirmary, supervised the choir, taught the novices to sing Gregorian chant, composed letters of official business for the mother abbess, wrote plays, and also performed in them. She saw as well to many personal needs of her famous father, Galileo Galilei, from mending his shirts to preparing the pastries and candies he loved to eat. When he stood trial in Rome for the crime of heresy, she managed his household affairs during the year of his absence, sending him lengthy, detailed reports at least once a week.

Had she not been Galileo's daughter, her correspondence surely would have disappeared in the lapse of centuries. But because he saved her letters, brushing them with his importance, they endure to repeat their evocative story, still speaking in the present tense, suspended in the urgency of their once current affairs.

The 124 letters span a decade, from 1623 to 1633. In that period, a pope came to power who battled the Protestant Reformation and filled Rome with artistic monuments. The Thirty Years' War embroiled all of Europe and Scandinavia. The bubonic plague erupted from Germany into Italy, where it ravaged the city of Florence until stemmed by a miracle.

And a new philosophy of science threatened to overturn the order of the universe. Suor Maria Celeste's evocative letters touch on all of these situations, but they dwell in the small details of everyday life. They tell who is sick, who has died, and who is getting well. They solicit herbs and fruits, fabric and thread. They beg for alms. They offer services, love, advice. They pray to the Lord for various blessings.

Except for the time Suor Maria Celeste chides Galileo for forgetting to send the telescope he promised, she does not discuss astronomy or physics. Her letters show she follows his studies by reading his books and asking him to describe what he is working on now. More important, the letters expose a relationship that redefines Galileo's character. Through them, the legend of a brilliant innovator becomes someone's loving father; the man generally thought to have defied the Catholic Church is seen to depend on the prayers of a pious daughter.

Suor Maria Celeste probably wrote Galileo many more than just these 124 letters, as she was already twenty-two years old by the date of the first in the series. Nor is there anything in that first letter of May 10, 1623, to suggest that it initiates their epistolary relationship. Another obvious gap occurs in the year 1624, which is represented by a single letter, dated April 26, just after Galileo set off at the height of his power to visit the new pope.

"What great happiness was delivered here, Sire, along with the news of the safe progress of your journey as far as Acquasparta," this one begins, "and we hope to have even greater occasion for rejoicing when we hear tell of your arrival in Rome, where persons of grand stature most eagerly await you." Galileo stayed in Rome through early June. No doubt the long separation occasioned a stream of news to pass back and forth in writing, of which no trace remains. But it is the nature of letters to go astray. At least an appreciable sample of Suor Maria Celeste's correspondence survives. Galileo's replies, on the other hand, have disappeared.

"I set aside and save all the letters that you write me daily, Sire," Suor Maria Celeste wrote on August 13, 1623, "and whenever I find myself free, then with the greatest pleasure I reread them yet again, so that I abandon myself to thoughts of you." His half of their dialogue thus vanished through no fault of hers. Someone else must have lost or destroyed Galileo's letters.

Little is known of Suor Maria Celeste beyond what she says herself in these letters. Her birth in Padua on August 13, 1600, was recorded in a baptismal notice dated the twenty-first of that month. The announcement named her mother, "Marina of Venice," but not her father. Although Galileo and Marina Gamba never married, their twelve-year union produced a second daughter in 1601 and a son in 1606.

As a child, Virginia lived in Padua with her mother and siblings, a short walk away from the house Galileo shared with his artisans and resident students. She may have attended school, though there is no record of her having done so. Possibly she acquired her perfect grammar and literary grace from her father, who is considered a giant of Italian prose. Her mother belonged to an undistinguished family and probably never learned to read or write. But Grandmother Giulia Ammannati Galilei had gone to school as a girl in Pisa, and when Giulia took the nine-year-old Virginia home to stay with her in Florence, she may have tutored her in rhetoric.

Soon after Virginia turned ten, Galileo became philosopher and mathematician to the grand duke of Tuscany, which enabled him to move to Florence. He brought Virginia's younger sister, Livia, along with him, and father and daughters lived a while in the grandmother's lodgings. He had left the boy, Vincenzio, back in Padua, since he was only four and therefore too young to leave his mother. Galileo sent money to Marina, and kept on cordial terms with the man she ultimately married. In time he sent for Vincenzio, had him legitimized by the grand duke, and enrolled him in the University of Pisa to study law.

Galileo's decision to cloister his daughters made sense in seventeenth-century Italy. Girls from good families either got married or entered one of dozens of convents in every city. In Florence alone, fifty-three convents promised refuge and employment to girls who could not arrange a marriage, or whose families could not afford to pay dowries for every daughter. Some number of the city's four thousand nuns must have felt a true religious calling; others actively sought the cloistered life for the opportunities it offered in playwriting, poetry, and musical composition, which struck some young women as preferable to the burden of marriage and the danger of childbirth. No one knows how many girls chose the convent of their own free will, and how many pursued a "forced vocation" at their parents' insistence. Either way, a nun's work held honor and value in society. During the plague, for instance, Suor Maria Celeste's convent was enjoined by the Florentine Magistracy of Public Health to keep a constant prayer vigil that would help drive the pestilence out of the city.

Virginia and Livia seemed predestined for the convent life because they were both "born of fornication" (out of wedlock, though not in adultery). Galileo might have found appropriate husbands for them had he been a wealthy man, but he spread his court stipend of one thousand *scudi* per year very thin by taking care of his widowed mother, making dowry payments for his two sisters, supporting his younger brother who had a wife and too many children, and helping out needy friends and neighbors who fell on hard times.

In the autumn of 1613, Galileo took his daughters to live at the Convent of San Matteo in Arcetri, about a mile south of Florence. Determined to keep them together, he had enlisted powerful friends—cardinals—to help him defy the local law barring the admission of natural sisters into the same convent. At thirteen and twelve, Virginia and Livia were not ready to be nuns, but girls as young as nine typically boarded at convents, awaiting the day they either took the veil at the canonical age of sixteen or were taken out to be married.

Virginia adopted the name Suor Maria Celeste when she professed her nuns' vows on the feast day of Saint Francis of Assisi (October 4) in 1616. Livia became Suor Arcangela on October 28th the following year. The girls now belonged officially to the Poor Clares, the second order of Franciscans, founded by Saint Clare of Assisi in the thirteenth century.

Secluded from ordinary affairs, the Poor Clares deprived themselves of earthly comforts to pray constantly for the souls of the world. The Convent of San Matteo in Arcetri was thus destitute by design, but sometimes the virtue of poverty put the nuns' lives at risk, forcing them to appeal for outside assistance. Most of Suor Maria Celeste's letters include a request of some sort, and each such supplication is followed, a few days later, by her thanks for the items received. It appears that her father never said no to her.

At no point in these letters does Suor Maria Celeste suggest that her father's science is irreligious or that the accusations made against him are valid. Never does she hint that her position in the convent is endangered by his revolutionary ideas or his interrogation at the Holy Office of the Inquisition. On the contrary, the other nuns and their father confessor all support her and anxiously track the progress of Galileo's trial: "I greet you lovingly on behalf of all these reverend mothers, to whom every hour seems like a thousand years on account of their great desire to see you again."

She makes no mention of her real mother, who died in 1619, four years before the date of the first extant letter.

The original pages penned by Suor Maria Celeste and carried across town or between cities to Galileo are retained today among the rare manuscripts in Florence's National Central Library. They fill a hand-bound book containing letters only from women, including Galileo's mother, his younger sister, and the Tuscan ambassadress to the Vatican, though Suor Maria Celeste is by far the most frequent and the most voluble contributor. The writing paper is not only yellowed (and the ink browned), but also furrowed where the sheets were folded for mailing—pleated lengthwise into thirds or quarters, then crosswise so the edges could be sealed with red wax, and Galileo's name and address written on the outside. Although his name easily stretched out to two or more lines with honorifics—"To the Very Illustrious Lord and My Most Worthy Father, Signor Galileo Galilei"—his address was a one-word affair: "Firenze," for example, or "Roma."

Suor Maria Celeste further distinguishes herself by having folded her pages into diamond patterns, at angles to the calendered ridges of the writing paper. And although she is the only regular correspondent to endure an arduous life of obedience, chastity, silence, and poverty, her handwriting fairly erupts into frills and flourishes, far more flamboyant than the scripts of the others. It is easy to imagine her letters arriving bathed in the now lost aromas of her apothecary work—nutmeg oil for nausea, dried rhubarb and crushed roses as purgatives.

All Suor Maria Celeste's letters are first drafts, as she had neither time nor paper to waste in copying. Yet they contain only a few mistakes—a word omitted here or there, with hardly any crossing out—and the long complex sentences never lose their balance.

Her tone of voice is consistently formal, respectful, even when she treats the intimate details of medical problems or family relationships. The Italian language allows a polite form of address, and Suor Maria Celeste always employs it. She begins each letter by saluting Galileo as "Most Illustrious Lord Father" or "Most Beloved Lord Father" or "Most Illustrious and Beloved Lord Father." In the body of the letters, she calls him "V. S." for "Vostra Signoria," which can be translated as "Your Lordship" when used by one gentleman to another, or, in her case, as "Sire." Closing, she identifies herself as "Your (or Your Most Excellent Lordship's) most affectionate daughter." This phraseology, which may strike the modern reader as a form of groveling, is perfectly consistent with the style of its time, when any ordinary business letter ended with the sender's cordially kissing the recipient's hands.

Twenty-seven of Suor Maria Celeste's letters first saw publication in Florence in 1852, in an early edition of Galileo's complete works. A free-standing collection of 121 of her letters followed in 1863, and all 124 appeared with an authoritative introduction and explanatory footnotes in 1891. Since then, Suor Maria Celeste's letters have been published more or less continually in Italy, constituting a little-known but well-loved classic of Italian literature.

Readers of English were introduced to her letters in 1870, when they served as the basis for a biography issued anonymously in London and Boston, called *A Private Life of Galileo. Compiled Principally from his Correspondence and that of his Eldest Daughter, Sister Maria Celeste, Nun in the Franciscan Convent of St. Matthew, in Arcetri.* The author, Mary Allan-Olney, no doubt translated all the letters into English, but included only selected excerpts from them in her book.

Until now, Suor Maria Celeste's letters have never been published in their entirety in any language other than Italian. This complete English edition of them includes the Italian originals, for although those have enjoyed a long history in print, they have not been readily available outside Italy.

The letters are presented in chronological order, thanks to Suor Maria Celeste's practice of ending almost every one with a dateline, such as, "From San Matteo in Arcetri, the 8th of July 1629." Often she fixed a time by naming the corresponding Catholic holiday, writing, for example, "the feast day of San Lorenzo," because of course she knew—and Galileo knew—that day was August 10. Eight of her letters, however, bear no indication of date, and their placement here represents the best thinking of all the researchers who have been captivated by Suor Maria Celeste over the past one hundred and fifty years.

Considering how many letters of hers may have been lost or discarded, it is fortuitous and remarkable that the surviving ones chronicle the ten most tumultuous years of Galileo's life. When read alongside the testimony of his trial, or the official reports of the plague in Florence, her letters create a stirring counterpoint. The jangling of affairs of state against household minutiae is enhanced by delays in the haphazard mail delivery system, which sometimes caused hope to rise on her end even as danger tightened around her father.

By all rights these letters should represent Suor Maria Celeste's middle years, from age twenty-two to thirty-three, but instead they mark the end of her life. The concern and responsibility she bore all through 1633 wore her down, so that the joy of Galileo's homecoming dissipated all too soon in a fatal illness, and she died during the night of April 2, 1634.

Letters to Father

Molto Ill.re Sig.r Padre,

Sentiamo grandissimo disgusto per la morte della sua amatissima sorella e nostra cara zia; ne habbiamo, dico, grave dolore per la perdita di lei et ancora sapendo quanto travaglio ne havrà havuto V. S., non havendo lei, si può dir, altri in questo mondo, nè potendo quasi perder cosa più cara, sì che possiamo pensare quanto gli sia stata grave questa percossa tanto inaspettata: e, come gli dico, partecipiamo ancor noi buona parte del suo dolore, se bene doverebbe esser bastato a farci pigliar conforto la consideratione della miseria humana et che tutti siamo qua come forestieri e viandanti, che presto siamo per andar alla nostra vera patria nel Cielo, dove è perfetta felicità e dove sperar dovi[a]mo che sia andata quell'anima benedetta. Sì che, per l'amor di Dio, preghiamo V. S. a consolarsi e rimettersi nella volontà del Signore, al quale sa benissimo che dispiacerebbe facendo altrimenti, et anco farebbe danno a sè et a noi, perchè non possiamo non dolerci infinitamente quando sentiamo che è travagliata o indisposta, non havendo noi altro bene in questo mondo che le[i].

Non gli dirò altro, se non che di tutto cuore preghiamo il Signore che la consoli e sia sempre seco. E con vivo affet[to] la salutiamo. Di S. M.o, li 10 di Mag.o 1623.

Di V. S. Molto Ill.re Aff.ma Fig.la

Suor M.a Celeste

Most Illustrious Lord Father,

We are terribly saddened by the death of your cherished sister, our dear aunt; but our sorrow at losing her is as nothing compared to our concern for your sake, because your suffering will be all the greater, Sire, as truly you have no one else left in your world, now that she, who could not have been more precious to you, has departed, and therefore we can only imagine how you sustain the severity of such a sudden and completely unexpected blow. And while I tell you that we share deeply in your grief, you would do well to draw even greater comfort from contemplating the general state of human misery, since we are all of us here on Earth like strangers and wayfarers, who soon will be bound for our true homeland in Heaven, where there is perfect happiness, and where we must hope that your sister's blessed soul has already gone. Thus, for the love of God, we pray you, Sire, to be consoled and to put yourself in His hands, for, as you know so well, that is what He wants of you; to do otherwise would be to injure yourself and hurt us, too, because we lament grievously when we hear that you are burdened and troubled, as we have no other source of goodness in this world but you.

Only yesterday Galileo's sister Virginia, dead at age fifty, was buried in Florence.

As cloistered nuns, Galileo's daughters dwell outside his world, while his mistress, his parents, and now his favorite sister have already gone to the next. His son is too young to be a comfort; his brother lives in another country; and he has never been close with his second sister, Livia, who entered a convent before her own marriage in 1601.

I will say no more, except that with all our hearts we fervently pray the Lord to comfort you and be with you always, and we greet you dearly with our ardent love. From San Matteo, the 10th of May 1623.

Sire's Most Affectionate Daughter,

Suor M. Celeste

Molt' Ill.re Sig.r Padre,

Il contento che m'apportato il regalo delle lettere che mi ha mandate V. S., scrittegli da quell'Ill.mo Cardinale, hoggi Sommo Pontefice, è stato inesplicabile, conoscendo benissimo in quelle qual sia l'affetione che le porta e quanta stima faccia delle sue virtù. Le ho lette e rilette con gusto particolare, et gliene rimando come m'impone, non l'havendo mostrate ad altri che a Suor Arcangela, la quale insieme meco ha sentito estrema allegrezza, per vedere quanto lei sia favorita da persona tale. Piaccia pure al Signore di concedergli tanta sanità quanta gl'è di bisogno per adempire il suo desiderio di visitar S. S.ta, acciò che maggiormente possa V. S. esser favorita da quella; et anco vedendo nelle sue lettere quante promesse gli faccia, possiamo sperare che facilmente havrebbe qualche aiuto per nostro fratello. In tanto noi non mancheremo di pregar l'istesso Signore, dal quale ogni gratia deriva, che gli dia gratia d'ottener quanto desidera, pur che sia per il meglio.

Mi vo inmaginando che V. S. in questa occasione havrà scritto a S. S.tà una bellissima lettera per rallegrarsi con lei della degnità ottenuta, et perchè sono un poco curiosa, havrei caro, se gli piacessi, di vederne la copia; et la ringratio infinitamente di queste che ci à mandate, et ancora dei poponi, a noi gratissimi. Le ho scritto con molta fretta, imperò la prego a scusarmi se ho scritto così male. La saluto di cuore, insieme con l'altre solite. Li 10 d'Agos.o

Di V. S. Aff.ma Fig.la

Suor M.a C.

Most Illustrious Lord Father,

The happiness I derived from the gift of the letters you sent me, Sire, written to you by that most distinguished Cardinal, now elevated to the exalted position of Supreme Pontiff, was ineffable, for his letters so clearly express the affection this great man has for you, and also show how highly he values your abilities. I have read and reread them, savoring them in private, and I return them to you, as you insist, without having shown them to anyone else except Suor Arcangela, who has joined me in drawing the utmost joy from seeing how much our father is favored by persons of such caliber. May it please the Lord to grant you the robust health you will need to fulfill your desire to visit His Holiness, so that you can be even more greatly esteemed by him; and, seeing how many promises he makes you in his letters, we can entertain the hope that the Pope will readily grant you some sort of assistance for our brother. In the meantime, we shall not fail to pray the Lord, from whom all grace descends, to bless you by letting you achieve all that you desire, so long as that be for the best.

Just last Sunday, on August 6, Maffeo Cardinal Barberini, long friendly to Galileo, was elected pope, taking the name Urban VIII.

I can only imagine, Sire, what a magnificent letter you must have written to His Holiness, to congratulate him on the occasion of his reaching this exalted rank, and, because I am more than a little bit curious, I yearn to see a copy of that letter, if it would please you to show it, and I thank you so much for the ones you have already sent, as well as for the melons which we enjoyed most gratefully. I have dashed off this note in considerable haste, so I beg your pardon if I have for that reason been sloppy or spoken amiss. I send you loving greet-

Molto Ill.re Sig.r Padre,

La sua amorevolissima lettera è stata cagione che io a pieno ho conosciuto la mia poca accortezza, stimando io che così subito dovessi V. S. scrivere a una tal persona, o per dir meglio al più sublime Signore di tutto il mondo. Ringratiola adunque dell'avvertimento, et mi rendo certa che (mediante l'affetione che mi porta) compatisca alla mia grandissima ignoranza et a tanti altri difetti che in me si ritrovano. Così mi foss'egli concesso il poter di tutti esser da lei ripresa et avvertita, come io lo desidero et mi sarebbe grato, sapendo che havrei qualche poco di sapere e qualche virtù che non ho. Ma poi che, mediante la sua continua indispositione, ci è vietato infino il poterla qualche volta rivedere, è necessario che patientemente ci rimettiamo nella volontà di Dio, il quale permette ogni cosa per nostro bene.

Io metto da parte e serbo tutte le lettere che giornalmente mi scrive V. S., e quando non mi ritrovo occupata, con mio grandissimo gusto le rileggo più volte; sì che lascio pensare a lei se anco volentieri leggerò quelle che gli sono scritte da persone tanto virtuose et a lei affetionate.

Per non la infastidir troppo, farò fine, salutandola affettuosamente insieme con Suor Arcangela e l'altre di camera, e ings along with the others here who always ask to be remembered to you. From San Matteo, the 10th of August.

Sire's Most Affectionate Daughter,

Suor M. C.

Most Illustrious Lord Father,

It was through your most gentle and loving letter that I became fully aware of my backwardness, in assuming as I did that you, Sire, would perforce write right away to such a person, or, to put it better, to the loftiest lord in all the world. Therefore I thank you for pointing out my error, and at the same time I feel certain that you will, by the love you bear me, excuse my gross ignorance and as many other flaws as find expression in my character. I readily concede that you are the one to correct and advise me in all matters, just as I desire you to do and would so appreciate your doing, for I realize how little knowledge and ability I can justly call my own. But since, considering your continuing indisposition, we are prohibited from seeing you again for some time, we must patiently submit ourselves to the will of God, who allows everything that contributes to our well-being.

Galileo has apparently explained to Suor Maria Celeste that protocol prevents him from writing directly to His Holiness.

I set aside and save all the letters that you write me daily, Sire, and whenever I find myself free, then with the greatest pleasure I reread them yet again, so that I abandon myself to thoughts of you, and equally as eagerly do I anticipate reading those letters written to you by persons of distinction who feel affection for you.

Suor Diamante ancora.   Li 13 d'Agosto 1623.

Di V. S. Aff.^ma^ Fig.^la^

Suor M.ª Celeste

Molto Ill.^re^ Sig.^r^ Padre,

Stamattina ho inteso dal nostro fattore che V. S. si ritrova in Firenze indisposta: et perchè mi par cosa fuora del suo ordinario il partirsi di casa sua quando è travagliata dalle sue doglie, sto con timore, et mi vo immaginando che habbia più male del solito. Per tanto la prego a darne ragguaglio al fattore, acciò che, se fossi manco male di quello che temiamo, possiam quietar l'animo. Et in vero che io on m'avveggo mai d'essar monaca, se non quando sento che V.S. è amalata, poi che allora vorrei poterla venire a visitare e governa[r] con tutta quella diligenza che mi fossi possible. Horsù, ringratiato sia il Signore Iddio d'ogni cosa, poi che senza il suo volere non si volta una foglia.

Io penso che in ogni modo non gli manchi niente; pure veda se in qua[l]che cosa à bisogno di noi, e ce l'avvissi, che non mancher[e]mo di servirla al meglio che possiamo. In tanto seguiteremo (conforme al nostro solito) di pregare nostro Signore per la sua desiderat[a] sanità, et anco che gli conceda la sua santa gratia. Et per fi[ne] di tuttto core la salutiamo, insieme con tutte di camera.   Di S. M.^o^, li 17 d'Agosto 1623.

Di V. S. Aff.^ma^ Fig.^la^

Suor M.ª Celeste

Not wanting to inconvenience or bore you, I will end here, sending you warmest greetings together with Suor Arcangela and the others in our room, and Suor Diamante, too. From San Matteo, the 13th of August 1623.

Sire's Most Affectionate Daughter,

Suor M. Celeste

Suor Arcangela is her natural sister, Livia, a year younger than she, and Suor Diamante one of their close friends.

Most Illustrious Lord Father,

This morning I learned from our steward that you find yourself ill in Florence, Sire: and because it sounds to me like something outside your normal behavior to leave home when you are troubled by your pains, I am filled with apprehension, and fear that you are in much worse condition than usual. Therefore I beseech you to send news of yourself via this steward, so that, if you are not faring as badly as we fear, we can calm our anxious spirits. And truly I never take notice of living cloistered as a nun, except when I hear that you are sick, because then I would like to be free to come to visit and care for you with all the diligence that I could muster. But even though I cannot, I thank the Lord God for everything, knowing full well that not a leaf turns without His willing it so.

The convent engages a steward who lives on the grounds with his wife, performing heavy work and running errands.

If there is anything you need, and you will only tell us what it is, we shall never fail to try to fulfill it in the very best way we know how. Meanwhile we continue, as is our custom, to pray the Lord for your coveted health, and ask that He grant you His holy grace. And I close with loving regards to you from all of us, with all our hearts. From San Matteo, the 17th of August 1623.

Sire's Most Affectionate Daughter,

Suor M. Celeste

Molto Ill.re et Amat.mo Sig.r Padre,

Desiderosa oltre modo d'haver nuove di V. S., mando costì il nostro fattore, e per un poco di scusa gli mando parecchi pescetti di marzapane, quali, se non saranno buoni come son quelli d'Arno, non penso che siano per esser cattivi a fatto per lei, e massimamente venendo da S. Matteo.

Non intendo già d'apportargli incomodo o fastidio con questa mia per causa dello scrivere, ma solo mi basta d'intender a bocca, come si sente, et perchè, se niente possiamo in suo servitio, ce l'avvisi. Suor Clara si raccomanda a suo padre e a suo fratello et a V. S. di tutto cuore; et il simile facciamo ambe dua noi, et dal Signor Iddio gli preghiamo et desideriamo la perfetta sanità. Di S. M.o, li 21 d'Agosto 1623.

Di V. S. molto Ill.re

Ricevemmo i poponi e'cocomeri bonissimi, e ve la ringratiamo.

Aff.ma Fig.la

Suor M.a Celeste

Molt' Ill.re Sig.r Padre,

Ci dispiace grandemente il sentire che per ancora V. S. non pigli troppo miglioramento, anzi che se ne stia in letto travagliata e senza gusto di mangiare, che tanto intendemmo hieri da Mess.r Benedetto. Niente di manco habbiamo ferma speranza che il Signore, per sua misericordia, sia per concedergli in breve qualche parte di sanità, non dico in tutto, parendomi

Most Illustrious and Beloved Lord Father,

Wishing above all else to have news of you, Sire, I dispatch our steward to you once again, and, as an excuse for the trip, I send several little fish-shaped pieces of marzipan, which, even if they do not taste quite as good as the ones you may find down along the banks of the Arno, still I think they will do you no harm, especially coming from San Matteo.

I do not, of course, mean to inconvenience or annoy you with this note, or to pressure you to write back, but only to hear a word carried from your lips about how you feel, and to learn whether there is anything we can do for you. Suor Chiara sends her love to her father and brother as well as to you, Sire; and the two of us do the same, praying to the Lord God in our longing for your perfect health. From San Matteo, the 21st of August 1623.

Sire's Most Affectionate Daughter,

Suor M. Celeste

Suor Chiara is Suor Maria Celeste's first cousin—the daughter of her uncle Benedetto Landucci and the recently deceased Aunt Virginia.

We received the delicious canteloupes and watermelons, and we thank you for them.

Most Illustrious Lord Father,

We are enormously disturbed to hear that you have not improved much as yet, Sire, that on the contrary your illness has left you bed-ridden and stripped you of your appetite, as we learned yesterday from Master Benedetto. Nonetheless we have firm hope that the Lord, through His mercy, is on the verge of restoring at least part of your health, I do not say all, quasi impossibile, mediante le sue tante indisposizioni, quali continuamente la molestano, et le quali, indubitatamente, gli saranno causa di maggior merito e gloria nell'altra vita, essendo da lei tollerate con tanta patientia.

Ho cercato di provveder quattro susine per mandargli, et gliene mando, se bene non sono di quella perfetione che havrei voluto: pure accetti V. S. il mio buon animo.

Gli ricordo che, quando riceve risposta da quei Signori di Roma, m'à promesso di concedermi che ancor io le possa vedere. Dell'altre lettere che m'aveva promesso mandarmi, non starò a dirgli niente, inmaginandomi che le tenga in villa. Per non l'infastidir troppo, non gli dico altro, se non che di tutto cuore la saluto insieme con Sr Arcangela e l'altre solite. Nostro Signore la consoli e sia sempre seco. Di S. M.^{o}, li 28 d'Agosto 1623.

Di V. S. Aff.^{ma} Fig.^{la}

Suor M.ª Celeste

Molto Ill.^{re} et Amatiss.^{mo} Sig.^{r} Padre,

Ho letto con gusto grandissimo le belle lettere da lei mandatemi. La ringratio e gliene rimando, con speranza però d'haverne per l'avvenire a veder dell' altre. Mandogli appresso una lettera di Vincenzio, acciò che con suo comodo gliela mandi.

as that seems almost impossible to me, considering the number of aggravations that continuously plague you, and which will undoubtedly earn you great reward and glory in the other life, since you tolerate all of this vexation with such patience.

I have searched everywhere to find you these four plums and I send them to you now, even if they are not at quite the level of perfection I would have wished; do please accept them, Sire, along with my best intentions.

Let this serve to remind you that, whenever you receive a response from those gentlemen in Rome, you did promise you would allow me to look at the letter; as for those other letters, which I know you have been meaning to let me read, I will not bother you about them now, as I imagine you do not have them with you. Not wanting to overburden you, I will say no more, except that I send you all my love together with Suor Arcangela and the others. May our Lord comfort you and be with you always. From San Matteo, the 28th of August 1623.

Sire's Most Affectionate Daughter,
Suor M. Celeste

Most Illustrious and Beloved Lord Father,

I have read with tremendous pleasure the beautiful letter that you sent to share with me. I thank you for that, and I return it to you with the hope, however, of being able to see it again sometime in the future, along with others and more. I enclose a letter I have written to Vincenzio, asking you, whenever it is convenient, to please see that it gets to him.

Suor Maria Celeste needs a letter carried to her seventeen-year-old brother, a university student in Pisa.

Ringratio il Signore, et mi rallegro con lei, del suo miglioramento, et la prego a riguardarsi più che gl'è possibile, fino a tanto che non raquista la desiderata sanità. La ringratio delle sue troppe amorevolezze, che in vero, mentre che à male, non vorrei che di noi si pigliassi tanto pensiero. La saluto con ogni affetto, insieme con S.r Arcangela, et da Nostro Signore gli prego abbondanza della sua gratia. Di S. Matteo, il dì ultimo d'Ag.to 1623.

Di V. S. molto Ill.re Aff.ma Fig.la

Suor M.a Celeste G.

Amat.mo Sig.r Padre,

Le mando la copiata lettera, con desiderio che sia in sua satisfatione, acciò che altre volte possa V. S. servirsi dell'opera mia, essendomi di gran gusto e contento l'occuparmi in suo servitio.

Madonna non si trova in comodità di comprar vino, fino che non sarà finito quel poco che habbiamo ricolto, sì che fa sua scusa appresso di lei, non potendo dargli satisfatione, et la ringratia dell'avviso datogli intorno al vino. Quello che ha mandato a S.r Arcangela è assai buono per lei, et ne la ringratia; et io insieme con lei la ringratio del refe et altre sue amorevolezze.

Per non tenere a bada il servitore, non dirò altro se non che la saluto caramente in nome di tutte et dal Signore gli prego ogni desiderato contento. Di S. M.o, il dì ultimo di 7mbre.

I give thanks to the Lord, rejoicing with you in your recovery, and I pray you to look after yourself as carefully as you possibly can, at least until you have regained your usual level of well-being. I thank you, too, for all the kindnesses of late, although truly, while you were ill, I almost wish you had not lavished so much thoughtfulness on us. I send you every loving greeting, together with Suor Arcangela, and I pray our Lord to bless you with the fullness of His grace. From San Matteo, the last day of August 1623.

Sire's Most Affectionate Daughter,

Suor M. Celeste G.

Most Beloved Lord Father,

Here is the copied letter, Sire, along with the wish that it meet with your approval, so that at other times I may again be able to help you by my work, seeing as it gives me such great pleasure and happiness to busy myself in your service.

Galileo has returned to his home on the hill called Bellosguardo.

Madonna is not in the best position to purchase wine just now, at least not until we have finished the little bit we have gathered, and therefore she makes her excuses to you accordingly, and thanks you for extending the offer even though she is unable to accept it. The wine you sent to Suor Arcangela is perfect as far as she is concerned and she thanks you for it: and I join her in thanking you for the thread and your many other loving gestures.

"Madonna" is the nuns' name for their mother abbess, in this case, Suor Laura Gaetani, who is nearing the end of her three-year term of office.

So as not to delay the servant I will say no more, except to send you most heartfelt greetings from all of us here and to pray the Lord God for the fulfillment of your every desire.

Sua Aff.^{ma} Fig.^{la}

Suor M.ª Celeste

Amatiss.^{mo} Sig.^{r} Padre,

Le frutte che V. S. ha mandate, mi sono state gratissime, per esser adesso per noi quaresima; sì come anco a Suor Arcangela il caviale: e la ringratiamo.

Vincenzio si ritrova molto a carestia di collari, se bene egli non ci pensa, bastandogli haverne uno imbiancato ogni volta che gli bisogna; ma noi duriamo molta fatica in accomodargli, per esser assai vecchi, e per ciò vorrei fargliene 4 con la trina, insieme con i manichini: ma perchè non ho nè tempo nè danari per farli, vorrei che V. S. supplissi a questo mancamento con mandarmi un braccio di tela batista e 18 o 20 lire almanco per comprar le trine, le quali mi fa la mia Suor Ortensia molto belle; et perchè i collari usano adesso assai grandi, vi entra assai guarnitione. Doppo che Vincenzio è stato così obediente a V. S. che porta sempre i manichini, per ciò, dico, egli merita d'havergli belli; sì che ella non si maravigli se domando tanti danari. Per adesso non dirò altro, se non che di cuore saluto ambe duoi, insieme con Suor Arcangela. Il Signor la conservi.

Sua Fig.^{la} Aff.^{ma}

Suor M.ª Celeste

From San Matteo, the last day of September.

Your Most Affectionate Daughter,

Suor M. Celeste

Most Beloved Lord Father,

The fruits you sent were most gratefully welcomed, Sire, and as it is now a period of fasting for us Franciscans, Suor Arcangela judged them the equal of caviar; and we thank you for them.

Vincenzio stands in desperate want of more collars, even though he may not think so, as it suits him to have his used ones bleached as the need arises; but we are struggling to accommodate him in this practice, since the collars are truly old, and therefore I would like to make him four new ones with lace trim and matching cuffs; however, since I have neither the time nor the money to do this all by myself, I should like for you to make up what I lack, Sire, by sending me a *braccio* of fine cambric and at least 18 or 20 *lire*, to buy the lace, which my Lady Ortensia makes for me very beautifully; and because the collars worn nowadays tend to be large, they require a good deal of trimming for properly finishing them; moreover, seeing as Vincenzio has been so obedient to you, Sire, in always wearing his cuffs, I maintain, for that reason, he deserves to have handsome ones; and therefore do not be astonished that I ask for this much money. Right now I will say no more, except that I send you both my love, together with Suor Arcangela. May the Lord bless you.

Your Most Affectionate Daughter,

Suor M. Celeste

Molto Ill.re et Amat.mo Sig.r Padre,

Gli rimando il resto delle sue camice, che abbiamo cucite, et anco il grembiule, quale ò accomodato meglio che è stato possibile. Rimandogli anco le sue lettere, che, per esser tanto belle, m'hanno accresciuto il desiderio di vederne dell'altre. Adesso attendo a lavorare ne i tovagliolini, sì che V. S. potrà mandarmi i cerri per metter alle teste; et gli ricordo che bisogna che siano alti, per esser i tovagliolini un poco corti.

Adesso ho rimesso di nuovo S.r Arcangela nelle mani del medico, per vedere, con l'aiuto del Signore, di liberarla della sua noiosa infermità, che a me apporta infinito travaglio.

Da Salvadore ho inteso che V. S. ci vuol venirci presto a vedere, il che molto desideriamo; ma gli ricordo che è obligat[o] a mantener la promessa fattaci, di venire per star una sera da noi, e potrà star a cena in parlatorio, perchè la scomunica è mandata alla tovaglia e non alle vivande.

Mandogli qui inclusa una carta, la quale, oltre al manifestargli qual sia il nostro bisogno, gli porgerà anco materia di ridersi della mia sciocca compositione; ma il vedere con quanta benignità V. S. esalta sempre il mio poco sapere, mi ha dato animo a far questo. Scusimi adunque V. S., e con la sua solita amorevolezza supplisca, al nostro bisogno. La ringratio del pesce, et la saluto affettuosamente insieme con S.r Arcangela. Nostro Signore gli conceda intiera felicità. Di S. M.o, li 20 d' 8bre 1623.

Di V. S. Aff.ma Fig.la

Suor M.a C.

Most Illustrious and Beloved Lord Father,

I am returning the rest of your shirts that we have sewn, and the leather apron, too, mended as best I could. I am also sending back your letters, which are so beautifully written that they have only kindled my desire to see more examples of them. Now I am tending to the work on the linens, so that I hope you will be able to send me the trim for borders at the ends, and I remind you, Sire, that the trimming needs to be wide, because the linens themselves are rather short.

I have just placed Suor Arcangela once more into the doctor's hands, to see, with God's help, if she can be relieved of her wearisome illness, which causes me no end of worry and work.

Salvadore tells me that you want to pay us a visit soon, Sire, which is precisely what we so desire; though I must remind you that you are obliged to keep the promise you made us, that is, to spend an entire evening here, and to be able to have dinner in the convent parlor, because we deliver the excommunication to the tablecloth and not the meals thereon.

Salvadore works as a servant for Galileo.

Here Suor Maria Celeste mocks a practice of the Poor Clares, whereby relatives may bring food to the convent and share it with the nuns, so long as they eat in the guest parlor, and not at the nuns' table.

I enclose herewith a little composition, which, aside from expressing to you the extent of our need, will also give you the excuse to have a hearty laugh at the expense of my foolish writing; but because I have seen how good-naturedly you always encourage my meager intelligence, Sire, you have lent me the courage to attempt this essay. Indulge me then, Lord Father, and with your usual loving tenderness please help us. I thank you for the fish, and send you loving greetings along with Suor Arcangela. May our Lord grant you complete

This composition has unfortunately disappeared.

Molto Ill.re et Amat.mo Sig.r Padre,

S'io volessi con parole ringratiar V. S. del presente fattoci, oltre che non saprei a pieno sadisfare al nostro debito, credo che a lei non sarebbe molto grato, come quella che, per sua benignità, ricerca più presto da noi gratitudine d'animo che dimostrationi di parole e cerimonie. Sarà adunque meglio che nel miglior modo che possiamo, che è con l'oratione, cerchiamo di riconoscere e ricompensare questo et altri infiniti, e di granlunga maggiori, benefitii che da lei ricevuti habbiamo.

Gl'havevo domandato dieci braccia di roba, con intenzione che pigliassi rovescio stretto, e non questo panno di tanta spesa e così largo e bello, quale sarà più che a bastanza per farne le camiciuole.

Lascio pensare a lei qual sia il contento che sento in legger le sue lettere, che continuamente mi manda; che solo il vedere con quale affetto V. S. si compiace di farmi partecipe e consapevole di tutti i favori che riceve da questi Signori, è bastante a riempiermi d'allegrezza; se bene il sentire che così presto deve partirsi, mi pare un poco aspro, per haver a restar priva di lei: et mi vado immaginando che sarà per lungo tempo, nè credo ingannarmi; e V. S. può credermi, poi che gli dico il vero, che, doppo lei, io non ò altri che possa darmi consolatione alcuna. Non per questo mi voglio dolere della sua partita, parendomi che più presto mi dorrei de i suoi con-happiness.   From San Matteo, the 20th of October 1623.

Sire's Most Affectionate Daughter,

Suor M. C.

Most Illustrious and Beloved Lord Father,

If I wanted to thank you with words, Sire, for these recent presents you sent us, I could not imagine how to begin to fully express our indebtedness, and what is more, I believe that such a display of gratitude would not even please you, for, as kind and good as you are, you would prefer true thankfulness of the spirit from us over any demonstration of speeches or ceremonies. We will therefore serve you better if we apply what we do best, and by that I mean prayer, in seeking to recognize and make recompense for this and all the other innumerable, and even far greater gifts that we have received from you.

I had asked you for six yards of material, expecting to work some narrow stuff inside out and upside down, and not this expensive bolt of flannel, so large and beautiful, which will be more than enough for making the winter undergarments.

I leave you to imagine what delight I derive from reading the continuous stream of letters you send me; when I see how affectionately you share these with me, Sire, and how you enjoy making me aware of all the favors bestowed upon you by the great lords, this alone is enough to fill me to the brim with happiness. No wonder the news that you must leave so soon seems a bit harsh to me, as it means being deprived of you, and I worry that this separation will be a long one, if I

Galileo plans to visit Rome for an audience with the new pope.

tenti; anzi me ne rallegro, et prego e pregherò sempre Nostro Signore che gli conceda perfetta sanità e gratia di poter far questo viaggio prosperamente, acciò che con maggior contento possa poi tornarsene in qua e viver felice molti anni: che così spero che sia per seguire, con l'aiuto di Dio.

Gli raccomando bene il nostro povero fratello, se ben so che non occorre, a la prego hormai a perdonargli il suo errore, scusando la sua poca età, che è quella che l'àindotto a commetter questo fallo, che, per esser stato il primo, merita perdono: si che torno a pregarla che di gratia Lo meni in sua compagnia a Roma, e là, dove non gli mancheranno l'occasioni, gli dia quegl'aiuti che l'obligo paterno et la sua natural benignità, et amorevolezza ricercano.

Ma perchè temo di non venirgli a fastidio, finisco di scrivere, senza finir mai di raccomandarmeli in gratia. E gli ricordo che ci è debitore di una visita, che ci ha promesso è molto tempo. Suor Arcangela e l'altre di camera la salutano infinite volte. Di S. M.º li 29 d' 8bre.

Di V. S. molt' Ill.re Aff.ma Fig.la

Suor M.a Celeste G.

am not mistaken. And you can believe me, Sire, because I always speak the truth, that, other than you, I have no one else in this world who can console me; yet it is for this very reason that I do not grieve over your departure, any more than I would grieve over your good fortune; on the contrary, I will cheer myself, and pray and continue to pray all the while for Our Lord to grant you the soundness of body and mind to undertake this journey most prosperously, so that with the greatest contentment you can later return to us, and live happily here for many more years: may all this that I hope for you come to pass with the help of God.

I want to offer you a good word on behalf of our poor brother, although I may be speaking out of turn, yet I beseech you to forgive him his mistake this time, blaming his youth as the real cause for his committing such a blunder, which, being his first, merits pardon: I therefore entreat you once again to take him with you to Rome, and there, where you will not lack for opportunities, you can give your son the guidance that your paternal duty and all your natural goodness and loving tenderness seek to provide him.

Because I fear I may be prattling on, I will stop writing now, though I will never stop striving to remain in your good graces. And I must remind you that you still owe us the visit you have been promising for so long. Suor Arcangela and the others in the room send you a thousand regards. From San Matteo, the 29th of October.

It takes Galileo nearly an hour, by mule or on foot, to reach San Matteo from Bellosguardo.

Sire's Most Affectionate Daughter,

Suor M. Celeste G.

Molto Ill.re Sig.r Padre,

L'infinito amore che io porto a V. S., et anco il timore che ho che questo così subito freddo, ordinariamente a lei tanto contrario, gli causi il risentimento de i suoi soliti dolori e d'altre sue indispositioni, non comportano ch' io possa star più senza haver nuove di lei: mando adunque costì per intender qualcosa, sì dell'esser suo, come anco quando pensa V. S. doversi partire. Ho sollecitato assai i[n] lavorare i tovagliolini, et sono quasi al fine; ma nell'appiccare le frange trovo che di questa sorte, che gli mando la mostra, ne manca per dua tovagliolini, che saranno 4 braccia. Havrò car[o] che le mandi quanto prima, acciò che possa mandarglieli avanti che si parta; chè per questo ho preso sollecitudine in finirgli.

Per non haver io camera dove star a dormir la notte, Suor Diaman[te], per sua cortesia, mi tiene nella sua, privandone la propria sorella per tenervi me; ma a questi freddi vi è tanto la cattiva st[an]za, che io, che ho la testa tanto infetta, non credo potervi stare, se V. S. non mi soccorre, prestandomi uno de i suoi padiglioni, di quelli bianchi, che adesso non deve adoprare. Havrò caro d'intender se può farmi questo servitio; et di più la prego a farmi gratia di mandarmi il suo libro, che si è stampato adesso, tanto ch'io lo legga, havendo io gran desiderio di vederlo.

Queste poche paste, che gli mando, l'havevo fatte pochi giorni sono, per dargliene quando veniva a dirci a Dio. Veggo che non sarà presto, come temevo, tanto che gliele mando acciò non indurischino. Suor Arcangela séguita ancora a purgarsi; se ne sta non troppo bene, con dua cauterii che se gli sono fatti nelle cosce. Io ancora non sto molto bene; ma per

Most Illustrious Lord Father,

Between the infinite love I bear you, Sire, and my fear that this sudden cold, which ordinarily troubles you so much, may aggravate your current aches and indispositions, I find it impossible to remain without news of you: therefore I beg to hear how you are, Sire, and also when you think you will be setting off on your journey. I have hastened my work on the linens, and they are almost finished; but in applying the fringe, of which I am sending you a sample, I see I will not have enough for the last two cloths, as I need almost another four *braccia*. Please do everything you can to get this to me quickly, so I can send them all to you before you leave; as it is for the purpose of your upcoming trip that I have gone to such lengths to finish them.

Since I do not have a room where I can sleep through the night, Suor Diamanta, by her kindness, lets me stay in hers, depriving her own sister of that hospitality in order to take me in; but the room is terribly cold now, and with my head so infected, I cannot see how I will be able to stand it there, Sire, unless you help me by lending me one of your bed hangings, one of the white ones that you will not need to use now while you are away. I am most eager to know if you can do me this service. And another thing I ask of you, please, is to send me your book, the one that has just been published, so that I may read it, as I am longing to see what it says.

The book she wants to read is ***The Assayer****, Galileo's treatise on comets and philosophy of science.*

Here are some cakes I made a few days ago, hoping to give them to you when you came to bid us adieu. I see that this will not happen quite as soon as I feared, and so I want you to have them before they turn hard. Suor Arcangela continesser ormai tanto assuefatta alla poca sanità, ne faccio poca stima: vedendo di più che al Signore piace di visitarmi sempre con qualche poco di travaglio, lo ringratio, e lo prego che a V. S. conceda il colmo d'ogni maggior felicità. Et per fine di tutto cuore la saluto, in nome mio e di S. Archangela. Di S. M.º, li 21 di 9mbre 1623.

Di V. S. molto Ill.re

S. M.a Celeste

Se V. S. à collari da imbiancare, potrà mandarceli.

Molto Ill.re et Amat.mo Sig.r Padre,

Pensavo di poter presentialmente dar risposta a quanto mi disse V. S. nell'amorevolissima sua lettera, scrittami già son parecchi giorni. Veggo che il tempo ne impedisce, sì che mi risolvo con questa mia notificargli il mio pensiero. Dicogli adunque che il sentire con quanta amorevolezza lei si offerisce ad aiutare il nostro monastero, mi apportò gran contento. Lo conferii con Madonna et con altre Madri più attempate, quali ne mostrorno quella gratitudine che ricercava la qualità dell'offerta; ma perchè stavano sospese, non sapendo in fra di loro a che risolversi, Madonna scrisse per questo al nostro Governatore; et egli rispose, che, per esser il monastero tanto bisognoso, gli pareva che ci fossi più necessità di adimandar qualche elemosina che altro. Fra tanto io ho discorso più volte ues still to purge herself, and she does not feel terribly well after having had the two cauteries on her thighs. I am still not very well either, but by now I am so accustomed to poor health that I hardly think about it, seeing how it pleases the Lord to keep testing me always with some little pain or other. I thank Him, and I pray that He grant you, Sire, the greatest possible well-being in all respects. And to close I send you loving greetings from me and from Suor Arcangela. From San Matteo, the 21st of November 1623.

Sire's Most Affectionate Daughter,

S. M. Celeste

If you have collars to be bleached, Sire, you may send them to us.

Most Illustrious and Beloved Lord Father,

I was hoping to be able to respond in person, Sire, to everything you said in your most solicitous letter of several days ago. I see, however, that time may prohibit us from meeting before you take your leave, and so I am resolved to share my thoughts with you in writing. Above all, I want you to know how happy you made me by offering so lovingly to help our convent. I conferred with Madonna and other elders here, all of whom expressed their gratitude for the nature of your offer; but because they were uncertain, not knowing how to come to a decision among themselves, Madonna wrote to our Governor, and he answered that, since the convent is so impoverished, alms were probably needed more than anything. Meanwhile I had several discussions with one particular nun, sopra questo con una monaca che e di giuditio e di bontà mi pare che sopravanzi tutte l'altre; et ella, mossa non da passione o interesse alcuno, ma da buon zelo, m'ha consigliato, anzi pregato, a domandargli cosa che a noi indubitatamente sarebbe molto utile, et a V. S. molto facile ad ottenere; ciò è che da S. S.^{tà} ci impetrassi gratia che potessimo tener per nostro confessore un regolare, o frate che dir lo vogliamo, con conditione di scambiarlo ogni 3 anni, come si costuma per l'altre, et per questo di non levarci dall'obedienza dell'ordinario, ma solo per ricever da questo i Santi Sacramenti: et è questo a noi tanto necessario che più non si può dire, e per moltissime cause, alcune delle quali ho qui notate nell'inclusa carta che gli mando. Ma perchè so che non può V. S. mediante una semplice mia parola muoversi a dimandar questo, oltre all'informarsene con qualche persona esperimentata, potrà, quando vien qui, cercar, così dalla lunga, d'intender qual sia, circa a questo, l'animo di Madonna, e di qualcun'altra di queste più attempate, senza però mai scoprir la causa per la quale gliene domanda. Et, di gratia, non ne parli niente con Mess.^{r} Benedetto, perchè senz'altro lo manifesterebbe a Suor Chiara, e lei poi a tutte le monache, et eccoci rovinati, perchè in fra tanti cervelli è impossibile che non ci siano variati humori, et per conseguenza qualcuna a chi potessi dispiacer questo et metter qualche impedimento acciò non si ottenessi: e pure anco non conveniente, per rispetto di dua o tre, privar tutte in comune di tanto utile, che di questo, sì per lo spirituale come per il temporale, ne potrebbe riuscire.

Resta adesso che V. S. con il suo retto giuditio (al quale ci apportiamo) vada esaminando se gli par lecito il domandar who seems to me to surpass all the others here in wisdom and goodwill; and she, moved not by passion or self-interest but by sincere zeal, advised me, indeed beseeched me to ask you for something which would undoubtedly be of great use to us and yet very easy for you, Sire, to obtain: that is to implore His Holiness to let us have for our confessor a Regular or Brother in whom we can confide, with the possibility that he may be replaced every three years, as is the custom at convents, by someone equally dependable; a confessor who will not interfere with the normal observances of our Order, but simply let us receive from him the Holy Sacraments: it is this that we require above all else, and so much so that I can hardly express its crucial importance, or the background circumstances that make it so, although I have tried to list several of them in the enclosed paper that I am sending along with this letter. But because I know, Sire, that you cannot, on the basis of a simple word from me, make such a demand, without hearing from others more experienced in such matters, you can look for a way, when you come here, to broach the question with Madonna, to try to get a sense of her feelings on the matter, and also to discuss it with any of the more elderly mothers, without, of course, exposing your reasons for mentioning such things. And please breathe not a word of this to Master Benedetto, since he would undoubtedly divulge it to Suor Chiara, who would then spread it among the other nuns, and thus ruin us, because it is impossible for so many brains to be of one mind; and as a consequence the actions of a single person who might be particularly displeased by this idea could thwart our efforts. Surely it would be wrong to let two or three individuals deprive everyone in the group

The Rule of Saint Clare calls for a "Visitator" from the Franciscan Order of Friars Minor to perform those functions forbidden to cloistered women, such as the celebration of the Mass. But in place of truly devout friars, the sisters of San Matteo have been visited by a series of unscrupulous priests, with no experience of monastic life, who probably won their positions through the common routes of apprenticeships or political connections.

questo, et in che modo si deva domandare per ottenerlo più facilmente; perchè, quanto a me, mi pare che sia domanda lecita, tanto più per haverne noi estrema necessità.

Ho voluto scrivergli oggi, perchè, essendo il tempo tanto quieto, penso che V. S. sia per venir da noi avanti che torni a rompersi, et acciò che già sia informata dell'uffitio che è necessario che faccia con queste vecchie, come già gl'ò detto.

Perchè temo d'infastidirla pur troppo, lascio di scrivere, riserbando molte cose che mi restano per dirgliene alla presenza. Oggi aspettiamo Monsr Vicario, che viene per l'eletione della nuova Abbadessa. Piaccia a Dio che sia eletta quella che è più conforme al Suo volere; et a V. S. conceda abbondanza della sua santa gratia. Di S. Matteo, li 10 di Xmbre 1623.

Di V. S. molto Ill.[re] Aff.[ma] Fig.[la]

Suor M.[a] Celeste G.

La prima e principal causa che ne muove a domandar questo, è il veder e conoscere che la poca cognitione et esperienza che ànno questi preti degl'ordini et oblighi che habbiamo noi altre religiose, ci dà grand'occasione, et, per dir meglio, buona licenza, che viviamo sempre più dilandite (*sic*) a con poca osservanza della regola nostra. E chi dubita che, mentre vivremo con poco timor di Dio, non siamo anco per viver in continua miseria quanto alle cose temporali? Dunque bisogna levar la prima causa, che è questa che già gl'ho detto.

La seconda è, che per ritrovarsi il nostro monastero nella poverta che sa V. S., non puo sodisfare a i confessori che ogni 3 anni si partono, dando loro il dovuto salario avanti che si partino: onde che io so, tre di quelli che ci sono stati, ànno a of all the benefits, both spiritual and practical, that could accrue from the success of this plan.

Now it is up to you, Sire, with your sound judgment, to which we appeal, to determine whether you deem it appropriate to pose our entreaty, and how best to present it so as to achieve the desired end most easily; since, as far as I am concerned, our petition seems entirely legitimate, and all the more so for our being in such dire straits.

I made it a point to write to you today, Sire, as this is rather a quiet time, and I think the right time for you to come to us, before things get stirred up again, so that you can see for yourself what may need to be done in respecting the stature of the older nuns, as I have already explained.

Because I fear imposing on you too heavily, I will leave off writing here, saving all the other things to tell you later in person. Today we expect a visit from Monsignor Vicar, who is coming to attend the election of the new Abbess. May it please God to see the one who bends most to His will elected to this post, and may He grant you, Sire, an abundance of His holy grace.   From San Matteo, the 10th of December 1623.

Sire's Most Affectionate Daughter,
Suor M. Celeste G.

[The enclosed paper reads as follows:]
The first and foremost motive, which drives us to make this plea, is the clear recognition and awareness of how these priests' paltry knowledge or understanding of the orders and obligations that are part of our religious life, allow us, or, to say it better, tempt us to live ever more loosely, with scant ob-

havere buona somma di danari, a con questa occasione vengano spesse volte qui a desina[re], e pigliano amicitia con qualche monaca, e, quel che è peggio, ci portano in bocca e si dolgon di noi dovunque vanno, sì che siam[o] la scorta di tutto il Casentino, di dove vengon questi nostri confes[s]ori, usi più a cacciar lepre che a guidar anime. Et credam[i] V. S. che se io volessi raccontargli le goffezze di questo che habbi[a]mo al presente, non verrei mai alla fine, perchè sono incredibili et infinite.

La 3ª sarà, che un regolare non sarà mai tanto ignorante che non sappia molto più che uno di questi tali; o se non saprà non andrà almanco, per ogni minimo caso che fra di noi occorra, a dimandar consiglio in vescovado o altrove, come si deva portare o governare, come tutt' il giorno fanno questi preti, ma ne addimanderà, a qualche Padre letterato della sua religione; e cosà le nostre cause si sapranno in un convento solo, e non per tutto Firenze, come si sanno al presente. Doppo che, se non altro per esperienza, saprà benissimo un frate i termini che deva tener con monache, acciò che vivino più quiete che sia possibile; dove che un prete, che vien qui senza haver, si può dir, cognition di monache, ha compito il tempo determinato di 3 anni, che ci deve stare, avanti che abbia imparato quali siano gl'oblighi et ordini nostri.

Non domandiamo già più i Padri di una religione che d'un'altra, rimettendoci nel giuditio di chi ne impetrerà e concederà, tal gratia. Ben è vero che quelli di S.ta Maria Maggiore, che molte volte sono venuti qui per confessori straordinarii, ci hanno dato gran satisfatione, e credo che sarebbano più il caso nostro: prima, per esser Padri molto osservanti et in buona servance of our Rule; and how can one doubt that once we begin to live without fear of God, we will be subject to continual misery with regard to the temporal matters of this world? Therefore we must address the primary cause, which is this one that I have just told you.

A second problem is that, since our convent finds itself in poverty, as you know, Sire, it cannot satisfy the confessors, who leave every three years, by giving them their salary before they go: I happen to know that three of those who were here are owed quite a large sum of money, and they use this debt as occasion to come here often to dine with us, and to fraternize with several of the nuns; and, what is worse, they then carry us in their mouths, spreading rumors and gossiping about us wherever they go, to the point where our convent is considered the concubine of the whole Casentino region, whence come these confessors of ours, more suited to hunting rabbits than guiding souls. And believe me, Sire, if I wanted to tell you all the blunders committed by the one we have with us now, I would never come to the bottom of the list, because they are as numerous as they are incredible.

The third thing will be that a Regular must never be so ignorant that he does not know much more than one of these types, or if he does not know, at least he will not flee the convent, as has been the constant practice of our priests here, on the occasion of any little happenstance, to seek advice from the bishopric or elsewhere, as though that were any way to comport oneself or counsel others; but rather he will consult some learned father of his own Order. And in this fashion our affairs will be known in only one convent, and not all over Florence, as they are now.

venerazione; e doppo questo, perchè non ambiscono a gran presenti, nè si curano (essendo usi a viver poveramente) di far una vita esquisita, come altri d'altra religione ànno voluto, quando ci son venuti, e come fanno i preti che ci son dati per confessori, che, venendo qui per 3 anni soli, in quel tempo non cercano altro che l'utile et interesse proprio, e quanta più roba posson cavar da noi, piu valenti si riputano.

Ma, senza ch'io stia ad estendermi più oltre con altre ragioni che gli potrei addurre, può V. S. informarsi in quale stat[o] si trovavano prima il monasterio di S. Iacopo, quello di S.ta Monaca, et altri, et in quale si trovano al presente, poi che son venute al governo di frati che ànno saputo ridurle per la buona strada.

Non per questo domandiamo di levarci dall'obedienza dell'ordinario, ma solo d'esser sacramentate e governate da persone esperimentate e che sappiano qualcosa.

More than this, if he has gained nothing else from his own experience, he will well understand the boundaries that a Brother must respect between himself and the nuns, in order for them to live as quietly as possible; whereas a priest who comes here without having, so to speak, knowledge of nuns, may complete the whole designated three years of his required stay without ever learning our obligations and Rule.

We are not really requesting fathers of one religious order in preference over another, trusting ourselves to the judgment of he who will obtain and grant us such a favor. It is very true that the Reformed Carmelites of Santa Maria Maggiore, who have come here many times as special confessors, have served us most satisfactorily in the offices we are prohibited from performing ourselves; and I believe that they would better conform to our need. First, being themselves very devout fathers and highly esteemed; and moreover, because they do not covet fancy gifts, nor concern themselves (being well accustomed to poverty) with a grandiose lifestyle, as members of some other Orders have sought here; certain priests sent to us as confessors spent the whole three years serving only their own interests, and the more they could wring out of us, the more skillful they considered themselves.

But, without straining to make further allegations, Sire, I urge you to judge for yourself the conditions at other convents, such as San Jacopo and Santa Monaca, now that they have come under the influence of Brothers who took steps to set them on the proper path.

Although Suor Maria Celeste never returns to this subject, several fond references to the convent's father confessor in subsequent letters show that Galileo must have succeeded in answering her plea.

We are by no means asking to shirk the obedience of our Order, but only to be administered the Sacraments and governed by persons of experience, who appreciate the true significance of their calling.

Molto Ill.re et Amat.mo Sig.r Padre,

Grandissimo contento c'ha apportato il sentire (per la lettera mandata d'ordine di V. S. a Mess.r Benedetto) il suo prospero viaggio fino in Acquasparta, e sommamente ne ringratiamo Dio benedetto. Godiamo anco de i favori che ha ricevuti dal Sig.r Prencipe Cesis, e stiamo con speranza d'haver occasione di molto più rallegrarci quando intenderemo il suo arrivo in Roma, essendo V. S. stata da gran personaggi tanto desiderata; ancorchè io mi persuada che questi suoi contenti sieno contrappesati con molto disturbo mediante l'improvvisa morte del Sig.r D. Virginio Cesarini, da lei tanto riverito et amato. Ne ho preso io molto disgusto, solamente pensando al travaglio che haverà havuto V. S. per la perdita di così caro amico, e tanto più che era così vicina a doverlo presto rivedere. È certo che questo caso ne dà materia da considerare quanto sieno fallaci e vane tutte le speranze di questo mondaccio.

Ma, perchè non vorrei che V. S. credessi ch'io voglia sermoneggiar per lettera, non dirò altro, salvo che, per avvisarla dell'esser nostro, gli dico che stiamo benissimo, et affettuosamente la salutiamo, in nome di tutte le monache. Et io gli prego da Nostro Signore il compimento d'ogni suo giusto desiderio.   Di S. Matteo, li 26 d'Aprile 1624.

Di V. S. molto Ill.re Aff.ma Fig.la

Suor M.a Celeste

Most Illustrious and Beloved Lord Father,

What great happiness was delivered here, Sire, along with the news (via the letter that you ordered sent to Master Benedetto) of the safe progress of your journey as far as Acquasparta, and for all of this we offer thanks to God, Master of all. We are also delighted to learn of the favors you received from Prince Cesi, and we hope to have even greater occasion for rejoicing when we hear tell of your arrival in Rome, Sire, where persons of grand stature most eagerly await you, even though I know that your joy must be tainted with considerable sorrow, on account of the sudden death of Signor Don Virginio Cesarini, so esteemed and so loved by you. I, too, have been saddened by his passing, thinking only of the grief that you must endure, Sire, for the loss of such a dear friend, just when you stood on the verge of soon seeing him again; surely this event gives us occasion to reflect on the falsity and vanity of all hopes tied to this wretched world.

*Prince Federico Cesi is Galileo's patron and publisher. The prince's cousin, Virginio Cesarini, to whom Galileo addressed **The Assayer**, has just died of tuberculosis.*

But, because I would not have you think, Sire, that I want to sermonize by letter, I will say no more, except to let you know how we fare, for I can tell you that everyone here is very well indeed, and all the nuns send you their loving regards. As for myself, I pray that our Lord grant you the fulfillment of your every just desire. From San Matteo, the 26th of April 1624.

Sire's Most Affectionate Daughter,

Suor M. Celeste

Molto Ill.re et Amatiss.mo Sig.r Padre,

Del cedro che V. S. m'ordinò ch'io dovessi confettare, non ne ò accomodato se non questo poco che al presente gli mando, perchè dubitavo che, per esser così appassito, non dovessi riuscir di quella perfezione ch'io havrei voluto, come veramente non è riuscito. Insieme con esso gli mando dua pere cotte per questi giorni di vigilia. Ma, per maggiormente regalarla, gli mando una rosa, la quale, come cosa straordinaria in questa stagione, dovrà da lei esser molto gradita, e tanto più, che insieme con la rosa potrà accettar le spine, che in essa rappresentano l'acerba passione di Nostro Signore; et anco le sue verdi fronde gli significheranno la speranza che (mediante questa santa passione) possiamo havere, di dover, doppo la brevità et oscurità dell'inverno della vita presente, pervenire alla chiarezza e felicità dell'eterna primavera del Cielo: il che ne conceda Dio benedetto per sua misericordia. Et qui facendo punto, la saluto insieme con S.r Arcangela affettuosamente; et stiamo ambe dua con desiderio di saper come stia V. S. al presente di sanità. Di S. Matteo, li 19 di Xmbre 1625.

Aff.ma Fig.la
Suor M.a Celeste

Gli rimando la tovaglia nella quale mandò involto l' agnello; et V. S. ha di nostro una federa, che mandammo con le camice, una paniera et una coperta.

Most Illustrious and Beloved Lord Father,

As for the citron, which you commanded me, Sire, to make into candy, I have come up with only this little bit that I send you now, because I am afraid the fruit was not fresh enough for the confection to reach the state of perfection I would have liked, and indeed it did not turn out very well after all. Along with this I am sending you two baked pears for these festive days. But to present you with an even more special gift, I enclose a rose, which, as an extraordinary thing in this cold season, must be warmly welcomed by you. And all the more so since, together with the rose, you will be able to accept the thorns that represent the bitter suffering of our Lord; and also its green leaves, symbolizing the hope that we nurture (by virtue of this holy passion), of the reward that awaits us, after the brevity and darkness of the winter of the present life, when at last we will enter the clarity and happiness of the eternal spring of Heaven, which blessed God grants us by His mercy. And ending here, I give you loving greetings, together with Suor Arcangela, and remind you, Sire, that both of us are all eagerness to hear the current state of your health. From San Matteo, the 19th of December 1625.

Most Affectionate Daughter,
Suor M. Celeste

The gap of eighteen months separating this letter from her last suggests that many others may have been lost or discarded, either by her father or his followers.

I am returning the tablecloth in which you wrapped the lamb you sent; and you, Sire, have a pillowcase of ours, which we put over the shirts in the basket with the lid.

Molto Ill.re et Amatiss.mo Sig.r Padre,

L' haver V. S. lasciato, li giorni passati, di venir a visitarne (essendo stato il tempo assai quieto, lei, per quanto' ho inteso, con sanità, et senza l'occupazione della Corte) sarebbe bastante a causar in me qualche timore che fossi in parte diminuito l'amore che grandissimo ne ha sempre dimostrato; se non che gl'effetti dell'amorevolezza sua in verso di noi tanto frequenti mi liberano da questo sospetto: sì che più presto m'inclino a credere ch'ella vada differendo la visita mediante la poca satisfazione che riceve dal venirci, tanto da noi che, mediante la nostra non so s'io mi dica dappocaggine, non sappiamo dargliene più, quanto dall' altre che per altre cagioni poca gliene danno. Et per questo lascio di lamentarmi con lei, come farei se non havessi questo pensiero; et solo la prego a conformarsi, con il lasciarsi da noi rivedere, se non in tutto al suo gusto, almeno al nostro desiderio, il qual sarebbe di star continuamente da lei, se ne fossi lecito, per farle quelli ossequii che i suoi meriti et il nostro debito ricercherebbono. Et poi che questo non ci è concesso, non mancheremo già di satisfare a questo debito con tenerla raccomandata al Signore, che gli conceda la sua grazia in questa vita et il Paradiso nell'altra.

Dubito che Vincenzio non si lamenti di noi, perchè indugiamo tanto a mandarli i collari che ci mandò a domandare, dicendo che ne haveva carestia. Di gratia, V. S. ci mandi un poca di tela batista, acciò gliene possiamo cucire, et anco ci dia qualche nuova di lui, chè lo desideriamo. Et se a lei occorre qualche cosa per suo servitio, nella quale possiamo impiegarci, si ricordi che ci è di gusto grandissimo il servirla. E qui facendo fine, a V. S. mi raccomando, insieme con Suor

Most Illustrious and Beloved Lord Father,

Your having let the days go by, Sire, without coming to visit us (this being an opportune time, as you, from what I hear, are in command of your health, and free from demands of the Court) would be enough to provoke some fear in me that the great love you have always shown us may be diminishing somewhat. Except that the expressions of your loving tenderness toward us come so frequently as to free me from this suspicion: therefore I am sooner inclined to believe that you keep putting off the visit because of the scarce satisfaction you derive from coming here, not only because the two of us, in what I suppose I would call our ineptitude, simply do not know how to show you a better time, but also because the other nuns, for other reasons, cannot keep you sufficiently amused. Given all that, I will leave off complaining, to act as though I had never entertained such thoughts; and I only pray you to bow (by allowing us to see you again) if not entirely to your own pleasure, at least partially to our wish; which would be to have you with us always, if only it were possible, in order to pay you that homage which your merits and our debt demand. Even though we are denied your presence, still we will not fail to remember our obligation to you by praising your name to the Lord so that He may grant you His grace in this life, and Paradise in the next.

I suspect that Vincenzio is complaining about us, because we lag so long in sending him the collars that he requested, insisting that he had great need of them. Please, Sire, get us a little bit of cotton batiste, so that we may sew them for him, and also give us some news of him, which we so desire. And if anything

Arcangela. Di S. Matteo, il primo giorno di Quaresima del 1625.

Di V. S. molto Ill.^{re} Aff.^{ma} Fig.^{la}

Suor M.ª Celeste

Molto Ill.^{re} et Amatiss.^{mo} Sig.^{r} Padre,

Desiderando io che in queste santissime feste di Natale et in molte altre ancora V. S. arrivi al colmo d'ogni bramata consolatione, vengo con questi pochi versi a fargliene felicissimo augurio; et prego il Signor Iddio che in questi benedetti giorni il suo animo goda tranquilla pace, et il simile a tutti di casa.

Mando alcune coserelle per i fanciullini del zio: il collare maggiore con i manichini sarà di Albertino, gl'altri due de gl'altri più piccoli, et il canino della bambina, le paste di tutti, eccetto i mostacciuoli che sono per V. S. Accetti la buona volontà, che sarebbe pronta per far molto più.

Ricevei il vino, et anco il rabarbaro: la ringratio, et prego il Signore che le rimeriti tante sue amorevolezze con l'aumento della Sua santa gratia. Con che per fine mi raccomando a tutti molto affettuosamente. Di S. Matt.^{o}, la vigilia di Natale del 1627.

Di V. S. molto Ill.^{re} Aff.^{ma} Fig.^{la}

Suor M.ª Celeste

occurs to you regarding some need of yours, in which we can engage ourselves, remember that it is our greatest pleasure to serve you. And ending here, Sire, I commend myself lovingly to you, together with Suor Arcangela. From San Matteo, first day of Lent 1625.

Sire's Most Affectionate Daughter,

Suor M. Celeste

Although the Christmas season has given way to the Lenten, the year is still 1625, as reckoned by the Florentine Calendar, which counts the 25th of March, the Feast of the Annunciation, as New Year's Day.

Most Illustrious and Beloved Lord Father,

Hopeful that in these most holy festivals of Christmas, and in much else besides, Sire, you will attain the summit of every longed-for consolation, I come to you with these few lines to wish you the happiest good fortune, and I pray the Lord God, that during these blessed days your spirit enjoys quiet peace, and likewise for all the members of your household.

I am sending a few little things for Uncle Michelangelo's children, the larger collar with the cuffs will be for Albertino, the other two for the two younger boys, and the teething bib for our baby girl, the pastry for everyone to enjoy, except the spiced cakes, as these are for you, Sire. Please also accept the good will with which I am ready to do much more.

The relatives Suor Maria Celeste favors with her Christmas gifts and wishes are the wife and children of Galileo's brother, Michelangelo, who all arrived from Munich the previous July.

I received the wine and also the rhubarb; I thank you; and I pray the Lord to reward you for all your loving tenderness with the fullness of His holy grace. To close I send my very loving regards to all of you. From San Matteo, Christmas Eve 1627.

Sire's Most Affectionate Daughter,

Suor M. Celeste

Amatiss.mo Sig.r Padre,

Con mio grandissimo contento intesi l'altro giorno che V. S. stava bene; il che non segue già di me, poi che da domenica in qua mi ritrovo in letto con un poca di febbre, la quale (secondo che dice il medico) saria stata di considerazione, se un poco di flusso di corpo sopraggiuntomi non gl'havessi tagliata la strada a ridotta di presente in poca quantità. Io, già, che Dio benedetto mi fa gratia di mantenermi V. S., prevalendomi di questa habilità, a lei ricorro in tutte le mie necessità, con quella confidenza che più un giorno dell'altro mi somministra la sua cordiale amorevolezza; a particolarmente adesso, che mi trovo bisognosa di governarmi mediocremente bene per rimediare alla mia estrema debolezza, havrei caro che V. S. mi somministrassi qualche quattrino per provvedere a i miei bisogni, che sono tanti che a me saria troppo faticoso l'annoverargli et a lei quasi impossibile in altra maniera il sovvenirgli. Solo gli dirò che la provvisione che ci dà, il monastero è di pane assai cattivo, di carne di bue, e di vino che va in fortezza. Io mi godo il suo, del quale ne ho ancora un fiasco e mezzo; e non me ne fa di bisogno per ancora, perchè bevo pochissimo. Basta, lo partecipo anco con le altre, come è il dovere, e particolarmente con Suor Luisa, alla quale gustò fuor di modo l'ultimo fiasco the V. S. mandò, che fu assai chiaro, ciò è di poco colore e assai valore.

Se nel suo pollaio si trovass[i] una gallina che non fossi buona per uova, sarebbe buona per farmi del brodo, che devo pigliar alterato. In tanto, non havendo altro, gli mando 12 fette di pasta reale, acciò se la goda per mio amore; e la saluto, insieme con tutte le amiche e particolarmente la Madre

Most Beloved Lord Father,

With the greatest happiness did I learn the other day that you fare well, Sire, although the same fortune has not followed me, as I have been confined to bed since Sunday with a fever, which (according to what the doctor says) would have been quite serious, had it not been for a sudden sweat that stopped the fever's rise and by this point has even lowered it some small amount. Now that blessed God has seen fit to keep me alive, Sire, I am availing myself of my ability, appealing to you in my neediness, confident that day after day you will minister to me with your gracious loving tenderness; and especially now that I find I must care for myself moderately well in order to overcome my extreme weakness, I would so appreciate it, Sire, if you could send me a few farthings to provide for my needs, which are so numerous that it would exhaust me just to count them, and perhaps impossible for you to assist me with them in any other fashion. I will say only that the provisions currently given to us in the convent consist of moldy bread, ox meat, and wine that has turned sour; I enjoy your wine, of which I still have one full flask and another half, and I do not need any more just yet, because I drink so little. There is enough for me to share it with the others as is proper, and in particular with Suor Luisa, who found the last flask you sent unusually good, being so very clear, by which I mean it was of little color and great quality.

Suor Luisa is Suor Maria Celeste's dearest friend and co-worker in the apothecary.

If you happen to have a hen in your poultry run that is no longer fit for laying eggs, I might make good use of her for soup, because it is helpful for me to drink weak broth. Meanwhile, not having any more to say, I send you twelve sweet pasbadessa, mia molto cortese e favorevole amicha. Nostro Signore la conser[vi].

Sua Fig.^{la} Aff.^{ma}

Suor M. Celeste

Amatiss.^{mo} Sig.^{r} Padre,

Credo veramente che l'amor paterno in verso de i figliuoli possa in parte diminuirsi mediante i mali costumi e portamenti loro; e questa mia credenza vien confermata da qualche indizio che me ne dà V. S., parendomi che più presto vadia in qualche parte scemando quel cordiale affetto che per l'addietro ha in verso di noi dimostrato, poi che sta tre mesi per volta senza venire a visitarne, che a noi paion tre anni, et anco da un pezzo in qua, mentre però si ritrova con sanità, non mi scrive mai mai un verso. Ho fatta buona esamina per conoscere se dalla banda mia ci fossi caduto qualche errore che meritassi questo castigo, et uno ne ritrovo (ancorchè involontario); e questo è una trascuraggine o spensieritaggine ch'io dimostro verso di lei, mentre non ho quella sollecitudine che richiederebbe l'obligo mio, di visitarla et salutarla più spesso con qualche mia lettera: onde questo mio mancamento, accompagnato da molti demeriti che per altro ci sono, è bastante a somministrarmi il timore sopra accennatoli, se bene appresso di me non a difetto può attribuirsi; ma più tosto a debolezza di forze, mentre che la mia continua indispositione m'impedisce il poter esercitarmi in cosa alcuna, e già più d'un mese ho travagliato con dolori di testa tanto eccessivi, che nè giorno nè notte trovavo riposo. Adesso che, tries for you to enjoy with my love; and I send you regards together with all my companions here and the Mother Abbess, my most kind and pleasant friend. May our Lord bless you.

Your Most Affectionate Daughter,

Suor M. Celeste

Most Beloved Lord Father,

I truly believe that the love of a father toward his sons and daughters may be diminished somewhat, on account of the children's own bad habits or behavior; and this belief of mine grows stronger in the light of several indications you give me, Sire, for I discern a waning of the warm affection you have shown us in the past; now that you have let three months go by without coming to visit us, which feels to us like three years, and all the more worrisome, since even now that you have recovered your good health, you never write to me. I have looked within myself, to see if some error committed on my part might call down this punishment, and I do see one (albeit involuntary), which I would call a heedlessness or thoughtlessness I may give way to, when I neglect my duty to visit you and greet you more often through my letters; this particular failing of mine, accompanied as it is by my many other shortcomings, surely justifies and sustains the fear that I mentioned to you above. Although, as I see it, my negligence should not be attributed to a weakness of my character, but rather to a lack of physical strength, precipitated by a long-standing indisposition that renders me unable to perform any of my duties; for more than a month now I have suffered headaches so severe that I could find no respite day or

Unbeknownst to Suor Maria Celeste, Galileo has just fallen gravely ill.

per gratia del Signore, sono mitigati, ho subito presa la penna per scriverle questa lunga lamentatione, che, per esser di carnevale, può più tosto dirsi una burla. Basta in somma che V. S. si ricordi che desideriamo di rivederla, quando il tempo lo permetterà; in tanto gli mando alcune poche confetioni che mi sono state donate: saranno alquanto indurite, havendole io serbate parecchi giorni con speranza di dargliene alla presenza. I berlingozzi sono per l'Anna Maria e suoi fratellini. Gli mando una lettera per Vincenzio, acciò questa gli riduca a memoria che siamo al mondo, perchè dubito ch'egli non se lo sia scordato, poi che non ci scrive mai un verso. Salutiamo per fime. V. S. e la zia di tutto cuore, et da Nostro Signore gli prego vero contento. Di S. Matteo, li 4 di Marzo 1627.

Di V. S. molto Ill.re Aff.ma Fig.la

S.r M.a Celeste

Amatiss.mo Sig.r Padre,

Perchè non saprei indovinare che cosa potessi mandargli che gli gustassi, ho pensato che forse gli sarà più grato qualche cosa per presentare alla Sig.ra Barbera et altre che la governano, alle quali ancora io (per amor di V. S.) mi confesso molto obligata. Per questo adunque gli mando queste poche paste, acciò le godino per amor nostro in questi giorni di digiuno; et se V. S. ne mandassi a chieder qualche cosa che gli fossi di gusto, non potrebbe farne maggior gratia di questa, che pur desideriamo d'esser buone in qualche minima cosa per lei.

night. But now that my pain has abated, by the Lord's grace, I take my pen in hand to write you this long lamentation, which, in the spirit of this Carnival season, may simply be dismissed as a joke. Suffice it to say that you recall, Sire, how much we are longing to see you again, when time will allow a visit; meanwhile I send you several little treats that were given to me. They will be somewhat hard, as I have set them aside for a few days in the hope of giving them to you in person. The ring cakes are for Anna Maria and her little brothers. I enclose a letter for Vincenzio, to jog his memory that we are still alive, which he seems to have forgotten, as he never writes us a line. Lastly we send loving regards to you and our Aunt with all our hearts, and from Our Lord I pray for your true happiness. From San Matteo, the 4th of March 1627.

Sire's Most Affectionate Daughter,

S. M. Celeste

The word "Carnival" derives from the Latin ***carnelevarium****, meaning abstention from meat, and refers to the weeks from Epiphany on January 6 through Mardi Gras ("Fat Tuesday") at the end of February, until Lent begins on Ash Wednesday.*

Most Beloved Lord Father,

Not knowing what in the world I might possibly send you to please you most, I thought perhaps you would like something you could present to Signora Barbera and your other caretakers, to whom I, too, confess (out of my love for you, Sire) that I am very much obliged. Therefore I send along these small pastries, for all of you to enjoy together with our love in these days of Lenten sacrifice; and if you would send us word, Sire, of whatever it is you might wish to have, you could do us no greater favor, since our hearts' desire is simply to be good to you in every way.

A letter from Michelangelo in Munich, written later this same week to Galileo in Florence, also salutes Signora Barbera, in whose lodgings Galileo seems to have taken refuge while ill.

Hieri mi cavai un altro dente, che mi dava grandissimo travaglio, sì che adesso, lo per gratia del Signore, resto libera da i dolori che per due mesi m'hanno tormentata, ancorchè resto ancora con la testa non troppo sana. Spero però, con progresso di qualche poco di tempo, di dover restarne libera, se piacerà a Dio, il quale io prego che a V. S. conceda perfetta sanità; et per fine a lei, a Vincenzio, alla zia et a tutti di casa mi raccomando, insieme con S.r Arcangela. Di S. Matteo, li 18 di Marzo 1627.

Di V. S. Fig.la Aff.ma

S.r M.a Celeste

Amatiss.mo Sig.r Padre,

Gli mando l'acqua di cannella, che, per esser fatta di fresco, non so se gli piacerà. Se non ha più stillato, potrà far render la guastada al nostro fattore, chè gliene manderò dell'altro; et se la pera cotta gl'è gustata, lo dica, chè ne accomoderò un'altra; ma dubito che, mediante la stagione, non siano adesso poco buone.

Saluto la zia et tutti di casa; non dico Vincenzio, perchè non so se sia partito; havrò ben caro d'intenderlo. V. S, stia allegramente, acciò posai guarir presto affatto et venir da noi, sì come lo desideriamo et ella c'ha promesso; et se gl'occorre qual cosa, avvisi. Il Signore gli doni la Sua santa gratia. Di S. Matteo, li 22 di Marzo 1627.

Di V. S Fig.la Aff.ma

S.r M.a Celeste

Yesterday I pulled a tooth of mine that had been causing me tremendous suffering, so that now by the grace of the Lord I am free of the pain that has tormented me the last two months, although I still have the remnants of my headache. I hope, however, with the passage of time, to be relieved of this, too, if it pleases God, whom I pray to grant you, Sire, a complete recovery; and in closing I send loving regards to you, to Vincenzio, to Aunt Chiara and to everyone else at home, from Suor Arcangela and me. From San Matteo, the 18th of March 1627.

Sire's Most Affectionate Daughter,

S. M. Celeste

Most Beloved Lord Father,

Here is the cinnamon water, which I fear may not be to your liking, as it is quite freshly made. If you have no more of the distilled, you can return the carafe via our steward so that I can send you the other; and if the cooked pear pleases you, only say so, and I will secure you another; but I doubt that, considering the season, they will be very good from now on.

Fragrant, utilitarian cinnamon water combats diarrhea, flatulence, and vomiting.

Please remember me to my aunt and the whole household; I do not mention Vincenzio because I am uncertain whether he is still with you; I would very much like to hear his whereabouts and how he is faring. Be happy, Sire, in the knowledge that you will soon effect a complete cure, and be able to come and see us, fulfilling both our desire and your promise to us, and, if you think of anything you need, do tell us what it is.

Amatiss.mo Sig.r Padre,

Non potendo io assisterle con la persona, sì come sarebbe il mio desiderio (che non per altro mi pare alquanto difficile la clausura), non tralascio già d'accompagnarla continuamente con il pensiero et desiderio di sentirne nuove ogni giorno; et perchè hier l'altro il fattore non potette vederla, lo rimando oggi, con scusa di mandargli due morselletti di cedro. In tanto V. S. potrà dirgli se vuol qual cosa da noi, et se la pera cotogna glè niente piaciuta, acciò possa accomodarne un'altra. Finisco, per non noiarla di soverchio, senza finir mai di raccomandarmeli e di pregar Nostro Signore per la sua intiera sanità; et il simile fa Suor Arcangela et l'altre amiche. Li 24 di Marzo 1627.

Sua Fig.la Aff.ma
S.r M.a Celeste

Amatiss.mo Sig.r Padre,

L'allegrezza che sentiamo del suo progresso in sanità é inestimabile, et con tutto il cuore ne ringratiamo il Signore Iddio, dator d'ogni bene.

May Our Lord grant you His holy grace. From San Matteo, the 22nd of March 1627.

Sire's Most Affectionate Daughter,

S. M. Celeste

Most Beloved Lord Father,

Prohibited as I am from tending to you in person, despite my great desire to do so (this separation being the only difficulty I experience in cloistered life), I never fail to keep you a constant companion in my thoughts and through my efforts to hear news of you every day; and because the steward was unable to see you the day before yesterday, I send him back today, with the excuse of delivering these two candied citron morsels. While he is there, Sire, you can let him know if you want anything from us, and whether the quince pear was at all to your liking, in which case I can furnish another. I will stop here, so as not to overburden you, though of course I never stop the flow of my loving regards, or my prayers for your perfect health, in which I am joined by Suor Arcangela and your many friends here. The 24th of March 1627.

Your Most Affectionate Daughter,

S. M. Celeste

Most Beloved Lord Father,

The happiness we feel at the news of your good progress in convalescence is inestimable, and with all our hearts we thank the Lord God, giver of every blessing.

Per non trasgredir al suo comandamento tanto amorevole, gli dico ch'io, per comandamento del medico, non fo quaresima, et che, per esser sdentata avanti tempo, havrò caro s'ella mi manderà un poca di carne di castrato, che sia grassa, chè pur di questa ne mangio qualche poca. Suor Arcangela si contenta di qualche cosetta per far colatione la sera; et particolarmente un poco di vino bianco ci sarà molto grato. Tanto gli dico per obedirla; e certo che resto confusa ch'ella mentre si ritrova indisposta, pigli di noi tanto pensiero: ma non si può dir altro se non ch'ella è padre, e padre amorevolissimo, nel quale, dopo Dio benedetto, è riposta ogni nostra speranza. Piaccia pur all'istesso Signore di conservarcelo ancora, se così è per sua salute. Et qui per fine me le raccomando di cuore. Di S. Matteo, li 25 di Marzo 1628.

Sua Fig.la Aff.ma

Suor M.a Celeste

Amatiss.mo Sig.r Padre,

I cedrati mandatimi da V. S. accomoderò conforme al suo gusto molto volentieri: et per farne l'agro et i morselletti penso che vi bisogneranno dua libre di zucchero e, caso che gli sia di gusto, un poco di musco buono. Il tutto mi sarà caro, perchè mi ritrovo assai scarsa di danari: et se vuole che gl'accomodi dei fiori di ramerino, che tanto soglion gustarli, potrà mandar più quantità di zucchero.

So as not to transgress against your commandment, so lovingly issued, for a full account of our health, I tell you that I am following the doctor's orders by not observing Lent, and that, being already mostly toothless at my age, I will be very pleased if you can send me some fatty mutton, for surely I can manage to eat that. Suor Arcangela contents herself with picking at a few little things for her evening meal; what she would particularly appreciate is a little white wine. This much I tell you to obey you, though I for one cannot fathom how you manage, even now while you find yourself indisposed, to think so much of us and our needs; but there is nothing to be said about it except that you are our father, our most tender, loving father, upon whom, after blessed God, we rely for our every hope. May it please that same blessed Lord to keep you with us still, in the fullness of health. And closing here I send you my love. From San Matteo, the 25th of March 1628.

In Tuscany, the New Year begins today.

Your Most Affectionate Daughter,

Suor M. Celeste

Most Beloved Lord Father,

The citrons that you sent me, Sire, I will transform to your taste most willingly: and in order to make them into marmalade and candies, I think I will need about two pounds of sugar, and, if you enjoy the flavor, a little bit of must wine; all of this will be too expensive for me because I find myself so short of money: also if you want me to prepare you a preserve of rosemary flowers, which has been such a favorite of yours, then please send even more sugar.

Must, or new wine, can be boiled into a syrup the thickness and sweetness of honey.

La sottocoppa non l'haviamo havuta; ma costì vi hanno bene di nostro una guastada et una piattellina bianca.

Non vorrei già ch'ella si prendessi tanto pensiero di noi, ma più tosto attenda a proccurar di conservarsi in sanità; et di gratia, quando ritorna in villa, lasci di star nell'orto, fino che non siano miglior tempi, perohè credo che questo gl'habbia nociuto assai. Perchè ho molta fretta, finisco, e la saluto con tutto il cuore. Il Signore gli conceda la Sua gratia.

Sua Fig.la Aff.ma
Suor M.a Celeste

Aspetto il zucchero quanto prima, perchè i cedri patirebbono; et se per sorte gliene venissi qualcun altro alle mani, mi sarà gratissimo per un altro mio bisogno, che gli dirò a bocca, che non vedo l'ora.

Amatiss.mo Sig.r Padre,

Il tempo d'oggi, tanto quieto, mi dava mezza speranza di riveder V. S. Poi che non è venuta, ci è stata molto cara la venuta del gratioso Albertino, havendoci egli dato nuova che V. S. sta bene et che presto verrà a vederci insieme con la zia; ma (questo *ma* guasta ogni cosa) quel sentire ch'ella sia ritornata così presto al solito esercitio dell'orto mi dispiace non poco, perchè, essendo ancora l'aria assai cruda e V. S. debole dal male, dubito che non gli faccia danno. Di gratia, V. S. non si scordi così presto in che termine ella sia stata, et habbia un

We did not have the saucer you are missing; but I do believe that you have a pitcher of ours, and a little white dish.

I would rather you not preoccupy yourself so soon with concern for us; but rather attend to regaining and conserving your own health; and please, when you return home, I implore you to leave the garden to its own devices, at least until the weather improves, because I fear that this working outdoors has done you considerable harm: since I am in a hurry, I end here, and send you regards with all my heart. May the Lord grant you His blessing.

Your Most Affectionate Daughter,
Suor M. Celeste

I await the sugar as soon as possible, lest the citrons spoil, and if per chance another one should come into your hands, I would be most happy to have that, as well, to fill another need of mine, which I will tell you about in person, and I can hardly wait to do so.

Most Illustrious Lord Father,

Something in the peaceful air today gave me half a hope of seeing you again, Sire. Since you did not come, we were most pleased with the arrival of adorable little Albertino, along with our aunt, giving us news that you are well and that you will soon be here to see us; yet my delight was all but destroyed when I learned that you have already returned to your usual labors in the garden, leaving me considerably disturbed; since the air is still quite raw, Sire, and you still weak from your recent illness, I fear this activity will do you harm.

Albertino, or Alberto Cesare Galilei, age ten, is the eldest of her cousins still staying with Galileo at Bellosguardo.

poco d'amore più a sè stessa che all'orto; ancor ch'io creda che non per amore che habbia all'orto, ma per il gusto che ne piglia, si metta a questo risico. Ma in questo tempo di quaresima par che si convenga far qualche mortificatione: V. S. facci questa, privisi per qualche poco di questo gusto.

Scrissi l'altro giorno a V. S., che se per sorte haveva qualche altro cedro, mi sarebbe stato grato; et hora di nuovo la prego, che se havessi comodità di provvedermene uno o due, mi farebbe grandissimo piacere; quando non fossino nostrali, non importerebbe; perchè, dovendo il Cavalier Marzi, che è tornato nostro governatore, venir a darne l'acqua santa questa settimana santa, siamo in obligo, Suor Luisa et io, di regalarlo di qualche galanteria nella nostra bottega, et vorremmo farli 4 di quei morselletti che tanto gli piacciono. Quelli di V. S. non sono ancora asciutti, perchè il tempo non mi ha servito se non oggi.

Gli mando parecchie uve accomodate, e 6 pine che saranno per i ragazzi. La ringratio della carne, e perchè sto adesso tanto bene, penso di ripigliar la quaresima venerdì prossimo; perciò V. S. non piglierà pensiero di mandarmene più. Per fine la saluto, insieme con la zia. Dio benedetto la feliciti.

Sua Fig.la Aff.ma

Suor M.a Celeste

Please, Sire, do not forget so quickly the dire straits you were in, and have a little more love for yourself than for the garden; although I suppose it is not for love of the garden per se, but rather the joy you draw from it, that you put yourself at such risk. But in this season of Lent, when one is expected to make certain sacrifices, make this one, Sire: deprive yourself for a short while of the pleasure of the garden.

I wrote to you the other day to say that if by chance you had any more citrons, I would be most happy to have them and now I entreat you again, Sire, for if you could provide me with one or two, I would really be extremely pleased; if they are not your own homegrown ones, that will not matter, for what with Cavalier Marzi, who has become our Governor, due here this holy week to give us the holy water, Suor Luisa and I feel obligated to make him a gift of some of the specialties of our shop; and we were hoping to make him 4 of those delicacies he likes so much; the ones we made for you, Sire, are not yet dry, because the weather has not cooperated until today.

I send you a few preserved grapes, and 6 pine cones for the children. I thank you for the meat, and because I am feeling so well now, I expect to resume the observance of Lent next Friday, and for that reason, Sire, you must not think of sending me any more: to close I offer my loving regards to you and to my Aunt; may blessed God grant you happiness.

Your Most Affectionate Daughter,

Suor M. Celeste

Amatiss.mo Sig.r Padre,

La ringratiamo infinitamente, Suor Luisa et io, de i cedri, a noi gratissimi, a sì perchè vengono da lei, sì anco perchè non havevamo miglior mezzo per haverli.

I cibi da quaresima ci sono stati gratissimi, e particolarmente a Suor Arcangela. Io vivo tanto regolatamente, per desiderio che ho di star sana, che V. S. non deve dubitare ch'io disordini; e dell'vuova ne mangerò per obedirla. Le immagini mi sono state molto care, et havrò caro che quando V. S. risponde alla Mechilde, la ringratii per nostra parte et gli renda dupplicate salute.

Rimando i collari de i regazzi, et nel fondo della paniera vi sono 8 morselletti, et due ne haviamo presi per noi, già ch'ella, per sua amorevolezza, ce li concede. Ho fatto anco (del zucchero che mandò) un poca di conserva di agro di cedro e di quella di fiori di ramerino, ma non sono ancora in ordine per poterli mandare.

Mi rallegro del suo progresso in sanità, et prego Nostro Signore che gliele renda perfettamente, se è per il meglio. Et per fine me le raccomando, insieme con Suor Arcangela e Suor Luisa. (La zia, ci si intende.) Li 8 d'Aprile 1628.

Sua. Fig.la Aff.ma

Suor M.a Celeste

Most Beloved Lord Father,

We thank you a thousand times (Suor Luisa and I) for the citrons that pleased us so much, partly because they came from you, and partly also because we could have had no better means of getting them.

We all enjoyed your Lenten dishes very much, and Suor Arcangela most of all. I am living in such a regimented manner, out of a desire to stay healthy, that you need not suspect any dietary infractions, Sire, and I promise I will obey your proscription against eating eggs. You can imagine how concerned I was, and how much it still means to me, that when you write back to Mechilde, you thank her on our behalf and return her good wishes doubled.

Mechilde, the eldest daughter of Uncle Michelangelo and Aunt Anna Chiara, has already returned to Munich.

I am returning the children's collars, and at the bottom of the basket there are 8 little sweetmeats, and knowing that you would want to share these with us in your loving way, we took the liberty of setting two aside for ourselves. I have also made (from the sugar you sent) a little bit each of the sour citron marmalade and the rosemary flower conserve, but they are not quite ready yet to send you.

I rejoice in the improvement of your health, and I pray our Lord to return you to a state of perfect well-being, if that be for the best. And, to end, I send you heartfelt greetings together with Suor Arcangela and Suor Luisa. (And of course we send regards to our aunt.)   The 8th of April 1628.

Your Most Affectionate Daughter,

Suor M. Celeste

Amatiss.mo Sig.r Padre,

La liberalità et amorevolezza di V. S. in alcuna maniera non compatisce d'esser paragonata con l'avaritia del Papazzoni, ma più tosto (quando ci fossin forze corrispondenti all'animo) a quella di Alessandro Magno; o, per dir meglio, io, quanto a me, assomiglierei V. S. al pellicano, che sì come egli per sostentar i suoi figliuoli sviscera sè stesso, così lei per sovvenire alle necessità di noi sue care figliuole non havrebbe riguardo di privar sè stessa di cosa a lei necessaria. Hor quanto meno dovrò io dubitare che gli dia molestia il pensiero di dovermi mandare 3 o 4 libre di zucchero, acciò ch'io possa condir per lei i cedri mandatimi? Certo ch'io non temo punto che questo pensiero et affanno habbia havuto forza di causargli una minima palpitation di cuore, et con questa sicurtà ho tardato a dargli risposta; oltre che, sopragiungendo il medico (appunto quando mi ero messa a scrivere), chiamato da me per causa della nostra maestra che si ritrova ammalata già sono parecchi giorni, e convenendomi assister a lei e doppo a tre altre ammalate, mi fu impossibile il poter all'hora satisfare all'obligo mio, già che in quell'atione non mi era lecito mandar altri in mio scambio. Scusimi per ciò V. S. della tardanza: et la prego che per carità mi mandi (per detta mia maestra) questo fiaschetto pieno di vino di casa sua; che basta che non sia agro, già che il medico glielo vieta, et il nostro del convento è assai crudo.

Ancora desidero di sapere se V. S. potessi farmi havere da Pisa, quando vi sarà fiera, parecchie braccia di calisse per due monache poverette che mi si raccomandano. Caso ch'ella possi farmi il servitio, manderò la mostra e otto scudi, che

Most Beloved Lord Father,

Your generosity and loving tenderness, Sire, represent the furthest possible remove from the avarice of Pappazzoni; indeed your virtue more closely recalls (if spirit could be equated with strength) that of Alexander the Great. Or better still, if it were up to me, I would compare you to the pelican, Sire, for just as he eviscerates himself in order to sustain his children, so do you, in like manner, deprive yourself of any necessity, without a thought for your own welfare, in order to cover every contingency for us, your beloved daughters. Now how could I not conclude that you are consumed by the thought of needing to send me three or four pounds of sugar, so that I can candy the citrons you sent me? Certainly I do not fear that this preoccupation and anxiety could be strong enough to cause you any palpitation of the heart, and thus assured I have held off responding to you. Not to mention being overtaken by the doctor (just when I had set myself to writing) whom I had called because my mistress is sick again, for several days now, and it is up to me to take care of her, as well as tend the three others who are ill, with the result that I have found it impossible to discharge my regular duties, since in this instance it would have been improper to send another to take my place. Therefore excuse me, Sire, for my tardiness, and pray be good enough to fill this little flask (according to my mistress's wishes) full of your house wine: as long as it is not sour it will do, since the doctor forbids her to drink much, and ours at the convent is surely worse.

Flaminio Papazzoni gained the chair of philosophy at Pisa with Galileo's help in 1610, and died there in 1614. Galileo apparently considered him a legendary miser.

I still want to know, Sire, if you might be able to get me a few yards of that inexpensive wool cloth from Pisa, when they hanno voluto già consegnarmi per questo effetto. Perchè ho molta fretta, non dico altro, se non che prego Nostro Signore che gli doni la Sua santa gratia; et a lei, alla zia e a tutti i rabacchini mi raccomando. Di S. Matteo, li 10 d'Aprile 1628.

Sua Fig.la Aff.ma

Suor M.a Celeste

Amatiss.mo Sig.r Padre,

I cedrati sono bellissimi, e della vista loro mi compiaccio assai, sì come anco della diligenza e manifattura che si ricerca in accomodarli, sì perchè questo esercitio mi gusta, e molto più perchè ho occasione d'impiegarmi in servitio di V. S., cosa a me più grata che altra del mondo.

Gli mando l'altro barattolo di conserva di fiori di ramerino, che appunto havevo fatto del zucchero avanzatomi de i morselletti, li quali non sono ancora in stagione ch'io glieli possa mandare, sì come anco l'agro, il quale non è però riuscito male affatto.

Quanto alla quantità del zucchero che ricercano i vasetti simili a questo che gli mando, non vuol esser manco di sei once per ciascuno, anzi che l'altro che gli mandai ne prese sette; e credami che non dico la bugia, se bene ho detto in caffo, come si suol dire in proverbio: ma V. S. vuol la burla meco, perchè sa bene che non gli direi bugie, in questo genere in hold the fair there, as a favor to two poor little nuns who have asked for my help. In the event that you can do me this service, I will send you the description and eight *scudi* that they have already insisted on giving me to pay for it. Because I am very rushed I will say no more, except that I pray our Lord to grant you His holy grace, and I send my loving wishes to you, to my aunt, and to all the little rabble-rousers. From San Matteo, the 10th of April 1628.

Your Most Affectionate Daughter,
Suor M. Celeste

Most Illustrious Lord Father,

The citrons you sent seem so very beautiful that I derive delight simply from beholding them, as well as from the diligence and workmanship required to prepare them properly; thus this endeavor brings me deep pleasure, and all the more so because I have occasion to employ myself in your service, Sire, which I find more agreeable than any other occupation in the world.

Here is the remaining jar of rosemary flower jam, just freshly made out of the sugar left over from the candied citrons, which I deem not quite ready yet to send to you, and the same is true for the citron marmalade, although I must say it turned out rather well.

As for the amount of sugar I need, it should fill several jars the size of this one I send you now, not less than six ounces each, although the other one I sent you held seven, and believe me I am not far wrong in my figures, even if I speak particolare. In tanto, se V. S. ha votati 3 vasi di vetro che ha di mio, potrà mandarmeli quando manderà i fiori, acciò li possa riempiere. Et vorrei anco che facessi una buona rifrusta per casa, adesso che si dà l'acqua santa, e se vi fossi qualche vasetto o ampolle vote, che siano per la spetieria, si levassi questo impaccio, che a noi servirebbono di gratia, o qualche scatola: basta, V. S. m'intende.

Quanto a i cantucci, faremo il conto che ne avvisa V. S., già che la quaresima è finita. Gli mando un poca di pasta reale per sè, e quattro pasterelle per i ragazzi. La ringratio del vino, il quale participerò con la nonna e amiche, chè veramente non è per me. La saluto con tutto l'affe[tto], insieme con la zia, e prego il Signore che la conservi. Li 19 d'Aprile.

Sua Fig.la Aff.ma

Suor M.a Celeste

Amatiss.mo Sig.r Padre,

Ringratiamo V. S. delle sue molte amorevolezze, le quali ci goderemo per suo amore.

I fiori che ha mandati, al mio conto faranno 4 barattoli; et perchè sono assai umidi, aspetteremo gl'altri, già che gl'adopriamo alquanto appassiti e V. S. dice volergli mandare. Vo appunto adesso lavorando intorno a i duoi cedri mandatimi ultimamente, che credo riusciranno meglio de gl'altri.

off the top of my head, as the saying goes: but surely you jest with me, Sire, for you well know I would not lie to you, especially in such a matter as this. Meanwhile, if you have emptied my three glass containers, you may return them when you send the additional flowers, so that I can refill them. And I would also like you to conduct a thorough search of your house, Sire, as it is time to make gifts of holy water, and if you were to find a few more empty bottles or vials that might do for the apothecary, I should gladly take them off your hands, for they would be most welcome here, or a few boxes: but enough, Sire, you understand me.

We made these *cantucci* according to your recipe, now that Lent is over. Here, too, is some marzipan pastry for you, Sire, and four little treats for the boys. I thank you for the wine, which I shall share with *la nonna* and our friends, because truly it is not my drink. I send you and aunt all my love, and I pray the Lord to bless you. The 19th of April.

Cantucci *are biscuits made of fine flour with sugar and egg whites.*

La nonna is the ailing mistress for whom she requested the wine.

Your Most Affectionate Daughter,

Suor M. Celeste

Most Beloved Lord Father,

We thank you, Sire, for your many expressions of thoughtfulness, all of which we will enjoy through your love.

The flowers that you sent, by my count, will make four jars of jam, and, because they are very damp, we will wait for the others to arrive, since we prefer to use somewhat drier ones, and you say, Sire, that you want to send more. Right now I am about to start work on the two citrons that came from you

Gl'annuntio felicissima la santissima Pasqua, questo e molti anni appresso, e me le raccomando di tutto cuore insieme con Suor Arcangela.

Sua Fig.la Aff.ma

Suor M.a Celeste

Amatiss.mo Sig.r Padre,

L'haver visto, qualche giorno adietro, il tempo assai quieto, e che V. S. non sia venuta da noi, mi fa sospettare, o ch'ella non si senta troppo bene, o vero che sia andata a Pisa. Per certificarmene mando questa donna costì, et con questa occasione gli mando tutti i morselletti che ho fatti: quelli cinque separati da gl'altri sono de i due cedrati che mandò ultimamente, e credo che saranno di maggior bontà de gl'altri, sì per esser stati migliori i cedri e più freschi, come anco perchè è il zucchero più raffinato, che perciò sono anco più bianchi; et me l'ha donato Suor Luisa, già che del suo non ne havevo più. Dubito che. V. S. non si sia scordata di mandarmi gl'altri fiori di ramerino, i quali aspetto ogni giorno, sì come mi disse V. S. nell'ultima sua: glieli ricordo, perchè penso che siano per durar poco.

Se V. S. va a Pisa avanti che venga a vederci, si ricordi del mio servitio, ciò è del calisse del quale già gl'ho trattato. Vorrei anco che V. S. vedessi se per sorte havessi in casa da mandarmi un pochetto di lucchesino, tanto che mi facessi un panno da stomaco, perchè adesso, che si cavano gl'altri panni most recently, which I believe will turn out better than the others.

I wish you great happiness for the most holy festival of Easter, this year and for many more to come, and I send you regards with all my heart together with Suor Arcangela.

Your Most Affectionate Daughter,

Suor M. Celeste

Most Beloved Lord Father,

Looking back over the past few days of this quiet time, and seeing that you have not yet come to us, Sire, makes me suspect that either you are not feeling very well or you have truly left for Pisa. To find out for certain, I dispatch this good woman to you, and seize the opportunity to have her carry along all the sweetmeats I have made; those five that are wrapped separately come from the two citrons you sent most recently, and I believe they will prove to be of much higher quality than the rest, since these particular citrons were the best and the freshest, and also the sugar I used was more refined, which makes the confection look whiter, and this sugar was a gift from Suor Luisa, now that I have no more of yours left. I wonder if you have forgotten, Sire, about the other flowers of rosemary, whose arrival I anticipate daily, since you said in your last letter that you would send them. I remind you now because I think they last only a short while.

And if you do go to Pisa before you come to see us, Sire, please remember the favor I asked you, regarding the fabric. I would also like for you to see if by chance you might have da verno, patisco assai, per haver lo stomaco fredo e debole. Perchè mi ritrovo molto occupata, non dico altro, se non che me le raccomando di tutto cuore, et prego il Signore che gli conceda vera felicità. Di S. Matteo, li 28 d'Aprile 1628.

Sua Fig.la Aff.ma

Suor M.a Celeste

Amatiss.mo Sig.r Padre,

Essendo io stata tanto senza scriverle, V. S. potrebbe facilmente giudicare ch'io havessi dimenticato, sì come potrei io sospettare ch'ella havessi smarrita la strada per venir a visitarci, poi che è tanto tempo che non ha per essa caminato; ma sì come son certa che non tralascio di scriverle per la causa sudetta, ma sì bene per penuria e carestia di tempo, del quale non ho mai un'hora che sia veramente mia, così mi giova di creder ch'ella non per dimenticanza, ma sì bene per altri impedimenti, lasci di venir da noi; e tanto più adesso che Vincenzio nostro viene in suo scambio, e con questo c'acquetiamo, havendo da esso nuove sicure di V. S., le quali tutte mi sono di gusto, eccetto quella per la quale o intendo ch'ella va la mattina nell'orto: questa veramente mi dispiace fuor di modo, parendomi che V. S. sì procacci qualche male stravagante e fastidioso, sì come l'altra invernata gl'intervenne. Di gratia, privisi di questo gusto che torna in tanto suo danno; et se non vuol farlo per amor suo, faccilo almeno per amor di noi suoi figliuoli, che desideriamo di vederla giugner alla about your house and could send me a bit of *lucchesino* big enough to make a stomach coverlet, because now that the time has come to put away the winter blankets, I suffer greatly from having a cold and weak stomach. Since I find myself very busy I will not say more, except that I greet you with all my heart, and pray the Lord to grant you true happiness. From San Matteo, the 28th of April 1628.

Your Most Affectionate Daughter,

Suor M. Celeste

Lucchesino *is a type of woolen fabric dyed red.*

Most Beloved Lord Father,

As I have not written to you in quite some time, Sire, you might easily assume I had forgotten, as in like manner I might suppose you had lost your way en route to visit us, since you have not walked that road in such a long while: but just as I know that I do not neglect writing to you for the aforesaid reason, but only on account of a constant and extreme shortage of time, of which I can never count a single hour truly mine, so in the same sense it behooves me to believe that you, not from forgetfulness, but under the pressure of other impediments leave off coming here; and this is easier to bear now that our Vincenzio visits in your stead, and we are appeased by having such a reliable source for good reports of you, all of which please me, except the part I hear about your going to the garden every morning; this news upsets me more than a little, as it seems to me that you will reap some strange and troublesome illness there, as came to pass last winter. Please renounce this recreation of yours that always repays you so ruinously; and if you will not do so out of love for yourself, decrepità; il che non succederà, s'ella così si disordina. Dico questo per pratica, perchè ogni poco ch'io stia ferma all'aria scoperta mi nuoce alla testa grandemente: hor quanto più farà danno a lei?

Quando Vincenzio fu ultimamente da noi, Suor Chiara gli domandò 8 o 10 melarance; adesso ella torna a dimandarle a V. S., se sono mediocremente mature, havendo a servirsene lunedì mattina.

Gli rimando il suo piatto, drentovi una pera cotta, che credo non le spiacerà, e questa poca pasta reale.

Se hanno collari da imbiancare, potranno mandarli insieme con un'altra paniera e coperta che hanno di nostro. Saluto V. S. e Vincenzio molto affettuosamente, et il simile fanno Suor Arcangela e le altre di camera. Il Signore gli conceda la Sua santa gratia. Di S. Matteo, il giorno di S. Martino del 1628.

Di V. S. Fig.^{la} Aff.^{ma}
Suor M.ª Celeste

Amatiss.^{mo} Sig.^{r} Padre,

Dovrei continuamente ringratiar Iddio benedetto, il quale, compiacendosi di visitarmi con qualche travaglio, insieme insieme mi dà molte consolationi; una delle quali, anzi la maggior in questo mondo, è il mantener in vita V. S., e mantenerla, dico, con pronta volontà di sovvenirmi in ogni mio bisogno:

then do it out of love for us, your children, who want to see you live to an advanced old age; which will not happen if you tax yourself thusly. I speak from personal experience, because every time I stay outdoors I suffer a terrible headache: think how much more harshly the air may punish you!

When Vincenzio was last here with us, Suor Chiara asked him for eight or ten Portuguese oranges; now she comes to ask them of you, Sire, if they are at all ripe, as she needs them for Monday morning.

I am returning your covered dish, with a cooked pear inside it, which I do not think will displease you, as well as this little bit of sweet almond pastry.

If you have collars to be whitened, you can send them together with that other covered basket you have of ours. I offer my loving greetings to you, Sire, and to Vincenzio, and Suor Arcangela does the same along with the others here. May the Lord grant you His holy grace. From San Matteo, St. Martin's Day of 1628.

Sire's Most Affectionate Daughter,

Suor M. Celeste

The date of the feast day of Saint Martin of Tours, the fourth-century champion of monastic life who performed acts of great charity, is November 11.

Most Beloved Lord Father,

I should be continuously thanking blessed God, who, seeing fit to visit me with a few pains, gives me at the same time many consolations, one of which, or rather the greatest one in the world, is keeping you in my life, Sire, and keeping you, I must add, with ready willingness to help me in my every need, chè veramente s'io non conoscessi in lei questa prontezza, malvolentieri mi arrisicherei ad infastidirla così spesso. Ma per finirla hormai, gli dico che Suor Arcangela da otto giorni in qua si ritrova ammalata; e se bene nel principio ne feci poca stima, parendomi che fossi il suo male d'infreddatura, finalmente vedo adesso ch'ella ha necessità di purgarsi, poi che, oltre al cader nella solita maninconia, è anco soprapresa da un catarro in tutta la vita, ma in particolare nelle gambe, che gli causa certi enfiati piccoli e rossi, sì che non può muoversi senza estrema fatica. Conosco che il suo bisogno è di cavarsi sangue (già che non ha mai il benefitio necessario), e per questa causa aspetto questa mattina il medico; ma perchè non ho assegnamento nessuno di danari per questo bisogno, la prego, per amor di Dio, che mi cavi di questo pensiero con mandarmene qualcuno, essendo io in molta necessità per molte cause, le quali sarei troppo tediosa se volessi raccontarle. Se il tempo lo concedessi, havrei caro che ci venissi Vincenzio, con il quale potrei dir liberamente i miei affanni, che non sono però superflui, venendo da Dio.

Gli mando una pera cotta, di quelle così belle che mi mandò ultimamente. Ho imparato questa nuova foggia di cuocerle, che forse più le piacerà; et havrò caro che mi rimandi la coperta, che non è mia. La saluto per fine affettuosamente, e prego il Signore che la conservi. Di S. Matteo, li 10 di Xmbre 1628.

Sua Fig.la Aff.ma

Suor M.a Celeste

because truly, if I did not recognize this quality in you, I would be reluctant to annoy you so often; but to come at last to the reason why I impose upon you now, I tell you that Suor Arcangela has been sick for the past eight days, and although at the outset I made little of it, as it seemed to me just a chill, I see now that she needs to be purged; because, in addition to falling under her usual melancholy, she is also overtaken by a catarrh that affects her entire body, but especially her legs, where she has so many small red swellings that she cannot move without extreme fatigue. I know the best course for her is bleeding (now that nothing else has helped) and this is why I await the doctor this morning: but because I have no expense allowance for such a contingency, I beg you, for the love of God, to free me from my worry by sending me some money, as we are in dire need for many reasons, so numerous that I would find it too tedious to relate them all. If time allows, I would dearly welcome a visit from Vincenzio, with whom I could speak freely of my troubles, which are not trifling, coming from God.

As apothecary, Suor Maria Celeste relies on herbal and dietary remedies, but when these fail she must call in a doctor for purging or bloodletting.

Here is a cooked pear, from among those very beautiful ones you sent me recently. I learned this new method of cooking them that you may prefer, and I will appreciate your returning the container, as it is not mine. I close here with loving regards, and I pray the Lord to bless you. From San Matteo, the 10th of December 1628.

Your most affectionate daughter,
Suor M. Celeste

Amatiss.mo Sig.r Padre,

Non saprei come meglio ringratiar V. S. di tante cortesie, se non con dirle che prego Nostro Signore che la rimeriti con l'aumento della Sua santa gratia, e le conceda felicissime le presenti Feste, questo a molti anni appresso, a similmente a Vincenzio nostro, al quale mando, per adesso, duoi collari e 2 para di manichini nuovi: la carestia del tempo non mi ha concesso che possa far il merlo da per me, e per ciò mi scuserà, se non saranno a sua intiera satisfatione; non mancherò anco di fargliene con la trina, si come ho promesso.

Suor Arcangela se la passa alquanto meglio, ma però se ne sta in letto; et hora appunto viene il confessore da lei, e per ciò non sarò più lunga. Si godino stasera questi pochi calicioni per colatione: et qui di tutto cuore mi raccomando ad ambeduoi.

Fig.la Aff.ma
Suor M.a Celeste

Amatiss.mo Sig.r Padre,

L'improvvisa nuova datami da Vincenzio nostro della conclusione del suo parentado, e parentado così honorato, ha causata in me tale allegrezza, che non saprei come meglio esprimerla, salvo che con dirle, che tanto quanto è grande l'amore che porto a V. S., tanto è il gusto che sento d'ogni suo contento, il quale suppongo che in questa occasione sia grandissimo; e per ciò vengo di presente a rallegrarmi seco, e prego Nostro Signore che la conservi per lungo tempo, acciò possa godere

Most Beloved Lord Father,

I would not know how better to thank you, Sire, for so many kindnesses, if not by telling you that I pray Our Lord may reward you with the fullness of His holy grace, and make these festive days the happiest for you, not only this year but for many years to come, and finally to our Vincenzio to whom I send, for now, two collars and two pairs of new cuffs: the great want of time prohibits me from doing my very best work, and for this reason he will excuse me if the gifts are not entirely to his satisfaction: nor will I fail to make him another pair with the trim, as I promised.

Suor Arcangela is faring a bit better, even though she is confined to bed, and just now the confessor is coming to see her, so that I must not tarry a moment: please enjoy these *calicioni* this evening for a sweet treat, and here with all my heart I send my love to you both.

__Calicioni__ are little square cakes made from sugar and almonds, similar to marzipan.

Your Most Affectionate Daughter,
Suor M. Celeste

Most Beloved Lord Father,

The unexpected news delivered here by our Vincenzio regarding the finalization of his wedding plans, and marrying into that esteemed family, has brought me such happiness that I would not know how better to express it, save to say that, as great as is the love I bear you, Sire, equally great is the delight I derive from your every joy, which I imagine in this instance to be immense; and therefore I come now to rejoice with you, and pray our Lord to protect you for a very

Vincenzio is betrothed to Sestilia Bocchineri, the sixth child of a fine family from Prato with strong connections to the Tuscan court.

quelle satisfationi che mi pare che gli promettino le buone qualità di suo figliuolo e mio fratello, al quale io accresco ogni giorno l'affetione, parendomi giovane molto quieto e prudente.

Havrei fatto con V. S. più volentieri questo offitio in voce; ma poi ch'ella così si compiace, la prego che almanco mi dica per lettera il suo gusto circa il mandar a visitar la sposa: ciò è se sia meglio il mandar a Prato quando vi andrà Vincenzio, o pure aspettar ch'ella sia in Firenze, già che questa è ceremonia solita di noi altre, e tanto più che per esser lei stata in monastero saprà queste usanze. Aspetto adunque la sua resolutione, e fra tanto la saluto di cuore.

Sua Fig.la Aff.ma
Suor M.a Celeste

Amatiss.mo Sig.r Padre,

Mi giova di creder che V. S., per ritrovarsi in questi giorni assai occupata, non habbia potuto altrimenti venir da noi; onde, desiderosa di saper qualcosa, mi son risoluta di scriverle di nuovo, dicendole che circa al visitar la sposa indugerò quando piacerà a V. S., bastandomi di saperlo qualche giorno avanti, e farò amco capitale dell'amorevole offerta ch'ella mi fa d'aiutarmi, poi che, come discreta, può giudicare, che, nel termine nel quale mi ritrovo, le forze non corrispondino nè all'animo nè al debito mio: onde gli mando in nota le cose di più spesa che per far un bacino di paste ci bisognano, la-sciando per me gl'ingredienti di minor costo. Oltre a ciò V. S. potrà vedere se long time, so that you can savor those satisfactions that seem guaranteed to you by the good qualities of your son and my brother, for whom my affection grows stronger every day, as he appears to me to be a calm and wise young man.

I would much rather have celebrated with you in person, Sire, but if you would be so kind, I implore you to at least tell me by letter how you plan to arrange your visit with Vincenzio's betrothed: meaning whether it may be well to meet in Prato when Vincenzio goes there, or better to wait until she is in Florence, since this is the usual formality among us sisters, and surely, given her experience of having been in a convent, she will know these customs. I await your resolution. And in the meanwhile I bid you adieu from my heart.

Your Most Affectionate Daughter,
Suor M. Celeste

Most Beloved Lord Father,

It suits me to believe, Sire, that you must be extremely occupied these days, or else you would have come to see us; wherefore, wanting to learn more, I have resolved to write to you again, telling you that I need not know the date of the betrothal visit until it pleases you, Sire, being content with hearing only a few days in advance, and also I will take advantage of your loving offer to help me, since, with discretion, and considering my circumstances, you can easily judge that my own powers fall far short of expressing my true feelings or giving my proper due. Here then is a list of the more costly items that we will need for making a platter of pastries, leavvuole che io gli faccia altre paste, come biscottini col zoccolo e simili, perchè credo senz'altro che spenderebbe manco che pigliandole dallo speziale; et noi le faremmo con tutta la diligenza possibile.

Desidero di più ch'ella mi dica il suo gusto quanto al presentar qualche cosa alla medesima sposa, perchè i[. . .]sidero se non di compiacer a V. S. Il mio pensier[. . .] farle un bel grembiule, sì perchè sarebbe cosa u[. . .] anco a noi di manco spesa, potendo lavorarlo da per [. . .]; e questi collari o grandiglie che usano adesso, non sappiamo farli.

Dubiterei di non far sproposito, domandando a V. S. di queste bagattelle, se non sapessi che ella, così nelle cose piccole come nelle grandi, ha di gran lunga più retto giuditio che non haviamo noi altre, et per ciò a lei mi rimetto. Et per fine mi raccomando, insieme con Suor Arcangela, et a Vincenzio ancora. Il Signor la feliciti. Di S. Matteo, li 4 di Gen.º 1628.

Potrà consegnare al fattore la [. . .] jiera de i collari con 3 coperte, [. . .] un grembiule sudicio, uno sciugatoio, [. . .] una pezzuola.

Sua Fig.la Aff.ma
Suor M.a Celeste

ing the less expensive ingredients to me. After this, Sire, you will be able to see if you want me to make other dishes for you, such as savory meat pastries, and the like; because I firmly believe you would spend less this way than buying them already prepared by the grocer, and we will apply ourselves to making them with the utmost possible care.

Her enclosed shopping list calls for three pounds of sugar, three also of almonds, and eight grams of fine confectioners' sugar.

What I want above all is for you to tell me your feelings about presenting a gift to the betrothed, because I do not want to do anything that is not to your liking, Sire. My thoughts lean toward making her a beautiful apron, so as to give her something that would be useful, and not require a great expenditure for us, since we could do all the work ourselves; not to mention that we have no idea how to make the high collars and ruffs that ladies are wearing nowadays.

I might think I had blundered, Sire, examining you on these many trifles, if I were not absolutely certain that you, in small details just as in great matters, exercise by far the soundest judgment of anyone. And therefore I leave everything to you. And to close I send you loving greetings together with Suor Arcangela and again to Vincenzio. May the Lord bless you. From San Matteo, the 4th of January 1628.

You will be able to send back with the steward the basket from the collars with the 3 covers, namely a dirty apron, a towel, and a handkerchief.

Your Most Affectionate Daughter,
Suor M. Celeste

Amatiss.mo Sig.r Padre,

Restammo veramente tutte satisfatte della sposa, per esser molto affabile e gratiosa; ma sopra ogn'altra cosa ne dà contento il conoscer ch'ella porti amore a V. S., poi che supponghiamo che sia per farle quegl'ossequii che noi le faremmo se ci fossi permesso. Non lasceremo già di far ancor noi la parte nostra in verso di lei, cioè di tenerla continuamente raccomandata al Signor Iddio; chè troppo siamo obligate, non solo come figliuole, ma come orfane abbandonate che saremmo, se V. S. ci mancassi.

Oh se almeno io fossi abile ad esprimerle il mio concetto, sarei sicura ch'ella non dubiterebbe ch'io non l'amassi tanto teneramente quanto mai altra figliuola habbia amato il padre; ma non so [si]gnificarglielo con altre parole, se non con dire ch'io l'amo più di me stessa, poi che, doppo Dio, l'essere lo riconosco da lei, accompagnato da tanti altri benefitii che sono innumerabili, sì che mi conosco anco obligata e prontissima, quando bisognassi, ad espor la mia vita a qual si voglia travaglio per lei, eccetuatone l'offesa di S. D. M.

Di gratia, V. S. mi perdoni se la tengo a tedio troppo lungamente, poi che talvolta l'affetto mi trasporta. Non mi ero già messa a scriver con questo pensiero, [ma sì] bene per dirle che se potessi rimandar l'orivolo sabato sera, la sagrestana, che ci chiama a matutino, l'havrebbe caro; ma se non si può, mediante la brevità del tempo che V. S. l'ha tenuto, sia per non detto: chè meglio sarà l'indugiare qualche poco, e riaverlo aggiustato, caso che ne habbia bisogno.

Most Beloved Lord Father,

We are truly perfectly pleased with the bride, as she is cordial and gracious; but above all else what makes us most happy is the recognition of the love she bears you, Sire, because we can readily see that she will be eager to perform all those services for you that we would undertake if we were permitted to. Not that we will ever stop doing our part on your behalf, by which I mean that we will continually commend you to the Lord God, because we are overwhelmingly committed to you, not only as daughters, but as the abandoned orphans we would be, Sire, if not for you.

Oh, if only I were capable of expressing to you my innermost thoughts! Then I could be certain that you would not doubt whether I loved you every bit as tenderly as ever a daughter loved a father: but I do not know how to convey these feelings to you in other words, if not by telling you that I love you more than myself: since, after God, the being I acknowledge most highly is you, and I perceive your good deeds toward me to be innumerable, so that I know I stand ever obliged and most willing, should the need arise, to risk my life in any sort of torment for your sake, except that which would offend His Divine Majesty.

Please, Sire, pardon me if I drive you to boredom by going on at such length, since sometimes I am transported by emotion. I did not set out to write you of these notions, but only to ask you if you could return the clock Saturday evening, as the sacristan who calls us to Matins would very much like to have

The clock chimes the midnight hour for the sacristan, who calls the sisters to Matins prayers.

Vorrei anco sapere s'ella si contentassi di far un baratto con noi, ciò è pigliarsi un chitarrone ch'ella ci donò parecchi anni sono, e donarci un breviario a tutte due; già che quelli che havemmo quando ci facemmo monache, sono tutti stracciati, essendo questi gl'instrumenti che adopriamo ogni giorno, ove che quello se ne sta sempre alla polvere e va a risico d'andar male, essendo costretta, per non far scortesia, a mandarlo in presto fuor di casa qualche volta. Se V. S. si contenta, me ne darà avviso, acciò possa mandarlo: e quanto a i breviarii, non ci curiamo che siano dorati, ma basterebbe che vi fossino tutti i Santi di nuovo aggiunti, et havessino buona stampa, perchè ci serviranno nella vecchiaia, se ci arriveremo.

Volevo fargli della conserva di fiori di ramerino, ma as[. . . che] V. S. mi rimandi qualcuno de'miei vasi di vetro, perchè non ho dove metterla; e così, se havessi per casa qualche barattolo o ampolla vota che gli dia impaccio, a me sarebbe grata per la bottega.

Et qui per fine la saluto di cuore, insieme con Suor Arcangela e tutte di camera. Nostro Signore la conservi in Sua gratia. Li 22 di Marzo 1628.

Di V. S. molto Ill.^{re} Fig.^{la} Aff.^{ma}

Suor M. Celeste

it; but if you cannot, on account of the short time it has been in your hands, Sire, do not concern yourself: for it will be better to keep us waiting a little longer, if that is what you need to have it running properly again.

I would also like to know if you would be interested in making an exchange with us, namely to take back the guitar you gave us several years ago, and give us each a new breviary; as the ones we have had since the time we became nuns are all torn, these being the instruments we use every day; while the guitar is forever gathering dust and runs the risk of damage, so that I feel compelled, to avoid being rude, to send it away from here sometime soon. If you like, Sire, give me some suggestions as to what I might send you: and as for the breviaries, we do not care whether they are gilded, but just that they contain all the newly added Saints, and that they be clearly printed, because they will serve us in our old age, should we reach that point.

Her much-consulted breviary contains the prayers for the hourly offices, psalms for daily recitation, feast days, hymns, and a catalog of saints.

I had wanted to make you some rosemary flower jam, Sire, but I am waiting for you to return one of my glass jars, because I have nothing to hold the jam; and so, if by chance you have a few empty bottles or vials lying about that are in your way, I would love to have them for the apothecary shop.

And here, to close, I send you my love together with Suor Arcangela and everyone else in the room. May Our Lord keep you in His grace. The 22nd of March 1628.

Sire's Most Affectionate Daughter,

Suor M. Celeste

Amatiss.^mo Sig.^r Padre,

L'incomodità che ho patita da poi che sono in questa casa, mediante la carestia di cella, so che V. S. in parte lo sa; et hora io più chiaramente glielo esplicherò, dicendole che una piccola celletta, la quale pagammo (conforme all'uso che haviamo noi altre) alla nostra maestra trentasei scudi, sono due o tre anni, mi è convenuto, per necessità, cederla totalmente a Suor Arcangela, acciò (per quanto è possibile) ella stia separata dalla sudetta nostra maestra, che, travagliata fuor di modo da i soliti humori, dubito che con la continua conversatione gl'apporterebbe non poco detrimento; oltre che, per esser Sr Arcangela di qualità molto diversa dalla mia, e più tosto stravagante, mi torna meglio il cedergli in molte cose, per poter vivere con quella pace et unione che ricerca l'intenso amore che scambievolmente ci portiamo: onde io mi ritrovo la notte con la travagliosa compagnia della maestra (se bene me la passo assai allegramente con l'aiuto del Signore, dal quale mi sono permessi questi travagli indubitatamente per mio bene), et il giorno sono quasi peregrina, non havendo luogo ove ritirarmi un'hora a mia requisitione. Non desidero camera grande o molto bella, ma solo un poca di stanzuola, come appunto adesso mi se ne porge occasione d'una piccolina, che una monaca vuol vendere per necessità di danari, et, mediante il buon uffitio fatto per me da Suor Luisa, mi preferisce a molte altre che cercano di comprarla; ma perchè la valuta è di scudi 35, et io non ne ho altro che dieci, accomodatimi pur da Sr Luisa, e cinque ne aspetto della mia entrata, non posso impossessarmene, anzi dubito di perderla, se V. S. non mi sovviene con la quantità che me ne mancano, che sono scudi 20.

Most Illustrious Lord Father,

The discomfort I have endured ever since I came to live in this house, for want of a cell of my own, I know that you know, Sire, at least in part, and now I shall more clearly explain it to you, telling you that two or three years ago I was compelled by necessity to leave the one small cell we had, for which we paid our novice mistress (according to the custom we nuns observe) thirty-six *scudi*, and give it over totally to Suor Arcangela, so that (as much as possible) she could distance herself from this same mistress, who, tormented to distraction by her habitual moods, posed a threat, I feared, to Suor Arcangela, who often finds interaction with others unbearable; beyond that, Suor Arcangela's nature being very different from mine and rather eccentric, it pays for me to acquiesce to her in many things, in order to be able to live in the kind of peace and unity befitting the intense love we bear each other. As a result I spend every night in the disturbing company of the mistress (although I get through the nights easily enough with the help of the Lord, who suffers me to undergo these tribulations undoubtedly for my own good) and I pass the days practically a pilgrim, having no place whatsoever where I can retreat for one hour on my own. I do not yearn for large or very beautiful quarters, but only for a little bit of space, exactly like the tiny room that has just become available, now that a nun who desperately needs money wants to sell it; and, thanks to Suor Luisa's having spoken well on my behalf, this nun prefers me over any of the others offering to buy it. But because its price is 35 *scudi*, while I have only ten, which Suor Luisa kindly gave me, plus the five I expect from my income, I cannot take possession of the room, and I rather fear I may lose it, Sire, if you do not assist me with the remaining amount, which is 20 *scudi*.

*One **scudo** equals seven **lire**—enough to feed a person for nearly two weeks.*

Esplico a V. S. il mio bisogno con sicurtà filiale e senza cerimonie, per non offender quell'amorevolezza da me tante volte esperimentata. Solo replicherò che questa è delle maggiori necessità che mi possino avvenire in questo stato che mi ritrovo, et che, amandomi ella come so che mi ama e desiderando il mio contento, supponga che da questo me ne deriverà contento e gusto grandissimo, e pur anco lecito et honesto, non desiderando altro che un poca di quiete e solitudine. Potrebbe dirmi V. S. che, per esser assai la somma che domando, io m'accomodi de i 30 scudi che tiene ancora il convento di suo; al che io rispondo (oltre che non è possibile l'haverli in questo estremo, essendo in molta necessità la monaca venditrice) che V. S. promesse alla Madre badessa di non gli domandare se non veniva qualche occasione, mediante la quale il convento fossi sollevato, e non astretto a sborsarli contanti: sì che non per questo penso che V. S. lascerà di farmi questa gran carità, la quale gl'adimando per l'amor di Dio, essendo ancor io nel numero de i poveri bisognosi, posti in carcere, e non solo dico bisognosi, ma anco vergognosi, poi che alla sua presenza non ardirei di dir così apertamente il mio bisogno, nè meno a Vincenzio; ma solo con questa mia a V. S. ricorro con ogni fiducia, sapendo che vorrà e potrà aiutarmi. E qui per fine me le raccomando con tutto l'affetto, sì come anco a Vincenzio e sua sposa. Il Signor Iddio la conservi lungamente felice. Di S. Matteo, li 8 di Lug.º 1629.

Di V. S. Molto Ill.re Fig.la Aff.ma

Suor M.a Celeste

I explain this need to you, Sire, with a daughter's security and without ceremony, so as not to offend that loving tenderness I have experienced so often. I will only repeat that this is of the greatest necessity, on account of my having been reduced to the state in which I find myself, and because, loving me the way that I know you love me, and desiring my happiness, you can well imagine how this step will bring me the greatest satisfaction and pleasure, of a proper and honest sort, as all I seek is a little quiet and solitude. You might tell me, Sire, that to make up the sum I require, I could avail myself of the 30 *scudi* of yours that the convent is still holding: to which I respond (aside from the fact that I could not lay claim to that money quickly enough in this extreme case, as the nun selling the room faces dire straits) that you promised the Mother Abbess you would not ask her for those funds until such time as the convent enjoyed some relief from the constraint of constant expenditures; given all that, I do not think you will forsake me, Sire, in doing me this great charitable service, which I beg of you for the love of God, numbering myself now among the neediest paupers locked in prison, and not only needy, I say, but also ashamed, since I would not dare to speak so openly of my distress to your face: no less to Vincenzio; but only by resorting to this letter, Sire, can I appeal with every confidence, knowing that you will want and be able to help me. And here to close I send you regards with all my love, and also to Vincenzio and his bride. May the Lord bless you and keep you happy always. From San Matteo, the 8th day of July 1629.

Most affectionate daughter,

Suor M. Celeste

Amatiss.mo Sig.r Padre,

Haviamo rihavuta l'ampolla d'olio con li scorpioni, e la ringratiamo Suor Luisa et io infinitamente. Volevamo parecchi giorni sono, mandargli un poca di acqua di cannella fatta da noi non è molto, che, avvicinandosi la stagione più fresca, pensiamo che gli deva esser grata; ma restiamo per l'incomodità che haviamo di chi la porti: che se V. S. havessi la casa più appresso (com'io desidererei), non ci sarebbano queste difficoltà. Basta, aspetteremo la prima occasione, et fra tanto havrò caro di sapere come stia la Lisabetta, et se vuol qualche cosa da noi.

Quando V. S. manda la tela per i collari per lei e pezzuola per la cognata, havrò caro che mandi la mostra di un collare che gli stia bene, e similmente il refe bresciano che m'ha promesso, che ne lavorerò con esso la pezzuola. Perchè ho gran sonno, non dirò altro, se non che ne vo al letto per cavarmelo, essendo assai notte. La saluto di cuore, insieme con Suor Luisa e Suor Arcangela, et similmente Vincenzio e la sposa. Nostro Signore la conservi. Di S. Matteo, li 6 di 7mbre 1629.

Di V. S. Molto Ill.re Fig.la Aff.ma

Suor M.a Celeste

Amatiss.mo Sig.r Padre,

Mi dispiace in estremo il sentire l'indispositione di V. S., e tanto più perchè ordinariamente è più travagliata quando viene da noi; et ardirei di dire, se credessi indubitatamente

Most Beloved Lord Father,

Now that we have back the ampule of oil with scorpions, Suor Luisa and I offer you profuse thanks. We have been wanting, for the past several days, to send you a little of our freshly made cinnamon water, which, what with the cold weather approaching, we think you must surely want to keep on hand; but we are still having trouble finding someone to deliver it to you. If you lived closer by (as I would wish) we might be spared these difficulties. But enough of that, we await the first opportunity and meanwhile we are eager to hear how La Lisabetta is faring, and if she wants anything from us.

Scorpion oil, actually prepared from the creature, serves as an antidote for its sting and sundry other purposes.

Galileo is paying for this young girl's maintenance in San Matteo. As Lisabetta is not yet a nun, she has apparently been sent to his home for treatment during an illness.

When you send the cloth for the collars for her and the handkerchief for our sister-in-law, Sire, do please let us see an example of one of the collars that suits her well, and likewise the Brescian cloth you promised me, out of which I will make the handkerchief: since I am extremely sleepy, I will say no more except that I am taking myself off to bed, as it is already late at night. I send you loving greetings together with Suor Luisa and Suor Arcangela, and the same to Vincenzio and his bride. May our Lord bless you. From San Matteo, the 6th of September 1629.

Sire's Most Affectionate Daughter,

Suor M. Celeste

Most Illustrious Lord Father,

I am extremely sorry to hear of your indisposition, Sire, and all the more so because ordinarily your illnesses tend to be especially troublesome when you catch them here; and I dare che questa gita tanto le nocessi, che più presto mi contenterei di privarmi di vista tanto cara e desiderata; ma veramente ne incolpo molto più la contraria stagione. La prego ad haversi cura più che sia possibile.

Non poteva Suor Luisa mia haver maggior gusto quanto che vedendo che V. S. faccia capitale (se bene in piccola cosa) della nostra bottega; solo ha timore che non sia l'oximele di quella esquisitezza ch'ella vorrebbe, dovendo servire per V. S. Gl'ene mandiamo on. V, come domanda, e se più gl'ene bisognerà, siamo prontissime; ma perchè ordinariamente si suol temperare con syroppo di scorza di cedro, anco di questo gli mandiamo, acciò veda se gli gusta: et se altro gl'occorre, dica liberamente.

La ringratio de i ritagli, e caso che ne habbia più, mi saranno gratissimi; et ancora io non lascerò di mandarle qualche amorevolezza per la Porzia. Gli mando un poco di marzapane, che se lo goda per mio amore, e la saluto, insieme con Vincenzio e la cognata, della quale molto mi duole che si ritrovi in letto, e se gli bisogna qualche cosa ch'io la possi servire, lo farò molto volentieri. Nostro Signore doni a tutti la Sua santa gratia. Li 10 di 9mbre 1629.

Sua Fig.^{la} Aff.^{ma}

S. Maria Celeste

to say, if I believed without a doubt that this excursion were that harmful to you, then how quickly would I consent to deprive myself of a sight so dear and desired; but in truth I put the blame on the contrary season. I beseech you to take care of yourself as well as you possibly can.

Nothing ever brought my Suor Luisa such great pleasure as seeing you take advantage (although in a small way) of our apothecary; her only fear is that the oxymel may not attain the excellence she would wish, Sire, for being of service to you. Here are V ounces of it as per your request, and if you find you need more we will be ready to provide it; and since the common practice is to mix it with syrup of citron rind, we are sending some of this, too, so you can see whether you like it: and, if anything else occurs to you, do please let us know.

Oxymel, a medicinal brew of vinegar and honey, treats a variety of ills.

Thank you for the cuttings, and should you perchance be able to spare some more, I will be most happy to have them, and still I will not neglect to send you some small loving tokens for La Porzia. I enclose a little marzipan, for you to enjoy with my love, and I give my best regards to you together with Vincenzio and my sister-in-law, and indeed I am very sad to hear that she, too, is sick in bed, and if she needs anything that I might be able to provide, I will be only too happy to do it. May Our Lord bless all of you with His holy grace. The 10th of November 1629.

La Porzia is Galileo's housekeeper.

Your Most Affectionate Daughter,

S. Maria Celeste

Amatiss.mo Sig.r Padre,

Hora che alquanto è mitigata la tempesta de i nostri molti travagli, non voglio tralasciar di farne consapevole V. S., sì perchè ne spero alleggerimento d'animo, come anco perchè desidero d'esser scusata da lei se già due volte gl'ho scritto così a caso e non in quella maniera che dovevo, perchè veramente ero mezza fuori di me, mediante il terrore causato a me et a tutte l'altre dalla nostra maestra, la quale, sopraffatta da quei suoi humori o furori, due volte ne i giorni passati ha cercato d'uccidersi: la prima volta con percuotersi il capo e il viso in terra tanto forte, che era divenuta deforme e mostruosa; la seconda, con darsi in una notte tredici ferite, due nella gola, due nello stomaco e l'altre tutte nel ventre. Lascio pensare a V. S. qual fossi l'orrore che ci soprapresе, quando la trovammo tutta sangue e così mal concia. Ma più ci dà stupore che, nell'istesso tempo che si era ferita, ella fa romore perchè si vadia là in cella, domanda il confessore, e in confessione gli consegna il ferro che adoprò, acciò non sia visto da alcuno (se bene, per quanto possiamo conghietturare, fu un temperino): basta che apparisce ch'ella sia pazza e savia nel medesimo tempo, e non si può concluder altro se non che questi sono occulti giuditii del Signore, il quale ancora la lascia in vita, quando per ragioni naturali doveva morire, essendo le ferite tutte pericolose, per quanto diceva il cerusico; che per ciò siamo state a guardarla continuamente, giorno e notte. Adesso siamo qui tutte sane, per gratia di Dio benedetto, et lei si tiene in letto legata, ma con le medesime frenesie, che per ciò stiamo in continuo timore di qualche altra stravaganza.

Most Beloved Lord Father,

Now that the tempest of our many torments has subsided somewhat, I want to make you fully aware of the events, Sire, without leaving anything out, for in so doing I hope to ease my mind, and at the same time to be excused by you, for dashing off my last two letters so randomly, instead of writing in the proper manner. For truly I was half beside myself, shaken by the terror aroused in me and in all of us by our novice mistress, who, overpowered by those moods or frenzies of hers, tried twice in recent days to kill herself. The first time she struck her head and face against the ground with such force that she became monstrously deformed; the second time she stabbed herself thirteen times, leaving two wounds in her throat, two in her stomach, and the others in her abdomen. I leave you to imagine, Sire, the horror that gripped us when we found her body all bloody and battered. But we were even more stupefied at how, as seriously injured as she was, she made the noise that drew us to enter her cell, asked for the confessor, and then in confession handed over to the priest the instrument she had used, so as to prevent any of us from seeing it (although, as far as we can conjecture, it was a pocket knife); thus it appears that she was crazy and cunning at the same time, and the only possible conclusion is that these are mysterious judgments of the Lord, Who still keeps her alive, when for every natural cause she should surely have died, as the wounds were all perilous ones, according to the surgeon; in the wake of these events we have guarded her continuously day and night. Now that the rest of us are recovered, by the grace of blessed God, and she is tied in her bed, albeit with the same deliriums, we continue to live in fear of some new outburst.

Doppo questo mio travaglio voglio accennarle un'altra inquietudine d'animo sofferta da me da poi in qua che V. S., per sua amorevolezza, mi donò i 20 scudi che gli domandai (poi che alla presenza non ardii di dirle liberamente l'animio, quando ultimamente mi domandò se ancora havevo bavuta la cella): e ciò è, che essendo io andata con i danari in mano a trovar la monaca che la vendeva, ella, che era in molta necessità, volentieri havrebbe accettati detti danari, ma di privarsi per ancora della cella non si risolveva; sì che, non essendo accordo in fra di noi, non ne segui altro, non pretendendo io altro che la presente comodità di quella stanzuola. La quale, per haver accertata V. S. che havrei havuta, e non essendo sortito, ne presi grandissimo affanno, non tanto per restarne priva, quanto perchè ho dubitato che V. S. non si tenga aggirata, parendomi d'haverle detto una cosa per un'altra, ancorchè tale non fossi il mio pensiero; nè mai havrei voluto haver questi danari, perchè mi davano molta inquietudine: che per ciò, essendo sopravvenuto alla Madre badessa certa necessità, io liberamente gliene prestai, et ella adesso, per gratitudine e sua amorevolezza, m'ha promesso la camera di quella monaca ammalata ch'io raccontai a V. S., la quale è grande e bella e valeva 120 scudi, et ella si contenta di darmela per 80, che in questo mi fa gratia particolare, sì come in altre occasioni m'ha sempre favorita. E perchè 4 essa sa benissimo che io non posso arrivare anco alla spesa di 80 scudi, s'offerisce di pigliar a questo conto i trenta scudi che già tanto tempo il convento ha tenuti di V. S., pur che ci sia il suo consenso; del che non mi par quasi di poter dubitare, parendomi che non sia da sfuggir questa occasione, essendo massime con molto mio comodo e satisfatione, la quale già so

Beyond this travail of ours, I want to apprise you of another anxiety that has been weighing heavily on my heart. The very moment you were so kind as to send me the 20 *scudi* I had requested (I did not dare to speak freely of this in person, when you asked me recently if I had obtained the cell yet) I went with the money in my hand to find the nun who was selling it, expecting that she, being in extreme necessity, would willingly accept that money, but she simply could not resign herself to relinquishing the cell she loved so much, and since we did not reach an agreement between ourselves, nothing came of it, and I lost the chance to purchase that little room. Having assured you, Sire, that I could indeed obtain it, and then not succeeding, I became greatly troubled, not just on account of being deprived of my own space, but also because I suspected you would get upset, Sire, believing me to have said one thing and done another, though such deceit was never my intention; nor did I even want to have this money, which was causing me such grief. As it happened, the Mother Abbess was confronted at that point with certain contingencies, which I gladly helped her through, and now she, out of gratitude and kindness, has promised me the room of that nun who is sick, the one whose story I told you, Sire, whose room is large and beautiful, and while it is worth 120 *scudi* the Mother Abbess will give it to me for 80, thus doing me a particular favor, just as she has on other occasions always favored me. And because she knows full well that I cannot pay a bill of 80 *scudi*, she offers to reduce the price by the 30 *scudi* that you gave the convent some time ago, Sire, so that with your consent, which I see no reason to doubt, as this seems to me an opportunity not to be missed, I will have quanto a V. S. sia di gusto. Pregola ad unque che mi dia qualche risposta, acciò io possa dar satisfatione alla Madre badessa, che, dovendo fra pochi giorni lasciar l'ofiitio, va di presente accomodando i suoi conti.

Desidero anco di sapere come V. S. si sente adesso che l'aria è alquanto rasserenata, e non havendo altro, gli mando un poco di cotognato, condito di povertà, ciò è fatto con mele, il quale se non sarà il caso per lei, forse non spiacerà a gl'altri. Alla cognata non saprei che mandarli, già che niente gli piace; pure, se havessi gusto a cosa alcuna fatta da monache, V. S. ce lo avvisi, chè desideriamo di dargli gusto. Non mi sono scordata dell'obligo che tengo con la Portia, ma per ancora non mi è possibile il far cosa alcuna. In tanto se V. S. havrà havuti gl'altri ritagli promessimi, havrò caro che me li mandi, aspettandoli io per metterli in opera con quelli che ho havuti.

Aggiungo di più che, mentre scrivo, la monaca sudetta ammalata ha havuto un accidente tale, che pensiamo che sia per morir in breve; a tal che mi bisognerà dar il restante de i danari a Madonna, acciò possi far le spese necessarie per il mortorio.

Mi ritrovo nelle mani la corona di agate donatami da V. S., la quale a me è superflua et inutile, e parmi che starebbe bene alla cognata. La mando adunque a V. S., acciò veda se si contenta di pigliarla et in cambio mandarmi qualche scudo per questo mio bisogno, che, se piacerà a Dio, credo pure che sarà l'ultimo di tanto gran somma, et per conseguenza non sarò più astretta ad infastidir V. S., ch'è quello che più mi preme. Ma in fatti non ho, nè voglio haver, altri a chi voltar-all that I could ever want in the way of comfort and satisfaction, which I already know to be of great importance to you. Therefore I entreat your consideration, so that I can give some response to our Mother Abbess, who will be relinquishing her office in a few days, and is currently settling her accounts.

I also want to know how you feel, Sire, now that the air is slightly more serene, and, not having anything better to send you, I offer a little poor man's candied quince, by which I mean that I prepared it with honey instead of sugar, so if it is not right for you, perhaps it will satisfy the others; I would not know what to give my sister-in-law now, in her condition. Surely if she had a taste for anything made by nuns, Sire, you would tell us, because we want so much to please her. Nor have I forgotten my obligation to La Porzia, but circumstances have prevented me from making anything as yet. Meanwhile if you have gathered the additional cuttings you promised me, Sire, I will be very happy to receive them, as I am holding off work on those I already have until the others arrive.

Sestilia is pregnant and near term.

I must add that, as I write, the sick nun I mentioned earlier has taken such a turn that we think she is on the verge of death; in which event I will be obliged to give the remainder of the money to Madonna right away, so that she can make the necessary purchases for the funeral.

In my hands I hold the agate rosary you gave me, Sire, which is excessive and vain for me, while it seems perhaps right for my sister-in-law. Let me therefore return it to you, so you can learn if she would like to have it, and in exchange send me a mi, salvo che a lei et a Suor Luisa mia fedelissima, la quale per me s'affatica quanto può; ma finalmente siamo riserrate, e non haviamo quell'habilità che molte volte ci bisognerebbono. Benedetto sia il Signore, che non lascia mai di sovvenirci; per amor del quale prego V. S. che mi perdoni se troppo l'infastidisco, sperando che l'istesso Signore non lascerà irremunerati tanti beni che c'ha fatti e fa continuamente, che di tanto lo prego con tutto l'affetto: et lei prego che mi scusi se qui saranno de gl'errori, chè non ho tempo per rilegger questa lunga diceria. Di S. Matteo, li 22 di 9mbre 1629.

Sua Fig.^{la} Aff.^{ma}

Suor Maria Celeste

Amatiss.^{mo} Sig.^{r} Padre,

Il timore che ho che la venuta qui di V. S. l'altro giorno non gl'habbia cagionato l'accidente solito di maggior indispositione, m'induce a mandarla a visitare di presente, con speranza però che non sia seguito quello che temo, ma sì bene quel che desidero, ciò è ch'ella stia bene: il che non segue già qua fra di noi, poi che la maestra di Sr Luisa, ciò è quella che V. S. non poteva creder l'altro giorno che havessi 80 anni, per esser così fiera, l'istessa sera fu soprapresa da male così repente di febbre, catarro e dolori, di tal maniera che si dà per few *scudi* for my present need, so that, if it please God, I believe I really will have the full sum; and in consequence I will no longer be forced to burden you, Sire, for that is what concerns me most. But in fact I do not have, nor do I want to have, others to whom I can turn, except for you and my most faithful Suor Luisa, who wearies herself doing everything she can for me; but in the end we depend upon each other because alone we lack the strength that circumstances so often demand of us. Blessed be the Lord Who never fails to help us; by Whose love I pray you, Sire, to forgive me if I vex you too much, hoping that God Himself will reward you for all the good things you have done for us and continue to do, for which I thank you with all my heart, and I entreat you to excuse me if you find any errors here, because I do not have time to reread this long litany. From San Matteo, the 22nd of November 1629.

Your Most Affectionate Daughter,
Suor Maria Celeste

Most Beloved Lord Father,

Galileo has just completed work on his masterpiece, ***Dialogue on the Two Chief Systems of the World.***

The dread I have, Sire, that your coming here the other day has perhaps occasioned a typical recurrence of your older indisposition, urges me to send this messenger to you now, with the hope, however, that what I fear has not come to pass, but only what I wish: namely, that you feel extremely well, which unfortunately cannot be said of everyone here, since Suor Luisa's teacher, Suor Giulia, the one you saw the other day, Sire, and could not believe to be eighty years of age, on account of her strong spirit, that very evening was stricken with spedita; et Sr Luisa per ciò si ritrova in molto travaglio, perchè l'amava lo grandemente. Oltre a ciò Sr Violante per ordine del medico se ne sta in letto, con un poca di febbre, et per quanto ne dice l'istesso medico si può sperarne poco bene: hiermattina prese medicina, et si va trattenendo. Se V. S. facessi carità di mandarmi per lei un fiasco di vino rosso ben maturo, l'havrei molto caro, perchè il nostro è assai crudo; et io voglio cercare, di quel poco che potrò, di aiutarla fino all'ultimo.

Tengo memoria del debito che ho con la Portia et per ciò gli mando queste pezzuole, che da per noi haviamo lavorate, e questa cordellina, acciò veda, se gli piace, di donargliene da nostra parte, et in tanto procurar di haver qualche altro ritaglio di drappo bello: basta, facci V. S. in quella maniera che più gli piace. Si goderà stasera quest'uova fresche per amor nostro; et per fine a lei di tutto cuore mi raccomando, insieme con tutte di camera. Il Signore la conservi in sua gratia. Li 4 di Gen.^o 1629.

Sua Fig.^la Aff.^ma
Suor Maria Celeste

Amatiss.^mo Sig.^r Padre,

In risposta della sua gratissima gli dico che Sr Arcangela sta bene, et io poco manco che bene, già che, per consiglio del medico Ronconi, fo di presente un poca di purga piacevole, per ovviare, se sarà possibile, ad una oppilatione duratami a sudden fever, catarrh, and pains of such gravity that the illness must surely kill her: and this has plunged Suor Luisa into extreme distress, because she has loved this teacher of hers so dearly. What's more, Suor Violante, following the doctor's recommendation, is now confined to bed with a fever; and, according to what this same doctor tells us, not much can be done or hoped for her: yesterday morning she took her medicine and we are waiting to see what happens. If you would be so kind, Sire, as to send a flask of well-aged red wine for her, I would be most grateful, because our wine is very harsh, and I want to try, in any small way I can, to help her to the last.

I keep remembering my debt to La Porzia, and so I offer you these handkerchiefs that we have embroidered ourselves, and this braided silk belt, so that you can see if you would like to present them to her as a gift from me, or wait until you can find another length of that fine cloth; enough: you will do as you see fit in this matter, Sire. Please enjoy these fresh eggs this evening with my love, and to close I greet you with all my heart together with the others in the room. May the Lord bless you with His holy grace. The 4th of January 1629.

Your Most Affectionate Daughter,
Suor Maria Celeste

Most Beloved Lord Father,

In response to your most welcome letter, I can tell you that Suor Arcangela fares well, and I am almost better, now that your Doctor Ronconi prescribed a modicum of mild purgative, in order to try to remove an obstruction that has troubled

Outside the convent, Giovanni Ronconi serves as physician to Galileo and to Vincenzio's family.

(fuor d' ogni mio solito) da 6 mesi in qua, e credo che domattina piglierò una presa di pillole. Non mi sento veramente indispositione particolare, ma stando in questa maniera dubito che mi verrebbe senz'altro. S.r Violante sta alquanto meglio, e va ancora purgandosi. S.r Giulia ci dà che fare assai, non agitandosi niente da per sè; et ogni volta che si leva dalletto, siamo tre o 4 a portarla. Non credo senz'altro che sia per scamparla, essendo la febbre continua, con andata di corpo. Io gl'assisto continuamente, parendomi adesso il tempo di dimostrare a S.r Luisa l' affettione che gli porto, con levarle quelle fatiche ch'io posso.

Vincenzio tenne parecchi giorni l'orivolo, ma da poi in qua suona manco che mai. Quanto a me, giudicherei che il difetto venissi dalla corda, che, per esser cattiva, non scorra; pure, perchè non me ne risolvo, glielo mando, acciò veda qual sia il suo mancamento e lo raccomodi. Potrebbe anco esser che il difetto fossi mio per non saperlo guidare, che perciò ho lasciato i contrappesi attaccati, dubitando che forse non siano al luogo loro. Ma ben la prego a rimandarlo più presto che potrà, perchè queste monache non mi lascerebbon vivere.

S.r Brigida le ricorda il servitio che gl'ha impromesso, ciò è la dote di quella povera fanciulla; et io harei caro di sapere se ha havuto per me dalla Portia il servitio che li domandai. Non lo nomino, accio V. S. non mi dica fastidiosa, ma solo glielo ricordo. Havrò caro anco di sapere se la lettera ch'io scrissi per S.r M.a Grazia fa conforme al desiderio di V. S., chè quando ciò non fossi, procurerei di emendar l'errore con scriverne un'altra, havendo scritta quella con molta penuria di tempo, il quale mi manca sempre per compire le mie facme (aside from my usual ailments) for the past six months, and I believe that tomorrow morning I am to take an assortment of pills. I do not really suffer any particular pain; but being in this condition, something is bound to strike me. Suor Violante feels much improved, and continues purging. Suor Giulia gives us quite enough to do, as she is unable to fend for herself at all, and, every time she gets out of bed, three or four of us are required to hold her up. I cannot believe that she will survive this illness, what with the unrelenting fever and her body always emptying itself. I help her constantly, as now seems to be the time to prove my affection for Suor Luisa, by relieving her of as much of the care of Suor Giulia as I can.

Vincenzio worked on our clock for a few days, but since then it sounds worse than ever. For my part, I would judge the defect to be in the cord, which, owing to its being old, no longer glides. Still, since I am unable to fix it, I turn it over to you, so that you can diagnose its deficiency, and repair it. Perhaps the real defect was with me, in not knowing the right action to take, which is the reason I have left the counterweights attached this time, suspecting that perhaps they are not in their proper place; but I beseech you to send it back as quickly as you possibly can, because otherwise these nuns will not let me live.

Suor Brigida reminds you of the favor you promised her, namely the dowry for that poor young girl, and I would love to know if you have received from La Porzia what I asked of her. I do not mention this to press you, Sire, but only as a helpful reminder. I would also very much like to hear if the cende, e per disgratia non posso tor alcun'hora al sonno, perché conosco che mi apporterebbe grandissimo nocumento alla sanità.

La ringratio del servitio fattomi della muletta, la quale feci instanza che m'accomodassi, acciò che Sr Chiara, che la ricercava, non dubitassi che io non volessi che fossi servita. Gli rimando il fiasco voto, essendo a Sr Violante molto gustato il buon vino che vi era dentro, e la ringratia.

Suor Arcangela, quando l'altro giorno vedde l'involto di caviale che V. S. mandò, restò ingannata, credendosi che fossi certo cacio di Olanda che è solita di mandarne; sì che, se V. S. vuol ch'ella resti satisfatta, di gratia ne mandi un poco, avanti che passi carnevale.

Adesso che ho buona vena di cicalare, non finirei così per fretta, se non dubitassi di venirle a fastidio, o più presto causarle stracchezza; che per ciò finisco, con raccomandarmeli per mille volte, insieme con Sr Luisa e tutte di camera. Il Signore la feliciti sempre.   Li 21 di Gen.^{o} 1629.

Sua Aff.^{ma} Fig.^{la}

Suor Maria Celeste

letter I wrote for Suor Maria Grazia met your expectations, Sire, because, if it were not suitable, I would attempt to correct any errors by writing another, having composed that one in a great rush, as I never find enough time even to finish my chores, and unfortunately I cannot wrench one additional hour from my sleep without seriously threatening my health.

I thank you for the use of the little mule, which I sat on this time, to save Suor Chiara the trouble of doing so, and thus show her that I want only to help her. I am returning the empty flask, as Suor Violante very much enjoyed the fine wine it contained, and she thanks you for that.

Suor Arcangela, when she saw the package of caviar that came from you the other day, felt cheated, convinced as she was that it must be the cheese from Holland you usually send at this time of year, so that, if you want her to rest easy, Sire, you will please send a little cheese before Carnival ends.

Now, seeing how I have chattered on, I would not sign off thus abruptly if I did not fear I were beginning to disturb you, or rather wear you out: therefore I close by sending all of you a thousand loving wishes, together with Suor Luisa and everyone else in the room. May the Lord bless you always. The 21st of January 1629.

Your Most Affectionate Daughter,
Suor Maria Celeste

Amatiss.mo Sig.r Padre,

So che V. S. è stata consapevole di tutti i miei disgusti, chè così mi fu dalla nostra Nora riferto; et io non ho voluto dargliene parte per non esser sempre annuntiatrice di cattive nuove: ma ben adesso gli dico che S.r Luisa, per la Dio gratia, sta assai bene, e S.r Arcangela et io stiamo benissimo, S.r Chiara ragionevolmente, e le due vecchie all'ordinario. Piaccia al Signore che anco V. S. stia con quella sanità ch'io desidero, ma non spero, mediante la crudezza del tempo; havrò caro d'haverne la certezza, et in tanto gli mando queste poche paste per far colatione la sera di queste vigilie.

Vincenzio c'inviò hiersera un buon alberello di caviale, del quale S.r Arcangela ringratia V. S., per esser questa sua e non mia portione, perchè non fa per me: io, in quel cambio, havrei più caro da far zuppa, e parecchi fichi secchi, che fanno per il mio stomaco. La consuetudine de gl'altri anni mi fa forse troppo ardita; ma il sapere che a V. S. non è discara simil domanda, mi dà sicurtà.

L'orivolo, che tante volte mandai in su e in giù, va adesso benissimo, essendo stato mio il difetto, che l'accomodavo un poco torto. Lo mandai a V. S. in una zanetta, coperta con uno sciugatoio, e non ho riavuto nè l'uno nè l'altra; se V. S. li ritrova per sorte in casa, havrò caro che li rimandi. Non dirò altro di presente, se non che la saluto per parte di tutte le sopra nominate, e prego Dio benedetto che la conservi lungamente felice. Di S. Matteo, li 19 di Febb.o 1629.

Di V. S. Fig.la Aff.ma

Suor Maria Celeste

Most Beloved Lord Father,

I know that you have heard all about my woes, Sire, from our Nora; and I was content to let her tell you, so as not to be always the bearer of bad news myself; but happily now I can say that Suor Luisa, by God's grace, is much better, and Suor Arcangela and I are extremely well: Suor Chiara reasonably so and the two old nuns their normal selves: may it please the Lord that you, too, Sire, enjoy the well-being that I desire, but dare not assume, considering the harshness of the weather: I am most eager to be assured of your good health, and meanwhile I send you these few cakes to break your fast during the long vigils of these winter nights.

Nora is the convent's gatekeeper.

Vincenzio came yesterday evening to deliver a fine pot of caviar, for which Suor Arcangela thanks you, Sire, this being her share not mine, as it does not suit me: I would much prefer to eat your soup, and a few dried figs to settle my stomach; the custom of all these years perhaps emboldens me too much; but knowing that such demands do not displease you, Sire, soothes and reassures me.

The clock that traveled back and forth between us so many times now runs beautifully, its flaw having been my fault, as I got it a little out of order; I sent it to you in a covered basket with a towel, and have not gotten either of those back; if you find them by chance about the house, Sire, please do return them. I will say no more for now, except that I send you loving regards on behalf of everyone I have mentioned here; and I pray blessed God to keep you happy always. From San Matteo, the 19th of February 1629.

Sire's Most Affectionate Daughter,

Suor Maria Celeste

Amatiss.mo Sig.r Padre,

S'io fui sollecita a domandare a V. S., non vorrei anco esser troppo tarda a ringratiarla dell'amorevolezza mandateci, le quali lunedì passato ci furno dalla cognata inviate, ciò è un cartoccio di zibaldone e tredici cantucci molto belli e buoni. Ce li andiamo godendo, con riconoscimiento dell'amorevolezza e prontezza di V. S. in satisfar sempre ad ogni nostro gusto. Hebbi anco alcuni pochi ritagli di drappi, che m'immagino che venghino dalla Portia.

Perchè so che V. S. gusta di sentire ch'io non stia in otio, gli dico che dalla Madre badessa (oltre alle mie solite faccende) sono assai esercitata, atteso che tutte le volte che gl'occorre scriver a persone di qualità, come Governatore, Operai e simili personaggi, impone a me tal carico, che veramente non è piccolo, mediante l'altre mie occupationi che non mi concedono quella quiete che per ciò mi bisognerebbe; onde, per mia minor fatica e miglior indirizzo, havrei caro che V. S. mi provvedessi qualche libro di lettere familiari, sì come una volta mi promesse, e so che m'havrebbe osservato se la dimenticanza non l'havessi impedito.

Vincenzio fu hiermattina da noi (forse per spatio di un'hora), insieme con la cognata e sua madre, e da lui intesi che V. S. voleva andar a Roma, il che mi dette alquanto disturbo; pure m'acqueto, supponendo ch'ella non si metterebbe in viaggio se non si sentissi in stato di poterlo fare. Credo che avanti che ciò segua ci rivedremo, e per ciò non replico altro, se non che la saluto con tutto l'affetto insieme con tutte di camera, e

Most Beloved Lord Father,

Just as I was quick to make requests of you, Sire, so in the same fashion I would surely not want to be tardy in thanking you for the loving gifts we have received, which were delivered here last Monday by my sister-in-law, namely a parcel of treats and thirteen very beautiful and delicious biscuits. We are busy enjoying them along with the awareness of your thoughtfulness and talent, Sire, for always finding the means to please us in every way. There were also some small lengths of fabric that I assume must come from La Porzia.

Because I know you like to hear that I do not sit idle, Sire, I tell you that I am kept extremely busy (aside from my usual duties) by the Mother Abbess, who, every time she needs to write to highly placed personages, such as our Governor, the Pious Workers, and people of that ilk, defers this burden to me, which is truly no trifle, considering my other responsibilities, and as a result I have no hope of obtaining the rest I need now more than ever; wherefore, to ease my labor and improve my skill, Sire, I would greatly appreciate your procuring me some books on letter writing, as you once promised, and which I know you would already have provided, if only your memory had served you.

The current mother abbess is Caterina Angela Anselmi.

Vincenzio came to see us yesterday morning (for perhaps the space of one hour) together with my sister-in-law and her mother, and from her we heard that you wanted to go to Rome, Sire, which put me into quite an agitated state. However, I calm myself with the thought that you would not prego il Signore che li conceda la Sua santa gratia. Di S. Matteo, li 14 di Marzo 1629.

Di V. S. molto Ill.re Fig.la Aff.ma

Suor Maria Celeste

Se ha collari da imbiancare, potrà mandarli; e si goda queste huova fresche per nostro amore.

Amatiss.mo Sig.r Padre,

Speravo di poter in voce satisfare al debito che tengo con V. S. di darle le buone Feste, et per ciò ho differito fino a questo giorno, nel quale, vedendo riuscir vane le mie speranze, vengo con questa a salutarla caramente e rallegrarmi che siano passate felicemente le Sante Feste di Pasqua, giovandomi di creder ch'ella stia bene non solo corporalmente, ma anco spiritualmente: e ne ringratio Dio benedetto. Solo mi dà qualche disturbo il sentire che V. S. stia ton tanta assiduità intorno a i suoi studii, perchè temo che ciò non sia con pregiuditio della sua sanità; e non vorrei che, cercando di immortalar la sua fama, accorciassi la sua vita, vita tanto riverita e tenuta tanto cara da noi suoi figliuoli, e da me in particolare, perchè, sì come ne gl'anni precedo gl'altri, così anco ardisco di dire che li precedo e supero nell'amore inverso di V. S. Pregola per canto che non si affatichi di soverchio, undertake such a journey if you did not feel well enough to do so. I believe that before this comes to pass we will see each other again, and therefore I make no other comment here. Except that I send you loving regards with all my heart together with everyone in the room, and I pray the Lord to grant you His holy grace. From San Matteo, the 14th of March 1629.

Sire's Most Affectionate Daughter,
Suor Maria Celeste

If you have collars to whiten you can send them to me, and please enjoy these fresh eggs with our love.

Most Beloved Lord Father,

I was hoping to convey in person, Sire, the holiday wishes I owe you, and therefore I waited until today, the day when, seeing those hopes end vainly, I come with this letter to greet you dearly, and to rejoice in the happy passage of the holy festival days of Easter, as it does me good to believe that you are well not only physically, but also spiritually, and I thank blessed God for that. The only thing that disturbs me is the report I hear of how assiduously you are attacking your scholarly work, Sire, because I fear that this behavior is not without risk to your health. And I would not want you, while seeking to immortalize your fame, to cut short your life; a life held in such reverence and treasured so preciously by us your children, and by me in particular. Because, just as I have precedence over the others in years, so too do I dare to claim that I precede and surpass them in my love for you, Sire. I acciò non causi danno a sè et afflitione e tormento a noi. Non dirò altro per non tediarla, se non che di cuore la saluto insieme con S.r Arcangela e tutte le amiche, e prego il Signore che la conservi in Sua gratia. Di S. Matteo, li 6 d'Aprile 1630.

Di V. S. Fig.la Aff.ma

Suor Maria Celeste

Amatiss.mo Sig.r Padre,

Non ho dubbio alcuno che V. S. non sia pronta a mandarmi molto volentieri quanto hier l'altro gli domandai; ma se per disgratia la memoria non gli servissi, ho stimato necessario il tenergli ricordato il fiasco di vino, due ricotte e quell'altra cosa per doppo l'arrosto; non limone o ramerino, come V. S. disse, ma cosa di fondamento, secondo il suo gusto, per domattina all'hora del desinare monache. La staremo aspettando, insieme con la cognata e Vincenzio, sì come ne promesse. Et fra tanto, pregandole da Nostro Signore ogni desiderato contento, la salutiamo di cuore. Li 14 d'Aprile 1630.

Sua Fig.la Aff.ma

Suor Maria Celeste

pray you therefore not to invite exhaustion through overexertion, so that you do no harm to yourself and cause neither anguish nor torment to us. I will say no more, so as not to bore you, save that I send you the loving regards of my heart together with Suor Arcangela and all our friends, and I pray the Lord to keep you in His grace. From San Matteo, the 6th of April 1630.

Sire's Most Affectionate Daughter,

Suor Maria Celeste

Most Beloved Lord Father,

I have no doubt whatsoever of your readiness, Sire, to send me most willingly all that I asked you for the other day; but in the unfortunate event that your memory may have failed you, I thought it wise to remind you of the flask of wine, the two buttermilk cheeses, and that other item to have after the roast meat; not lemons, or rosemary, as you said, Sire, but something fundamental according to my tastes for tomorrow morning at the hour when the Nuns dine. That is, we will be expecting you, Sire, together with my sister-in-law and Vincenzio, just as you promised us. And meanwhile, praying to Our Lord for the fulfillment of your every desire, we send you loving regards. The 14th of April 1630.

Galileo leaves for Rome soon after this family gathering, arriving May 3 for a two-month stay to arrange publication of his ***Dialogue****.*

Your Most Affectionate Daughter,

Suor Maria Celeste

Amatiss.mo Sig.r Padre,

Ho preso infinito contento, insieme con S.r Arcangela, di sentire che V. S. sta bene, il che più mi preme che altra cosa del mondo. Io sto ragionevolmente, ma non interamente bene, poi che ancora sono in purga mediante la mia oppilatione; e per questo e per le molte faccende che haviamo in bottega in questo tempo, non ho prima scritto a V. S. et alla S.r Ambasciatrice. Mi perdoni la negligenza, e veda se l'inclusa sia a proposito; se no, ne aspetto la corretione.

S.r Arcangela e tutte l'altre stanno bene, eccetto S.r Violante, che se ne sta con il suo solito flusso di corpo.

La Madre badessa saluta V. S., e le tien ricordato quanto in voce le disse: ciò è che, se per sorte se li porgessi qualche occasione di procurar qualche elemosina per il nostro monastero, facci questa carità d'affaticarsi per amor di Dio e nostro sollevamento: et io di più aggiungo che veramente par cosa stravagante il domandare a persone così lontane, le quali, quando habbiano a far benefitio ad alcuno, lo vorranno fare a i loro vicini e compatriotti; non dimeno io so che V. S. sa, aggiustando il tempo, trovar dell'occasioni da poter ottener l'intento suo; e per ciò gli raccomando caldamente questo negotio, perchè veramente siamo in estrema necessità, e se non fossi l'aiuto che haviamo di qualche elemosina, andremmo a risico di morirci di fame. Ma sia pur sempre lodato il Signore, che con tutta la nostra povertà non permette che patiamo d'altro che di afflitione d'animo, per veder la nostra Madre badessa continuamente afflitta per questa causa; et io particolarmente molto gli compatisco e vorrei poterla aiutare, portandoli affetione più che ordinaria. Le ricordo ancora le

Most Beloved Lord Father,

I took the greatest delight, along with Suor Arcangela, in hearing that you are well, Sire, which matters more to me than anything else in the world. I feel reasonably, but not entirely well, since I am still taking the purgative on account of my blockage; and it is for this reason, as well as all the pressing duties to be tended to in the apothecary shop just at this juncture, that I have not written sooner to you, Sire, or to Her Ladyship the Ambassadress. But please pardon my negligence, and see if the enclosed letter suits the purpose; if not, I will await your correction.

Caterina Riccardi Niccolini, wife of the Tuscan ambassador to Rome, has taken an interest in Suor Maria Celeste.

Suor Arcangela and all the others fare well, except Suor Violante who struggles against her ongoing dysentery.

The Mother Abbess sends her regards to you, Sire, and reminds you of what she told you in person: that is, if chance should offer you the opportunity there in Rome to obtain some charitable help for our Monastery, to please extend yourself in this effort for the love of God and for our relief; although I must add that truly it seems an extraordinary thing to ask of people living so far away, who, when doing a good deed for someone, would prefer to favor their own neighbors and compatriots. Nonetheless I know that you know, Sire, by biding your time, how to pick the perfect moment for implementing your intentions successfully; and therefore I eagerly encourage you in this endeavor, because indeed we really are in dire need, and if it were not for the help we have received from several donations of alms, we would be at risk of starving to death; but may the Lord be ever praised, for, despite the depth of our poverty, He protects us from suffering anyreliquie che gli domandai, e per non tediarla finisco, salutandola insieme con tutte affettuosamente. E prego Nostro Signore che la conservi. Di S. Matteo, li 25 di Mag.º 1630.

Di V. S. molto Ill.re Fig.la Aff.ma

Suor Maria Celeste

Amatiss.mo Sig.r Padre,

Quando appunto andavo pensando di scriver a V. S. una carta di lamentationi per la sua lunga dimora o tardanza in visitarne, mi è comparsa la sua amorevolissima, la quale mi serra la bocca di maniera che non ho replica. Solamente me gl'accuso per troppo timorosa o sospettosa, poi dubitavo che l'amore che V. S. porta a quelli che gli sono presenti, fossi causa che si intepidissi e, diminuissi quello che porta a noi, che gli siamo assenti. Conosco veramente che in questo mi dimostro di animo vile e codardo, poi che con generosità dovrei persuadermi che, sì come io non cederei ad alcuno in questo particolare, ciò è nell'amar lei, così, all'incontro, che lei ami più di ciascun altro noi sue figliuole; ma credo che questo timore proceda da scarsezza di meriti. E questo basti per hora.

Ci dispiace il sentire la sua indispositione, e veramente, per haver V. S. fatto viaggio nella stagione che siamo, non poteva thing other than the sorrow of the spirit, which we feel for seeing our Mother Abbess continually afflicted by our difficulties; and I for one sympathize with her a great deal, and would like to be able to help her, as I am especially fond of her. I remind you again of the relics that I requested, and so as not to tire you I will finish by sending you loving greetings, from me and from everyone here. And I pray our Lord to bless you. From San Matteo, the 25th of May 1630.

Sire's Most Affectionate Daughter,

Suor Maria Celeste

Most Beloved Lord Father,

This letter is addressed to Galileo at Bellosguardo, as he had left Rome by the end of June.

The very moment I was thinking of writing you a list of lamentations upon your long absence, or delay in visiting me, Sire, your loving tenderness is made manifest to me, locking my lips against complaint. I suppose I only accuse myself of being too shy and distrustful, whenever I suspect that the love you demonstrate to those in your presence, Sire, could diminish and degrade that which you bear us who are absent. I see very well that such thoughts display a vile and cowardly spirit, because with generosity I would have to persuade myself that, just as I could never cede to another in the matter of loving you, thus must you love us your daughters more than anyone else you might meet face to face; but I believe that my apprehension springs from my own lack of merit; and this explanation will have to suffice for now.

We are sorry to learn of your illness, and truly, Sire, this was the inevitable outcome of your having traveled about in the esser altrimenti; anzi che mi stupivo, sentendo che V. S. andava ogni giorno in Firenze. La prego per tanto a starsene qualche giorno in riposo, nè pigli fretta di venir da noi, perchè ci è più cara la sua sanità che la sua vista. In tanto veda se per sorte gl'è restata una corona per portarmi, la quale vorrei mandar alla mia S.r Ortensia, essendo un gran pezzo che non gl'ho scritto, sì come anco ho mancato non scrivendo prima a V. S., mediante l'esser ancor io stata sopraffatta da una estrema lassezza, e tale che non mi dava il cuore di muover la penna, per così dire. Ma da poi in qua che è alquanto cessato il caldo, sto benissimo, per gratia del Signor Iddio, il quale non lascio di continuamente pregar per la salute e sanità di V. S., premendomi non meno la sua che la mia propria.

La ringratiamo del vino e frutte, così a noi oltremodo gratissime: e perchè serbavamo questi pochi marzapanetti, numero 12, per quando veniva da noi, adesso glieli mandiamo, acciò non indurischino; i biscottini saranno per la Virginia. Per fine la salutiamo, insieme con la Madre badessa e tutte, affettuosamente. Di S. Matteo, li 21 di Luglio 1630.

Sua Fig.la Aff.ma

Suor M.a Celeste

hot weather that oppresses us: I was rather astonished to hear how you were going to Florence every day. I beg you therefore to take a few days of rest, and not rush yourself here for a visit, because your health is even more dear to us than the sight of you. Meanwhile please see if by chance you have a rosary you could bring me, for I would like to send one to my Lady Ortensia, as I have not written to her in a very long time, just as I have also been remiss in not writing sooner to you, Sire, on account of still feeling oppressed by an extreme lassitude, such that drained me of the will even to move my pen, so to speak. But now that the heat has let up somewhat, I am feeling very well, by the grace of the Lord God, to whom I pray unceasingly for your health and well-being, Sire, as yours matters no less to me than my own.

We thank you for the wine and the fruits which we were even more delighted than usual to receive, and although we have been saving these few pieces of marzipan (12 in number) for when you came here, we are sending them now, so that they do not grow stale: the little cookies are for La Virginia. I close by sending you loving greetings from all of us including the Mother Abbess. From San Matteo, the 21st of July 1630.

This young Virginia is Galileo's grandniece, the daughter of Vincenzio Landucci and his wife, Anna di Cosimo Diociaiuti.

Your Most Affectionate Daughter,

Suor M. Celeste

Amatiss.mo Sig.r Padre,

Per mia buona sorte mi è accaduto il poter in qualche parte supplire alla minore delle molte disgrazie che V. S. mi disse esserle accadute, ciò è d'esserseli guasto 2 barili di aceto, in vece de i quali io ne ho provvisti questi due fiaschi che gli mando; il quale, in questi tempi, ho havuto per gratia, e mi par ragionevole. Accetti V. S. la mia buona volontà, desiderosa di poter, se fossi possibile, supplire e concorrere con gl'effetti ad ogni suo bisogno.

S.r Violante, e noi insieme, la ringratia assai de i ranocchi e zatta, gustando non solamente del dono in sè, ma molto più della diligenza e sollecitudine di V. S.

Madonna hiermattina m'impose ch'io dovessi domandar a V. S., se credeva che della elemosina havuta dal Ser.mo G. Duca si dovessi far ringratiamento, poi che, per havercela portata qui un lavoratore che sta al Barbadoro, non se ne fece ricevuta. Io me lo scordai, et hora prego V. S. a darmene indizio con suo comodo, et in tanto spero di sentir anco buon esito della supplica che si fece hiermattina. La saluto in nome di tutte, e prego Nostro Signor che la conservi. Li 4 7mbre 1630.

Sua Fig.la Aff.ma
Suor M. Celeste.

Nel fiasco più vecchio dell'aceto vi sono state alcune poche roselline.

Most Beloved Lord Father,

By my good fortune it has befallen me to be able in some measure to make up for the most minor of the many mishaps you tell me have befallen you, Sire, meaning the spoiling of the two *barili* of vinegar, in place of which I have provided these two *fiaschi* which I send you now, as we had them on hand and they appear to be fine; do accept my sincere willingness, Sire, if only it were possible for me, to meet your every need.

*A **barile** contains about ten gallons of vinegar, or twenty **fiaschi**; thus a single **fiasco** holds about four pints.*

Suor Violante, and we along with her, thank you so much for the frogs and melon, enjoying not only the gift itself, Sire, but your diligence and solicitude even more so.

Madonna yesterday morning enjoined me, Sire, saying that I must ask you whether you believe we still owe some formal thanks for the alms we received from the Grand Duke, because, as the gift was brought here to us by a workman who still remains at Barbadoro, we have not yet acknowledged its receipt; I forgot about it, and now I beseech you, Sire, to give me some guidance at your convenience, and meanwhile I hope to hear also of a good outcome to the appeal that you made yesterday morning. I send you regards from everyone, and I pray our Lord to bless you. The 4th of September 1630.

Twenty-year-old Medici scion Ferdinando II currently rules the Grand Duchy of Tuscany.

Your Most Affectionate Daughter,

Suor M. Celeste

In the older *fiasco* of vinegar there were a few small damask roses.

Amatiss.^{mo} Sig.^{r} Padre,

Non detti risposta all'ultima sua per non trattener troppo il suo servitore; adesso, con più comodità, ringraziandola delle sue tante amorevolezze, gli dico che in presentando le bellissime susine a Sr Violante, hebbi gusto grandissimo per veder l'allegrezza e gratitudine che ella ne dimostrò, sl come anco Sr Luisa delle due pesche, quali gli donai, perchè queste più di tutte l'altre frutte gli gustano.

Ricevo per mortificazione il non esser sortito il negozio di Madonna, perchè forse havevo troppo desiderio che, col mezzo e favore di V. S., ella ricevessi qualche benefizio: pazienza; staremo aspettando l'esito dell'altro di Roma.

Hiersera la Ser.^{ma} ci mandò a presentare una bella cervia, e qua si fece tanta allegrezza e tanto romore quando fu portata, che non credo che tanto ne facessero i cacciatori quando la presero.

Adesso che comincia a rinfrescare, Sr Arcangela et io, insieme con le nostre più care, facciamo disegno di star a lavorare nella mia cella, che è molto capace; ma perchè la finestra è assai alta, ha bisogno d'esser rimpannata, acciò si possi veder un poco più lume. Io vorrei mandarla (cioè li sportelli) a V. S., acciò me la accomodassi con panno incerato, che, quando sia vecchio, non credo che darà fastidio; ma prima havrò caro di sapere s'ella si contenti di farmi questo servizio. Non dubito della sua amorevolezza; ma perchè l'opera è più tosto da legnaiuoli che da filosofi, ho qualche temenza. Dicami adunque liberamente l'animo suo, ch'io in tanto, insieme con la Madre badessa e tutte le amiche, la salu-

Most Beloved Lord Father,

I offered no reply to your last letter, not wanting to detain your servant too long; now with more leisure, thanking you for all your loving thoughtfulness, I tell you that I took the greatest pleasure in proffering those exquisite plums to Suor Violante, seeing the happiness and gratitude that she showed me, as did Suor Luisa, too, for the two peaches you gave her, because she loves these more than all the other fruits.

I am mortified to hear that Madonna's appeal did not succeed, because I had perhaps too strong a wish that, with your assistance and favor, Sire, she would have received some good return: never mind, we shall await the outcome of that other effort in Rome.

Yesterday evening her highness the Grand Duchess sent over a beautiful doe to be presented to us, and everyone here made such merriment and so much noise when the deer was brought in, that I do not believe the hunters who caught it could have been more excited.

This largesse comes from the mother of the grand duke, Archduchess Maria Maddalena of Austria.

Now that the weather is beginning to turn cool, Suor Arcangela and I, together with our dearest friends, are planning to do our work in my cell, which is so spacious; but because the window is very high, it needs to be newly covered in a way that will admit a little more light. I would like to send it to you, Sire, meaning the windowpanes themselves, in the hope that you could help me by fitting them with waxed linen, which I believe will give us no trouble as it ages, but first I need to know if you will agree to do me this service. I do not doubt your loving attention; but because the work is to di cuore, e prego Dio benedetto che la conservi nella Sua gratia.   Di S. Matteo, li 10 di 7mbre 1630.

Sua Fig.[la] Aff.[ma]

Suor M. Celeste

Amatiss.mo Sig.r Padre,

Sto con l'animo assai travagliato e sospeso, immaginandomi che V. S. si ritrovi molto disturbata, mediante la repentina morte del suo povero lavoratore. Suppongo ch'ella procurerà con ogni diligenza possibile di guardarsi dal pericolo, del che la prego caldamente; et anco credo che non gli manchino i rimedii e difensivi proportionati alle presenti necessità, onde non replicherò altro intorno a questo. Ma ben, con ogni debita reverenza e confidenza filiale, l'esorterò a procurar l'ottimo rimedio, quale è la grazia di Dio benedetto, col mezzo d'una vera contrizione e penitenza. Questa, senza dubbio, è la più efficace medicina non solo per l'anima, ma per il corpo ancora; poi che se è tanto necessario, per ovviare al male contagioso, lo star allegramente, qual maggior allegrezaa può provarsi in questa vita di quella che c'apporta una buona e serena conscienza? Certo che quando possederemo questo tesoro, non temeremo nè pericoli nè morte; e poi che il Signore giustamente ne gastiga con questi flagelli, cerchiamo noi, con l'aiuto Suo, di star preparati per ricever il colpo da quella potente mano, la quale, havendoci cortesemente donarather more suited to a carpenter than a philosopher, I hesitate to ask. Therefore speak your mind freely to me on this matter, while I in the meantime send you loving greetings along with the Mother Abbess and all your friends here, and I pray blessed God to keep you in His holy grace. From San Matteo, the 10th of September 1630.

Your Most Affectionate Daughter,

Suor M. Celeste

Most Beloved Lord Father,

I am heartsick and worried, Sire, imagining how disturbed you must be over the sudden death of your poor unfortunate worker. I assume that you will use every possible precaution to protect yourself from the danger, and I fervently urge you to make great effort in this endeavor; I further believe that you possess remedies and preventatives proportionate to the present threat, wherefore I promise not to dwell on the subject. But still with all due respect and filial confidence I will exhort you to procure the best remedy of all, which is the grace of blessed God, by means of a thorough contrition and penitence. This, without doubt, is the most efficacious medicine, not only for the soul, but for the body as well: since, given that living happily is so crucial to the avoidance of contagious illness, what greater happiness could one secure in this life than the joy that comes of a clear and calm conscience? It is certain that when we possess this treasure we will fear neither danger nor death; and since the Lord justly chastises us with these whips, we try, with His aid, to stand ready to receive the blow from that mighty hand, which, hav-

Galileo's glassblower falls early victim to the bubonic plague epidemic that has recently invaded Florence.

to la presente vita, è padrona di privarcene come e quando gli piace.

Accetti V. S. queste poche parole profferite con uno svisceratissimo affetto, et anco resti consapevole della disposizione nella quale, per grazia del Signore, io mi ritrovo, ciò è desiderosa di passarmene all'altra vita, poi che ogni giorno veggo più chiaro la vanità e miseria della presente: oltre che finirei d'offender Iddio benedetto, spererei di poter con più efficacia pregar per V. S. Non so se questo mio desiderio sia troppo interessato: il Signore, che vede il tutto, supplisca per Sua misericordia ove io manco per mia ignoranza, et a V. S. doni vera consolazione.

Noi qua siamo tutte sane del corpo, eccetto S.r Violante, la quale va a poco a poco consumandosi; ma ben siamo travagliate dalla penuria e povertà, ma non in maniera che ne patiamo detrimento nel corpo, con l'aiuto del Signore.

Havrei caro d'intender se V. S. ha mai havuta risposta alcuna di Roma, circa la elemosina per noi domandata.

Il Sig.r Corso mandò il peso di seta di lib. 15, del quale Suor Arcangela et io haviamo havuta la nostra parte.

Scrivo a hore 7: imperò V. S. mi scuserà se farò degl'errori, perchè il giorno non ho un'hora di tempo che sia mia, poi che all'altre mie occupazioni s'aggiugne l'insegnare di canto fermo a 4 giovanette, e per ordine di Madonna ordinare l'offizio del coro giorno per giorno; il che non mi è di poca fatica, per non haver cognizione alcuna della lingua latina. È ben vero che questi esercizii mi sono di molto gusto, s'io non havessi anco necessità di lavorare. Ma di tutto questo ne cavo ing magnanimously granted us the present life, retains the power to deprive us of it at any moment and in any manner.

Please accept these few words proffered with an overflowing heart, Sire, and also be aware of the situation in which, by the Lord's mercy, I find myself, for I am yearning to enter the other life, as every day I see more plainly the vanity and misery of this one: in death I would stop offending blessed God, and I would hope to be able to pray ever more effectively, Sire, for you. I do not know but that this desire of mine may be too selfish. I pray the Lord, who sees everything, to provide through His compassion what I fail to ask in my ignorance, and to grant you, Sire, true consolation.

All of us here are in good physical health, save for Suor Violante, who is little by little wasting away: although indeed we are burdened by penury and poverty, which take their toll on us, still we are not made to suffer bodily harm, with the help of the Lord.

I am eager to know if you have had any response from Rome, regarding the alms you requested for us.

Signor Corso sent a weight of silk totaling 15 pounds, and Suor Arcangela and I have had our share of it.

Signor Corso is the brother of Suor Giulia.

I am writing at the seventh hour: I shall insist that you excuse me if I make mistakes, Sire, because the day does not contain one hour of time that is mine, since in addition to my other duties I have now been assigned to teach Gregorian chant to four young girls, and by Madonna's orders I am responsible for the day-to-day conducting of the choir: which last creates considerable labor for me, with my poor grasp of the Latin lan-

Since the counting of the day's hours begins at sunset, the seventh hour arrives about midnight this time of year.

un bene non piccolo, ciò è il non stare in ozio un quarto d'hora mai mai, eccetto che mi è necessario il dormire assai per causa della testa. Se V. S. m'insegnassi il secreto che usa per sè, che dorme così poco, l'havrei molto caro, perchè finalmente 7 hore di sonno ch'io mando male, mi par pur troppo.

Non dico altro per non tediarla, se non che la saluto affettuosamente insieme con le solite amiche. Di S. Matteo, li 18 8bre 1630.

Sua Fig.la Aff.ma

Suor M. Celeste

Il panierino ch'io gli mandai ultimamente con alcune paste, non è mio, e per ciò desidero che me lo rimandi.

Amatiss.mo Sig.r Padre,

Non havevo alcun dubbio che V. S. non dovessi farmi la grazia domandatale circa la copia della lettera per il nuovo Arcivescovo; e con tutto che ella dica di non haver fatto cosa buona, sarà non dimeno molto meglio di quello ch'io havessi mai poturofare da per me. La ringrazio infinitamente, e con questa occasione gli mando 6 pere cotogne, quali ho provviste per haver inteso da lei che gli gustano e che non ne trovava, che veramente di simili frutti ne è gran carestia, per quanto intendo; con tutto ciò, se mi sarà osservata la promessa che mi è stata fatta, credo che gliene manderò qualcun'altra.

guage. It is certainly true that these exercises are very much to my liking, if only I did not also have to work; yet from all this I do derive one very good thing, which is that I never ever sit idle for even one quarter of an hour. Except that I require sufficient sleep to clear my head. If you would teach me the secret you yourself employ, Sire, for getting by on so little sleep, I would be most grateful, because in the end the seven hours that I waste sleeping seem far too many to me.

I shall say no more so as not to bore you, adding only that I give you my loving greetings together with our usual friends. From San Matteo, the 18th of October 1630.

Your Most Affectionate Daughter,
Suor M. Celeste

The little basket, which I sent you recently with several pastries, is not mine, and therefore I wish you to return it to me.

Most Beloved Lord Father,

I never doubted that you would find a way, Sire, to do me the favor I asked of you regarding the copy of your letter for the new Archbishop, and despite all you may say about not having turned a good deed, it will nonetheless turn out to be much better than anything I could ever have done by myself. I thank you from the bottom of my heart, and take this occasion to send you six quince pears I prepared, having heard from your own lips that they are a particular favorite of yours and yet you have not found any, for truly there is a great dearth of such fruits, as everyone knows: and on that score, if the promise

Havrò caro di intender se Vincenzio sia poi andato a Prato. Io havevo pensiero di scrivergli l'animo mio intorno a questo, esortandolo a non partirsi o almeno a non lasciar la casa impedita, chè questa mi par veramente cosa strana, per gl'accidenti che potrebbono occorrere; ma dubitando di far poco frutto e molto scompiglio, ho lasciato di farlo, e tanto più che tengo speranza indubitabile che Dio benedetto sia per supplire con la Sua provvidenza ove mancano gl'huomini, non voglio dire per poca affezione, ma per poca intelligenza e considerazione. Saluto V. S. con tutto l'affetto insieme con le amiche, e l'accompagno sempre con le mie povere orazioni.

Li 28 di 8bre 1630.

Sua Fig.la Aff.ma

Suor M. Celeste

Amatiss.mo Sig.r Padre,

So che V. S. sa meglio di me che le tribolazioni sono la pietra del paragone, ove si fa prova della finezza dell'amor di Dio; sì che tanto quanto le piglieremo pazientemente dalla sua mano, tanto potremo prometterci di posseder questo tesoro, ove consiste ogni nostro bene. La prego a non pigliar il coltello di questi disturbi e contrarietà per il taglio, acciò da quello non resti offesa, ma più tosto, prendendolo a dritto, se ne serva per tagliar con quello tutte le imperfezioni che per avventura conoscerà in sè stessa, acciò, levati gl'impedimenti, sì come con vista di Linceo ha penetrato i cieli, così, pemade to me is honored, I believe I will be sending you another one.

I shall be most eager to learn whether Vincenzio has taken refuge in Prato: I had thought of writing him my honest opinion on this, exhorting him not to go, or at least not to leave the house unguarded; because this seems to me a truly rash act, considering all the mishaps that could occur; but, suspecting such efforts on my part to bear little fruit and cause much fuss, I let it go: and all the more do I cling to the indubitable hope that blessed God will make up through His providence what men fail to do, if not for lack of feeling, then for want of intelligence and consideration. I greet you with all my love together with our friends, and I accompany you always with my humble prayers.   The 28th of October 1630.

Your Most Affectionate Daughter,
Suor M. Celeste

Vincenzio and Sestilia have fled the city to escape the plague, taking refuge in a villa the Bocchineri family keeps at Montemurlo, in the countryside between Prato and Pistoia.

Most Beloved Lord Father,

I am sure you know better than I, Sire, that tribulations are the touchstone where we test the quality of God's love. Thus, to whatever extent we can patiently bear the trials He doles out, then in that same measure do we promise ourselves possession of the treasure of His love, which comprises our every good. I beseech you not to grasp the knife of these current troubles and misfortunes by its sharp edge, lest you let it injure you that way; but rather, seizing it by the blunt side, use it to excise all the imperfections you may recognize in yourself; so that you rise above the obstacles, and in this fashion, just as you penenetrando anco le cose più basse, arrivi a conoscerti la vanità e fallacia di tutte queste cose terrene; vedendo e toccando con mano che nè amor di figliuoli, nè piaceri, onori o ricchezze, ci posson dar vera contentezza, essendo cose per sè stesse troppo instabili, ma che solo in Dio benedetto, come in ultimo nostro fine, possiamo trovar vera quiete. O che gaudio sarà il nostro, quando, squarciato questo fragil velo che ne impedisce, a faccia a faccia goderemo questo gran Dio! Affatichiamoci pure questi pochi giorni di vita che ci restano, per guadagnare un bene così grande e perpetuo. Ove parmi, carissimo S.r Padre, che V. S. s'incamini per diritta strada, mentre si vale dell'occasioni che se gli porgono, e particolarmente nel far di continuo benefizii a persone che la ricompensano d'ingratitudine; azione veramente che quanto ha più del difficile, tanto è più perfetta e virtuosa: anzi che questa più che altra virtù mi pare che ci renda simili all'istesso Dio, poi che in noi stessi esperimentiamo che, mentre tutto il giorno offendiamo S. D. M., egli all'incontro va pur facendone infiniti benefizii; e se pur tal volta ci gastiga, fa questo per maggior nostro bene, a guisa di buon padre che per corregger il figlio prende la sferza: sì come par che segua di presente nella nostra povera città, acciò che almeno, mediante il timore del soprastante pericolo, ci emendiamo.

Non so se V. S. haverà intesa la morte di Matteo Ninci, fratello della nostra S.r M.a Teodora, il quale, per quanto ne scrive M.r Alessandro suo fratello, non ha havuto male più che 3 o 4 giorni, et ha fatto questo passaggio molto in grazia di Dio, per quanto si è potuto comprendere. Gl'altri credo che siano sani, ma ben assai travagliati per haver fatta la lor casa una gran perdita. Credo che V. S. ne sentirà disgusto, come lo sentrated the heavens with the vision of a Lyncean, so will you, by piercing also through baser realms, arrive at an awareness of the vanity and fallacy of all earthly things: seeing and touching with your own hands the truth that neither the love of your children, nor pleasures, honors or riches can confer true contentment, being in themselves ephemeral; but that only in blessed God, as in our final destination, can we find real peace. Oh what joy will then be ours, when, rending this fragile veil that impedes us, we revel in the glory of God face to face! By all means let us struggle hard through these few days of life that we have left, so as to be deserving of a blessing so vast and everlasting. Wherefore it appears to me, my dearest Lord Father, that you must keep to your own right path, availing yourself of opportunities as they present themselves, and especially those that allow you to perpetuate your beneficence toward those who repay you with ingratitude, for truly this action, being so rife with difficulty, is all the more perfect and virtuous: indeed I think such behavior, far above any other virtue, renders us in God's image, since, as we know from experience, while we go about offending His Divine Majesty all through the day, He responds by constantly showering us with blessings: and if He chastises us now and then, He does so for our greater well-being, in the manner of a good father who keeps his son in line with the whip. Something of the same seems to be happening now in our poor city, where, spurred on as we are by our dread of the danger hanging over us, at least we amend ourselves.

Galileo belongs to a scientific society, the ***Accademia dei Lincei,*** *or Lyncean Academy, whose members observe nature with the sharp eyes of the lynx.*

I do not know whether you have heard, Sire, of the death of Matteo Ninci, brother of our Suor Maria Teodora, who, according to what her brother Alessandro writes, had not tiamo noi, perchè era veramente giovane di grandissimo garbo e molto amorevole.

Ma non voglio però darle solamente le nuove cattive, ma dirle anco che la lettera ch'io scrissi per parte di Madonna a Ms.r Arcivescovo, fu da lui molto gradita, e se n'hebbe cortese risposta, con offerta d'ogni suo favore et aiuto. Similmente due suppliche che feci la settimana passata per la Serenissima e per Madama hanno havuto buon esito, poi che da Madama havemmo la mattina d'Ogni Santi elemosina di 300 pani e ordine di mandar a pigliar un moggio di grano, con il quale s'è alleggerito l'affanno di Madonna, perchè non haveva da seminare.

V. S. mi perdoni se troppo l'infastidisco con tanto cicalare, perchè (oltre ch'ella mi innanimisce col darmi indizio che gli siano grate le mie lettere) io fo conto ch'ella sia il mio devoto (per parlare alla nostra usanza), con il quale io comunico tutti i miei pensieri e partecipo de i miei gusti e disgusti, e, trovandolo sempre prontissimo a sovvenirmi, gli domando, non tutti i miei bisogni, perchè sariano troppi, ma sì bene il più necessario di presente; perchè, venendo il freddo, mi converrà intirizzarmi, s'egli non mi soccorre mandandomi un coltrone per tener addosso: poi che quello ch'io tengo non è mio, e la padrona se ne vuol servire, come è dovere; quello che havemmo da V. S. insieme con il panno, lo lascio a S.r Arcangela, la quale vuol star sola a dormire et io l'ho caro; ma resto con una sargia sola, e se aspetto di guadagnare da comprarlo, non l'haverò nè manco quest'altro inverno: sì che io lo domando in carità a questo mio devoto tanto affezionato, il quale so ben io che non potrà comportar ch'io patisca.

been ill more than 3 or 4 days, and made his passage very much in God's grace, as far as could be determined. The others in the household still have their health, I believe, but they are all sorely tried by their great loss. I suspect you must feel as shocked as we do, Sire, remembering what a well-mannered youth he was, and how very lovable.

But then, not wanting to give you only the bad news, I must tell you also that the letter I wrote, on Madonna's behalf, to Monsignor Archbishop, was very well received by him, and she had a courteous reply with an offer of all his protection and aid. Similarly, two requests made last week to the Grand Duke and the Grand Duchess have both produced a good outcome, as we received from Her Highness on the morning of All Saints' Day [November 1] a donation of 300 loaves of bread, and orders that we send someone to collect a *moggio* of grain for us, which greatly alleviates Madonna's anxiety, for she did not have so much as a seed to sow.

Madama Cristina of Lorraine, though she is grandmother to the current grand duke, still keeps her title of grand duchess—and an active hand in the Tuscan government.

*One **moggio** is the equivalent of twenty-four bushels.*

Pardon me, Sire, if I annoy you excessively with my lengthy chatter, but, beyond your encouraging me through demonstrations of proof that you enjoy my letters, I consider you my *devoto* (to speak in our parlance of patron saints) in whom I confide my every thought, and share all my joys and sorrows; and, finding you always ready and willing to assist me, I ask you, not to fill all my needs, because they are too numerous, but to please see to those that are most pressing at present: for, with the chill weather coming on, I will surely grow numb with cold, unless you help by sending me a warm quilt to protect me, since the one I have now is not mine, and its owner wants to use it herself, as is only right. The one that you sent,

Piaccia al Signore (se è per il meglio) di conservarmelo ancora lungo tempo, perchè doppo di lui non mi resta bene alcuno nel mondo. Ma è pur gran cosa ch'io non sia buona per rendergli il contraccambio in cosa alcuna. Procurerò almeno, anzi al più, d'importunar tanto Dio benedetto e la Madonna Santissima che egli si conduca al Paradiso; e questa sarà la maggior ricompensa ch'io possa darle per tutti i beni che mi ha fatti e fa continuamente.

Gli mando due vasetti di lattovaro preservativo dalla peste. Quello che non vi è scritto sopra, è composto con fichi secchi, noci, ruta e sale, unito il tutto con tanto mele che basti. Se ne piglia la mattina a digiuno quanto una noce, con bervi dietro un poco di greco o vino buono; e dicono che è esperimentato per difensivo mirabile. È ben vero che ci è riuscito troppo cotto, perchè non avvertimmo alla condizione dei fichi secchi, che è di assodare. Anco di quell'altro se ne piglia un boccone nell'istessa maniera, ma è un poco più ostico. Se vorrà usare o dell'uno o dell'altro, procureremo di farli con più perfezione. V. S. mi dice nella sua lettera di mandarmi l'occhiale; m'immagino che dipoi se lo scordassi, e per ciò gliene ricordo insieme con il canestro nel quale mandai le cotogne, acciò possi mandargliene dell'altre, facendo pur diligenza di trovarne. Con che per fine me le raccomando con tutto il cuore, insieme con le solite. Di S. Matteo, il giorno dei Morti del 1630.

Sua Fig.la Aff.ma

Suor M. Celeste

Sire, along with the woolen blanket, I leave with Suor Arcangela, who wants to sleep alone, and I respect her wishes. But I am left with only one cotton coverlet, and if I wait until I have earned enough to buy a quilt, I will neither get one, nor survive this winter: therefore I beg this benevolence of my beloved *devoto*, who, as I know so well, will not be able to bear the thought of my suffering: and may it please the Lord (if it be for the best) to keep him with me for a long time to come, because, after he goes, I am left all alone in this world. But indeed it weighs heavily on me that I cannot offer him a proper exchange for his generous gifts! I will endeavor at least, or rather more than ever, to importune blessed God and the Most Holy Virgin that he be conducted into Paradise; and this will be the greatest reward that I can give him for all the good he has done and continues to do for me.

Here are two small jars of electuary for safeguarding against the plague. The one that has no written label is composed of dried figs, nuts, rue and salt, held together with as much honey as was needed. You may take it every morning, before eating, in a dose about the size of a walnut, followed immediately by drinking a little Greek or other good wine, and they say it provides a marvelous defense. I must admit that it has been overcooked, because we did not consider the tendency of the figs to harden. The other mixture is also to be taken by mouthful in the same manner as the first, but it has a harsher taste. If you decide to make regular use of either one, we will try to prepare them with greater skill. You say in your letter, Sire, that you mean to send me the telescope; I suppose that you have since forgotten, and therefore I remind you of it, as well as the basket in which I sent the quinces, because

Amatiss.mo Sig.r Padre,

Desidero di sapere se V. S. sta bene, e per ciò mando costì, con occasione anco di mandarle un poca di acqua delta Madre S.r Orsola di Pistoia. Io l'ho ottenuta per grazia, già che, per haver proibizione le monache di darne, chi ne ha la tiene come reliquia. Prego V. S. che la pigli con gran fede a devozione, come preservativo efficacissimo mandatoci da Nostro Signore, il quale si serve di soggetti debolissimi per dimostrar maggiormente la sua grandezza e potenza; sì come apparisce di presente in questa benedetta Madre, che, di una povera servigiale che era e senza saper pur anco leggere, si è ridotta a governar il suo monastero tanti anni e ridurlo così ordinato quanto è adesso. Io tengo 4 o 5 lettere di suo et altri scritti [. . . .] molto profitto, et ho altre relazioni di lei da persone degne di fede, che danno manifesto indizio della sua gran perfezione e bontà. Prego V. S. per tanto ad haver fede in questo rimedio, perchè se tanta ne dimostra nell'orazioni mie, che sono così miserabile, molto maggiormente può haverla ad un'anima tanto santa, assicurandola che per i suoi meriti scamperà, ogni pericolo. Con che a lei affettuosamente mi

I am diligently working to find more of them for you. With that, to close, I send you greetings with all my heart together with our usual friends. From San Matteo, All Souls' Day 1630.

All Souls' Day, devoted to prayer for souls in purgatory, is celebrated on November 2, the day after All Saints' Day.

Your Most Affectionate Daughter,

Suor M. Celeste

Most Beloved Lord Father,

I want to know if you are well, Sire, and so I am sending for word from you, also taking this opportunity to give you a small quantity of the healing potion made by Abbess Orsola of Pistoia. I was able to get some as a very special favor, since, as the nuns of that convent are prohibited from giving it out, whoever obtains any clings to it like a holy relic. I implore you to take it with great faith and devotion, Sire, as the most effective preventive sent to us by Our Lord, He who works through the weakest persons in order to demonstrate all the more forcefully His majesty and power. Thus He makes Himself manifest now in this blessed nun, who started out as a poor servant girl, not even knowing how to read, yet was obliged to govern her entire monastery for many years, bringing it to the state of order it currently enjoys. I keep 4 or 5 letters from her as well as several other very inspirational writings of hers, and I have further reports about her from people deigned faithful who give clear indication of her extreme perfection and goodness. Therefore I beseech you, Sire, to put your faith in this remedy, because if you believe

Suor Orsola Fontebuoni distills her rare elixir at the Convent of San Mercuriale in Pistoia.

raccomando, e sto con ansietà di saper nuove di lei. Li 8 di 9mbre 1630.

Sua Fig.la Aff.ma

Suor M. Celeste

Amatiss.mo Sig.r Padre,

Domenica mattina a hore 14 passò a miglior vita la nostra Suor Violante, la quale, per haver sofferta così lunga e fastidiosa infermità con molta pazienza e conformità con il volere di S. D. M., possiamo piamente sperare che sia andata in luogo di salute. E veramente da un mese in qua ella era ridotta a tanta miseria, non potendosi nè anco voltar in letto da per sè, e pigliando con estrema pena pochissimo cibo, che pareva esserle quasi desiderabile la morte, come ultimo termine di tutti i nostri travagli. Volevo prima farne consapevole V. S., ma non mi è stato possibile il trovar tanto tempo, del quale ho scarsezza anco adesso, per scrivere; onde non dirò altro, se non che siamo qua tutte sane, per grazia di Dio, e desidero di sapere se il simile segue di lei e della sua poca compagnia, e particolarmente del nostro Galileino.

Devo anco ringraziarla del coltrone mandatomi, il quale è stato pur troppo buono per me. Prego il Signore che gli renda il merito di tutto il bene che mi ha fatto e fa continuamente, con aumentarle la Sua santa grazia in questa vita e concederle la gloria del Paradiso nell'altra. E qui a lei di tutto cuore as strongly as you have indicated in my poor prayers, then all the more greatly can you trust in a soul so saintly, assuring yourself that by her merits you will escape every danger. With that I lovingly greet you and anxiously await receiving news of you. The 8th of November 1630.

Your Most Affectionate Daughter,

Suor M. Celeste

Most Beloved Lord Father,

Sunday morning at the fourteenth hour, our Suor Violante passed on to the other life; seeing how she suffered her long and debilitating illness with great patience and compliance with the will of His Divine Majesty, we can piously hope that she has gone to her salvation; and indeed for the past month she had been reduced to such a miserable state, unable even to turn over in bed by herself, and struggling so to swallow the tiniest bit of food, that death seemed almost desirable to her as the final end of all these trials: I wanted to let you know before now, Sire, but it was impossible for me to find the time, which remains scarce even now, to write; wherefore I will say no more except that we are all well here by the mercy of God; and I want to know if the same is true of you, and of those close to you and especially of our little Galileino.

The long-suffering Suor Violante died at daybreak.

I must also thank you for the quilt you sent me, which was really more than I deserve: I pray the Lord to reward you for all the good you have done for me and do continually, by blessing you with His holy grace in this life and granting you the glory of Paradise in the next: and here with all my heart

In fleeing Florence, Vincenzio and Sestilia left their infant son, nicknamed Galileino, in the care of his grandfather and a neighborhood wet nurse.

mi raccomando insieme con Suor Arcangela e Suor Luisa.
Di S. Matteo, li 26 di 9mbre 1630.

Sua Fig.la Aff.ma

Suor M.a Celeste

Amatiss.mo Sig.r Padre,

La venuta di Madonna Piera mi fu di grandissima consolazione, poi che da lei hebbi certezza della sanità di V. S.; et in conoscer ch'ella sia donna assai prudente e discreta, trovo quella quiete d'animo che per altro non troverei, mentre considero V. S., in tempo tanto pericoloso, priva d'ogn'altra più cara compagnia et assistenza: onde, per ciò io giorno e notte sto con il pensiero fisso in lei, e molte volte mi dolgo della sua lontananza, che impedisce il poter giornalmente sentirne nuove, sì come io grandemente desidererei. Spero non dimeno che Dio benedetto, per Sua misericordia, la deva liberare da ogni sinistro accidente, e di tanto con tutto il cuore Lo prego. E chi sa se forse più copiosa compagnia gli fossi occasione di maggior pericolo? So ben questo, che quanto a noi succede, tutto è con particolar provvidenza del Signore e per maggior nostro bene: e con questo m'acquieto.

Questa sera haviamo havuto comandamento da Monsig.r Arcivescovo di metter in nota tutti i più stretti nostri parenti e domani mandargliela, volendo S. S. Ill.ma procurare che tutti concorrino a sovvenire il nostro monastero, tanto che campiamo quest'invernata così penuriosa. Io ho domandata et ottenuta licenza dalla Madre badessa di poterne far consapevole V. S., acciò non le sia improvvisa tal cosa. Non posso qui

I send you my love together with Suor Arcangela and Suor Luisa. From San Matteo, the 26th of November 1630.

Your Most Affectionate Daughter,

Suor M. Celeste

Most Beloved Lord Father,

The arrival of Dame Piera gave me indeed welcome consolation, Sire, since she assured me of your health; and in recognizing her as the prudent and considerate woman she seems to be, I feel a peace of mind that I would not otherwise find, whilst I think of you in these dangerous times, Sire, deprived of all other more beloved companionship and assistance. For all that, my thoughts stay fixed on you day and night, and many times I rue the great remove that bars me from being able to hear daily news of you, as I would so desire. Nonetheless I hope that blessed God, by His mercy, sees fit to deliver you from every grim misfortune, and so I pray Him with all my heart. And who can tell whether the presence of more plentiful society around you might not occasion greater peril? This much I know, whatever happens to us, everything proceeds from the particular providence of the Lord, and for our best: and with this thought I calm myself.

Piera has replaced Porzia as Galileo's housekeeper.

This evening we received a command from Monsignor Archbishop to set down the names of all our closest relatives, and to send them to him tomorrow, as His Most Illustrious Lordship wishes them all to take part in assisting our Convent, so that we can get through this long wintertime of want. I asked for and obtained permission from the Mother

The new Archbishop, Cosimo Bardi, has taken an interest in the Convent's welfare in response to Suor Maria Celeste's letters.

dir altro, se non raccomandar il negozio al Signor Iddio, e nel resto rimettermi nella prudenza di V. S. Mi dorrebbe assai s'ella restassi aggravata; ma da l'altra banda so che io non posso con buona conscienza cercar d'impedire l'aiuto e sollevamento di questa povera casa, veramente desolata. Questa sola replica (per esser assai universale e nota) gli dico che potrà far a Mons. Arcivescovo, ciò è che sarebbe cosa molto utile e conveniente il cavar di mano a molti parenti di nostre monache i dugento scudi che tengono delle loro sopradote, e non solamente i 200 de i capitali di ciascuna, ma molti ancora de gl'interessi che gli devono di più anni: fra i quali ci s'intende anco Mess.r Benedetto Landucci, debitore a Suor Chiara sua figliuola; e dubito che V. S., per esserli mallevadore, o per lo manco Vincenzio nostro, non deva esserne pagatore, se non si piglia qualche termine. Con questo assegnamento credo che si andrebbe aiutando comodamente il convento, e molto più di quello che potranno far i parenti, poi che sono pochi quelli habbino facultà da poterlo fare. L'intenzione de i superiori è bonissima, e c'aiutano quanto è possibile, ma è troppa grande il nostro bisogno. Io per me non invidio altri in questo mondo che i Padri Cappuccini, che vivono lontani da tante sollecitudini et ansietà quante a noi monache ci conviene havere necessariamente, convenendoci non solo supplire a gl'offizzii per il convento e dar ogn'anno e grano e danari, ma anco pensare a molte nostre necessità particolari con il nostro guadagno, il quale è così scarso che si fanno pochi rilievi. E se io havessi a dir il vero, credo che sia più la perdita, mentre, vegliando fino a sette hore di notte per lavorare, progiudichiamo alla sanità, e consumiamo l'olio che è tanto caro.

Abbess to be allowed to give you fair warning, Sire, so that you are not unduly surprised by such an act. I can say nothing else here except that I leave this affair to the Lord God, and for the rest I entrust myself to your wisdom. It would grieve me very much if you were to be overburdened by the decree; but on the other hand I know that I cannot in good conscience try to impede the succor and support of this poor, truly desolate house. The only possible rejoinder you could offer Monsignor Archbishop (on account of its being sufficiently widespread and well known) is the one I tell you here: namely that it would be a very useful and profitable matter to take out of the hands of many relatives of our nuns the two hundred *scudi* that they control of the sisters' dowries, and not only the two hundred *scudi* of capital for each one, but also the large sums of interest that have accrued to these individuals over the passing years. Among this company, as we gather, even Master Benedetto Landucci is a debtor to Suor Chiara his daughter, and I doubt that you, Sire, on account of serving as guarantor to him, no less to our Vincenzio, can be expected to pay their shares unless you are granted certain terms. With this [assessment], I believe that you would set about helping the Convent comfortably, and do much more than any of the relatives ever could, since so few of them are in a position to make such a suggestion. The intention of the Superiors is extremely good, and they help us as much as possible, but our need is too great. For my part I envy no one else in this world except the Capuchin Fathers, who live far removed from the cares and anxieties that are part and parcel of our lives as nuns, obliging us not only to pay our duty to the Convent by giving donations every year of both grain

Sentendo oggi da Madonna Piera che V. S. diceva che domandassimo se havevamo bisogno di qualcosa, mi lasciai calare a domandarli qualche quattrino per pagare alcuni miei debitelli che mi danno pensiero: chè nel resto, se haviamo tanto che ci possiamo sostentare, è pur assai; che questo, per grazia di Dio, non ci manca.

Del venirci a vedere sento che V. S. non ne tratta, et io non la importuno, perchè ad ogni modo ci sarebbe poca satisfazione, non potendosi parlare liberamente per hora. Ho havuto gran gusto di sentire che i morselletti di cedrato gli siano piaciuti: quelli fatti a forma di cotognato erono di un cedro che con molta instanza havevo provvisto, e d'intenzione di S.r Luisa confettai l'agro insieme con la parte più dura di esso cedrato, chiamandola confezione di tutto cedro; gl'altri gli feci del suo, al modo solito; ma perchè non so quali più gli sieno gustati, non metterò in opera quest'altro cedrato s'ella non me lo dice, desiderando di accomodarlo con ogni esquisitezza, acciò più gli piaccia. La rassegna che desidero che V. S. faccia per la nostra bottega, di scatole, ampolle e simil cose, l'accennai alla sua serva; onde non replicherò altro, se non che vi si aggiugne anco due piatti bianchi che ha di nostro. Con che gli do la buona notte, essendo 9 hore della 4.a notte di Xmbre 1630.

Quando V. S. sarà stata da Ms.r Arcivescovo, mi sarà grato sentir ragguaglio del seguito.

Sua Fig.la Aff.ma

Suor M.a Celeste

and money, but also to see to our many personal needs with earnings too meager to provide more than the barest necessities. And to tell the truth, I believe that we lose more than we gain by staying awake seven hours of the night to work, for in doing so we jeopardize our health, and waste the oil that is so expensive.

Hearing today from Dame Piera that you wanted to know if we need anything, Sire, I lower myself to request a few *quattrini* to pay several small debts of mine that weigh on my mind. For the rest, if we have enough to sustain us, that is surely sufficient; this much the grace of God provides.

*A **quattrino** is a pence-like fraction of the base currency, the **lire**—about one-tenth its value.*

Of your coming here to see us, Sire, I hear you say nothing, and I do not importune you, because in any case it would bring us small satisfaction, not being able to speak freely for now. I was most eager to learn whether you liked the citron candy morsels; the ones made in the form of a quince came from a citron that I had procured with much entreaty, and at Suor Luisa's suggestion I preserved the flesh together with the rind of the same fruit, calling it total citron confection; the others I made from your citron, in the usual manner; but because I do not know which ones you may find more tasty, I shall prepare this other large citron the way I always do, unless I hear from you, wanting to spare no effort in making it exactly to your liking.

The list of items that I desire you to prepare for our apothecary, Sire, of boxes, glass vials, and such things, I explained to your servant and therefore I will not go over it again, except to add to it two white plates that you have of ours. With that I bid you goodnight, as it is now the ninth hour of

Amatiss.mo Sig.r Padre,

Veggo che questa tramontana così gagliarda non permette che V. S. possi esser da noi così presto come ne haveva promesso, anzi dubito che non progiudichi alla sua sanità; che per ciò mando a vederla, e mandogli i cedri accomodati, ciò è i morselletti fatti con la scorza, senza l'agro, di quel cedro più bello. L'altre fantasie sono con l'agro ancora, de gl'altri più piccoli; ma il meglio di tutti credo che sia quel tondo più grande, perchè vi ho messo il zucchero più a misura e dovizia.

Fo disegno di far un poco di ceppo alla Virginia e a Madonna Piera. Havrò caro che V. S. ce le mandi avanti le Feste, acciò possi dargliene; et per chè vorrei anco far un poca di burla, a Suor Luisa, vorrei che V. S. concorressi ancor lei, vedendo se per sorte havessi in casa tanta roba che facessi una portiera all'uscio della sua cella: o sia cuoio o panno di colore, non mi darebbe fastidio; la lunghezza sarebbe 3 braccia e la larghezza poco meno di 2, et io vi aggiugnerò alcune bagattelle per farla ridere, come sarebbe arcolai da incannare, una filza di zolfanelli per accender il lume la notte, stoppino, aghetti e simili coserelle, più per darle una volta segno di gratitudine per tanti oblighi che gli tengo, che per altro. Se V. S. ha in the fourth night of December 1630.

Your Most Affectionate Daughter,

Suor M. Celeste

The time is roughly 2 A.M.

When you have been to see Monsignor Archbishop, I will be happy to hear a report.

Most Beloved Lord Father,

I see that this *tramontana* will not allow you, Sire, to be with us as soon as you had promised me; on the contrary I doubt that you could brave it without compromising your health; however I send to see how you are, and to give you the candied citron peel, these morsels having been made from the rind alone without the flesh of that most beautiful citron. The other fanciful shapes are prepared from both the flesh and the rind of the smaller fruits: but the best of all these I believe you will find to be the big round one, owing to the more than generous measure of sugar I heaped into it.

*The cold north wind called the **tramontana** blows from the Apennines through the winter.*

I intend to make a little *ceppo* for Virginia and La Piera. I will be most pleased if you can send the two of them here before the holy day, so I can give them their gifts; and because I also want to make a little joke present for Suor Luisa, I would love it if you could share in its preparation, Sire, by seeing if per chance you have around your house some material that I might make into a curtain for the door of her cell; whether it is hide or dyed cloth makes no difference to me: the length should be two yards and the width a little more than one, to which I will add various odd trifles to make her laugh; these would include bobbins, a string of sulphur matches for light-

*In Tuscany, the word **ceppo** refers to Christmas, from the expression **ceppo di Natale**, or Yule log.*

casa da farmi il servizio, l'havrò caro; se no, non cerchi già haverlo di fuora, acciò non si mettessi a qualche pericolo, desiderando io troppo che ella si conservi, e per ciò la prego a riguardarsi quanto sia possibile.

Del negozio di Monsig.r Arcivescovo non ho inteso altro per ancora; havrò caro di sapere se V. S. è stata chiamata. Con che me le raccomando di cuore, insieme con S.r Arcangela e le solite amiche. Il Signore la conservi. Di S. Matteo, li 15 di Xmbre 1630.

Di V. S. Fig.la Aff.ma
Suor M.a Celeste

Amatiss.mo Sig.r Padre,

Speravo di riveder V. S. avanti che si dessi principio alla quarantena; visto che non mi è sortito, desidero almeno di sapere come stia di sanità di corpo e di quiete di animo, chè quanto all'altre cose necessarie per il suo vivere mi persuado ch'ella stia comodamente, per haverne fatta provvisione o almeno con haver largità di poter romper clausura tanto che vadia alla busca, sì come ha fatto per il passato, il che mi sarà grato d'intendere; chè per altro non credo ch'ella si curi di allontanarsi dal suo caro tugurio, particolarmente in questa stagione. Piaccia a Dio benedetto che vaglino queste tante ing the lamps at night, wick taper, bootlaces, and other little items such as these, more than for anything else to give her, just once, a sign of gratitude for all I feel I owe her. If you have the things at home to do me this favor, Sire, I will be delighted, if not, never mind trying to get them from outside, lest you risk some peril, as I desire above all that you maintain your health, and therefore I beg you to take care of yourself as well as you possibly can.

I have heard nothing more yet regarding the business of Monsignor Archbishop; please do let me know when you have been called, Sire. With that I send you greetings from my heart together with Suor Arcangela and our usual friends. May Our Lord bless you. From San Matteo, the 15th of December 1630.

Sire's Most Affectionate Daughter,
Suor M. Celeste

Most Beloved Lord Father,

I was hoping to see you again, Sire, before the imposition of the quarantine; given that things have not turned out as I expected, do please let me know how you stand with regard to your physical health and peace of mind; as for the other necessities of life, I feel certain that you manage comfortably on account of having made proper provisions, or at least having the freedom of being able to break cloister to go in search of whatever you need, as you have done in the past, which would be welcome news to me, nonetheless I do not believe that you find much reason to stray from your beloved shelter,

The Florentine Magistracy of Public Health has declared a general quarantine of forty days' duration, beginning on the tenth of this month, limiting travel in or out of the city as well as visits among neighbors and friends.

diligenze per conservazione universale di tutti, ma particolare per V. S., sì come spero che seguirà con l'aiuto divino, il quale non manca a quelli che fermamente in esso oonfidano; sì come è riuscito a noi, poi che Nostro Signore c'ha provviste in questo tempo con una buona elemosina, ciò è di dugento quattro scudi, cinque lire e quattro crazie, dispensatici, credo io, da i Signori della sanità per comandamento dell'AA. SSer.^{me}, le quali si dimostrano molto benevole al nostro monastero: tanto che viveremo qualche mese senza tanta afflizione della nostra povera Madre badessa, la quale credo che habbia ottenuto questo bene con le sue molte orazioni e con supplicare e raccomandarci a diverse persone.

Del cedrato che V. S. mi mandò ultimamente, ne ho fatto questo girello che gli mando; l'altro in forma di mandorla è di scorza di arancio, acciò senta se gli gustano. La pera cotogna sarebbe stata più bella alcuni giorni in dietro, ma non hebbi comodità di mandarla. Mi manca la carta, onde non dirò altro, se non che la saluto di cuore insieme con le solite. Li 24 di Gen.^{o} 1630.

Sua Fig.^{la} Aff.^{ma}

Suor M.ª Celeste

especially at this season. May it please blessed God for the best of these earnest efforts to promote the universal preservation of all, but you above all others, Sire, as I hope will follow with divine help: that aid never fails those who put their faith in Him; thus it has come to pass here for us, since Our Lord has now provided a great sum of alms, namely two hundred four *scudi*, five *lire* and four *crazie*, donated to us, I believe, by the Commissioners of Health following an order from their Most Serene Highnesses, who show themselves to be extremely benevolent toward our monastery, so much so that we will live through this month without grieving our poor Mother Abbess, who I believe has obtained this goodness through her constant prayers, as well as by petitioning and pleading our cause to various people.

*One **scudo** is worth 7 **lire**, and one lira equals 12 **crazie**.*

From the citron that you sent me most recently, Sire, I have made this little ring I send you now: the almond-shaped piece I made from orange rind, for you to taste and see if you like it. The quince pear would have been better a few days ago, but I had no means of getting it to you. I have run out of paper, wherefore I will say no more, except that I greet you from the bottom of my heart together with my usual companions. The 24th of January 1630.

Your Most Affectionate Daughter,

Suor M. Celeste

Molto Ill.re et Amatiss.mo Sig.r Padre,

Il disgusto che ha sentito V. S. della mia indisposizione dovrà restar annullato, mentre di presente gli dico che io sto ragionevolmente bene circa il male sopraggiuntomi in questi giorni passati; chè quanto alla mia antica oppilazione, credo che farà bisogno di una efficace cura a miglior stagione. In tanto mi andrò trattenendo con buon governo, sì come ella mi esorta. È ben vero ch'io desidererei che del consiglio che porge a me si valessi anco per sè stessa, non immergendosi tanto ne i suoi studii che progiudicassi troppo notabilmente alla sua sanità: chè se il povero corpo serve come instrumento proporzionato allo spirito nell'intender et investigar novità con sua gran fatica, è ben dovere che se le conceda la necessaria quiete; altrimenti egli si sconcerterà di maniera, che renderà anco l'intelletto inhabile per gustar quel cibo che prese con troppa avidità.

Non ringrazierò V. S. de i due scudi et altre amorevolezze mandatemi, ma sì bene della prontezza e liberalità con la quale ella si dimostra tanto, e più, desiderosa di sovvenirmi, quanto io bisognosa di esser sovvenuta.

Godo di sentire il buon essere del nostro Galileino, et in questa quaresima, quando sarà miglior tempo, havrò caro di rivederlo. Ho anco caro d'intender la credenza che ha che Vincenzio stia bene, ma non mi gusta già il mezzo con il quale viene in questa cognizione, ciò è con il non saperne nulla; ma queste sono frutte dell'ingrato mondo.

Resto confusa sentendo ch'ella conservi le mie lettere, e dubito che il grande affetto che mi porta gliele dimostri più

Most Illustrious and Beloved Lord Father,

The disturbance you have suffered over my indisposition shall have to be annulled, Sire, for at this moment I tell you that I feel reasonably well rid of the illness that recently came over me; as far as my long-standing blockage, however, I believe that will require an effective cure at a better time. Meanwhile I will go on taking good care of myself, as you urge me to do. In truth I would desire you to heed some of the same advice you offer me, by not immersing yourself so deeply in your studies that you jeopardize your health too markedly; for if your poor body is to serve as an instrument capable of sustaining your zest for understanding and investigating novelties, it is well that you grant it some needed rest, lest it become so depleted as to render even your powerful intellect unable to savor that nourishment it devours with such relish.

I will thank you not only for the two *scudi* and other loving tokens you sent me, Sire, but also for the readiness and generosity by which you show yourself ever more willing to help me, as needy as I am of being helped.

I am delighted to hear of the good health of our little Galileino, and in this coming period of Lent, when better times arrive, I will dearly love to see him again. I also yearn to share your belief that Vincenzio is all right, although I am not at all pleased with the way you come to this conclusion, namely without knowing anything for certain about him; but these are the fruits of a thankless world.

Although Galileo hears no news from Vincenzio, Sestilia has already given birth to their second son, Carlo, on January 20.

I am confounded to hear that you save my letters, and I suspect that the great love you bear me makes them seem more compite di quello che sono. Ma sia pur come si voglia; a me basta ch'ella se ne sodisfaccia. Con che gli dico a Dio, il quale sia sempre con lei, e gli fo le solite raccomandazioni. Di S. Matteo in Arcetri, li 18 di Feb.º 1630.

Di V. S. molto Ill.re Fig.la Aff.ma

Suor M.ª Celeste

Amatiss.mo Sig.r Padre,

Perchè credo infallibilmente che V. S. haverà ricevuta l'ultima mia lettera, che scrissi molti giorni sono, non replicherò altro del contenuto di essa, se non che gli significherò di nuovo il mio bene stare, e similmente di tutte le amiche, per grazia di Dio. È ben vero che questi tanti ritiramenti e quarantene mi danno, o più presto hanno dato, per la fantasia, mentre mi hanno vietato il poter haver spesse nuove di V. S. Credo pure che adesso dovranno terminare, e per conseguenza che potremo presto rivederla. In tanto desidero di sapere s'ella sta bene, che è quello che più d'ogn'altra cosa mi preme, et anco se ha nuove di Vincenzio e della cognata.

Rimando due fiaschi voti, e mandogli questi pochi mostacciuoli, che credo che non gli spiaceranno, pur che non siano, come dubito, cotti un poco più di quello che richieggono i suoi denti.

Questo tempo così piovoso non mi ha concesso il fargli un poca di conserva di fiori di ramerino, come havevo dissegnato; ma subito che potrò haver i fiori asciutti, la farò e gliela accomplished than they really are. But be that as it may, it is enough for me that you find satisfaction in them. With that I commend you to God, that He may be with you always, and I send you my usual loving greetings. From San Matteo, the 18th of February 1630.

Sire's Most Affectionate Daughter,

Suor M. Celeste

Most Beloved Lord Father,

Because I am absolutely certain that by now you must have received my last letter, Sire, which I wrote many days ago, I will not repeat its content, except to assure you again of my well-being, and the good health of all my friends, by the grace of God. It is quite true that all these retreats and quarantines give, or rather have given, my imagination too much play, while they prevented me from receiving frequent news of you, Sire. However, I do believe that any day now they shall have to come to an end, and as a result we will soon be able to see you again. Meanwhile I want to know if you are well, because that is what matters to me above all else, and also if you have word of Vincenzio and my sister-in-law.

I am returning two empty flasks, and I send you these little spiced cakes which I think you will enjoy, being, as I suspect, cooked a bit longer than that other one, which your teeth may still recall.

The rainy weather of late has kept me from making you any of the rosemary flower jam, which I have been meaning to do, manderò. In tanto a lei di cuore mi raccomando, insieme con Suor Arcangela e le solite. Prego N. S. che la conservi in Sua santa grazia, e desidero che dia un bacio di più a Galileino per mio amore.   Di S. Matteo, li 9 di Marzo 1630.

Di V. S. molto Ill.re Fig.la Aff.ma

Suor M.a Celeste

Molto Ill.re et Amatiss.mo Sig.r Padre,

La lettera di V. S. mi ha apportato molto disgusto per più ragioni: e prima, perchè sento la nuova della morte del zio Michelagnolo, del quale mi duole assai non solo per la perdita di lui, ma anco per l'aggravio che per ciò ne viene a lei, chè veramente questa non credo che sarà la più leggieri fra l'altre sue poche sodisfazioni, o, per dir meglio, tribolazioni. Ma, poi che Dio benedetto si dimostra prodigo con V. S. di lunghezza di vita e di facoltà più che con suo fratello e sorelle, è conveniente ch'ella spenda l'una e l'altre conforme al beneplacito di Sua D. M., che ne è padrone.

Così havessi ella qualche ripiego per Vincenzio, acciò, con guadagnar egli qualcosa, a V. S. si alleggerissino i fastidii e le spese, et a lui si tagliassino l'occasioni del potersi lamentare. Di grazia, Sig.r padre, poi che V. S. è nata e conservata nel mondo per benefizio di tanti, procuri che fra questi il primo sia suo figliuolo: parlo nel trovarli avviamento, chè quanto al resto so che non ci bisognano raccomandazioni; e di questo but the moment I am able to dry the flowers, I will prepare some and send it to you. For now I offer you loving greetings together with Suor Arcangela and the usual friends. I pray Our Lord to keep you in His holy grace, and I want you to give yet another kiss to little Galileino with my love. From San Matteo, the 9th of March 1630.

Sire's Most Affectionate Daughter,

Suor M. Celeste

Most Illustrious and Beloved Lord Father,

Your letter brought me deep distress for many reasons, Sire, and primarily because it bears the news of Uncle Michelangelo's death, for which I feel so sorry, not only over the loss of him, but also anticipating the burden that consequently must fall on you, which I truly fear will not be the lightest to bear among your other considerable worries, or, to say it better, tribulations. But, since blessed God lavishes upon you His gifts of long life and great ability, Sire, far more generously than He favored your brother or sisters, it is only fitting that you expend the one and bend the other to the absolute power of His Divine Majesty, who is our Master.

Following a long illness, Michelangelo died in Munich in early January, but the letter announcing his death was not written till a month later, and then took another month to reach Galileo.

Thus if you had some expedient for Vincenzio, then, by his earning an income, your difficulties and expenses would be lightened, Sire, while at the same time his opportunities for complaining could be curtailed. Please, my lord father, since you were born and kept in this world for the benefit of so many, endeavor to put your own son first ahead of all these particolare discorro solo per interesse di V. S., per il desiderio che ho di sentire ch'ella stia in pace e unione con il medesimo Vincenzio e sua moglie, e viversene nella sua quiete: il che non dubito che sortirà, s'ella gli farà ancora questo benefizio, molto desiderato da lui, per quanto ho potuto comprendere tutte le volte che gl'ho parlato.

Sento anco grandissimo disgusto di non poterle dar quella sodisfazione che vorrei circa il tener qua in serbo la Virginia, alla quale sono affezionata per esser ella stata di sollevamento e passatempo a V. S.; già che i nostri superiori si sono dichiarati non voler in modo alcuno che pigliamo fanciulle nè per monache nè per in serbo, perchè, essendo tale la povertà del convento quale V. S. sa, si rendono difficili a provveder da vivere per noi che già siamo qua, non che voglino aggiugnercene dell'altre. Essendo adunque questa ragione molto probababile, et il comandamento universale per parenti et altre, io non ardirei di ricercare da Madonna o da altre una tal cosa. Assicurisi bene che provo una pena intensa, mentre mi trovo priva di poter in questo poco sodisfarla; ma finalmente non ci veggo verso.

Dispiacemi anco grandemente il sentire ch'ella si trovi con poca sanità; e se mi fossi lecito, di molto buona voglia piglierei sopra di me i suoi dolori. Ma poi che non è possibile, non manco almeno dell'orazione, nella quale la preferisco a me stessa. Così piaccia al Signore di esaudirle.

Io sto tanto bene di sanità, che vo facendo quaresima, con speranza di condurla fino al fine; sì che V. S. non si pigli pensiero di mandarmi cose da carnevale. La ringrazio di quelle già mandatemi, e per fine di tutto cuore me le raccomando others; I speak of finding a means to ease his way. Because, as for the rest of your dealings with him, I know that no recommendations are needed, but on this particular matter I speak for your ears only, Sire, compelled by my own yearning to hear that you are at peace and joined in union with our Vincenzio and his wife, and that you all live together in tranquility. I have no doubt that this will come to pass, if you will do him this additional kindness, so strongly desired by him, as I know from the many times I have talked to him about it.

I am terribly disturbed by my inability to grant you satisfaction as I would have liked to do taking custody here of La Virginia, for whom I feel such fondness, considering all the sweet relief and diversion she has been to you, Sire. However I know that our superiors have declared themselves totally opposed to our admitting young girls, either as nuns or as charges, because the extreme poverty of our Convent, with which you are well acquainted, Sire, makes it a struggle to sustain those of us who are already here, let alone consider the addition of new mouths to feed. This being the most likely response, and also the general rule regarding relatives and outsiders, I could not dare to propose such a thing to Madonna or the other elders. Be assured that I suffer great anguish in disappointing you on this score, but in the end I see no alternative.

Young Virginia Landucci eventually took the veil at the Convent of San Giorgio, where she became Suor Olimpia.

It also upsets me greatly to learn that you find yourself in poor health; and if I were allowed, how willingly I would take your burdens on my shoulders. But since that is impossible, I shall not fail to pray, for you more than for myself. Thus may it please the Lord to hear my prayer.

insieme con S.r Arcangela e le amiche. Di S. Matteo, li 11 di Marzo 1630.

Di V. S. molto Ill.re Fig.la Aff.ma

Suor M.a Celeste

Se V. S. non ha a chi dispensar la carne che gli avanza, io haverò bene a chi distribuirla, essendo stata molto gradita quella che mi ha mandata. Sì che se havessi occasione, potrebbe talvolta mandarmene.

Amatiss.mo Sig.r Padre,

Ringrazio V. S. dell'amorevolezze a noi gratissime, poi che quest'anno cosi penurioso è causa che passiamo la presente quaresima assai magramente; se bene, quando si ha la sanità, l'altre cose si tolerano facilmente.

La venuta di V. S. e di Galileo piccino è da noi grandemente desiderata, quanto prima sia possibile. In tanto mi rallegro di sentire ch'ella stia assai bene, sì come di nuovo mi dolgo dell'impedimento che ho nel poter giovare alla Virginia e sodisfare a V. S. Spero non dimeno che Dio benedetto la provvederà in qualche altra maniera.

Se Vincenzio ha ancora V. S. in sospet[toJ, a lei sarà di utilità, già che non si pigliano danari da persone che siano

My health is good enough for me to observe Lent, with the hope of seeing it through to the end, so that you must abandon all thoughts of sending me any more treats for Carnival, Sire. I thank you for those you have already sent, and to close I offer you loving greetings with all my heart together with Suor Arcangela and our friends. From San Matteo, the 11th of March 1630.

Sire's Most Affectionate Daughter,

Suor M. Celeste

If you have no one to whom you can give your leftover meat, Sire, I will be very happy to have it, as I so appreciated it last time. Thus, if you were to have the opportunity, you could send me more of it sometime.

Most Beloved Lord Father,

I thank you, Sire, for your most welcome loving attention to us, since this year of hardships causes us to pass the present Lenten season so meagerly supplied, although, when one has one's health, everything else is more easily tolerated.

We are all eagerly awaiting your arrival, Sire, along with little Galileo, just as soon as you can possibly come. Meanwhile I cheer myself with the news that you are faring reasonably well, even though I regret anew the obstacle that prevented me from helping Virginia and pleasing you: I trust nonetheless that blessed God will provide for her in some other manner.

If Vincenzio remains suspicious of your possible contagion, Sire, that will be to your advantage, since no one takes money appestate; e così egli, che ne ha tanto timore, non ne domanderà a V. S. Alla quale di cuore mi raccomando: N. S.re la conservi. Di S. Matteo, li 12 di Marzo 1630.

Sua Fig.la Aff.ma

Suor M.a Celeste

Amatiss.mo Sig.r Padre,

Non resto maravigliata del cordialissimo affetto ch'ella mi porta, già, che troppi sono gl'indizii e contrassegni che ne tengo; ma ben stupisco che l'amore arrivi tant'oltre che la faccia indovinare, con mandarmi V. S. una vivanda più conforme al gusto e sanità mia di qual si voglia altra quadragesimale. La ringrazio pertanto infinitamente, e mi preparo a goderla con gusto raddoppiato, per esser accomodata da quelle mani tanto da me amate e reverite. E già che mi ordina ch'io domandi altro di mio gusto, io domanderò qualcosa per far colazione la sera; e nel re[s]to, di grazia, V. S. non si pigli altro pensiero, chè quando mi bisognerà qualcosa mi lascerò intendere, sapendo che posso farlo con ogni sicurtà.

Non vedo l'hora di rivederla insieme con il bambino, pur che non sia in giorno di festa, chè non ci saria sodiafazione.

Lascio giudicar a lei se mi sarà di consolazione la grazia che V. S. pretende di ottener da Monsig.r Arcivescovo; ma non posso in questo punto risolverla. Sarò con la Madre badessa, e quanto prima gli significherò quel che ne havrò potuto ritrarre. In tanto finisco, senza finir mai di raccomandarmele, from a person infected with the plague; and thus he, who has such great fear of the disease, will demand no funds from you, Sire, to whom I send my loving greetings. God bless you. From San Matteo, the 12th of March 1630.

Your Most Affectionate Daughter,

Suor M. Celeste

Most Beloved Lord Father,

I no longer stand astonished by the extreme fervor of the affection you bear me, Sire, for you have given me too many signs and expressions of it; but I am indeed amazed that the love reaches so far beyond what I am capable of predicting, by your sending me a delicacy better suited to my taste and my health than any other Lenten food whatsoever. Therefore I thank you from the bottom of my heart, and I am prepared to enjoy it with doubled pleasure, knowing it was made by those hands I love and respect so much. And now that you order me to ask for another dish I like, I would request something for the evening meal, and as for the rest, please, Sire, put it out of your thoughts; because when I do have need of something, I will let it be known, confident that I can do so with complete security.

I cannot wait to see you again together with the baby, provided that it is not on a feast day because duties would prohibit us from welcoming you properly then.

I leave it to you to judge, Sire, whether the favor you intend to obtain from Monsignor Archbishop will console me; but I e prego Nostro Signore che la conservi. Di S. Matteo, li 13 di Marzo 1630.

Sua Fig.[la] Aff.[ma]
Suor M.[a] Celeste

Amatiss.[mo] Sig.[r] Padre,

La risposta che riporto dalla Madre badessa, circa il servizio del quale mi scrisse V. S. l'altro giorno, è che senza dubbio sarà di molto gusto a tutte universalmente il procurar la grazia da Monsr Arcivescovo non solo per i padri, ma per i fratelli ancora, ma che giudica esser conveniente l'indugiar a domandarla doppo Pasqua. In tanto V. S. sarà da noi e potrà in voce trattarne con lei, che veramente è persona molto prudente e discreta, ma assai timida.

Rimando i collari imbiancati, che, per esser tanto logori, non saranno accomodati con quella esquisitezza che havrei desiderato: se altro gli fa bisogno, si ricordi che non ho il maggior gusto nel mondo quanto che d'impiegarmi in cosa di suo servizio, sì come all'incontro mi pare che lei non l'habbia in altro se non nel compiacermi e sodisfare a tutte le mie domande, già che con tanta sollecitudine provvede ad ogni mio bisogno. La ringrazio di tutte in generale, et in particocannot resolve the matter just yet. I will spend some time with the Mother Abbess, and as soon as it becomes possible I shall let you know what I have been able to find out. Meanwhile I come to the end of this letter, without ever coming to the end of my loving regards for you. And I pray Our Lord to bless you. From San Matteo, the 13th of March 1630.

Your Most Affectionate Daughter,

Suor M. Celeste

Most Beloved Lord Father,

The response that I report from the Mother Abbess, regarding the service of which you wrote the other day, Sire, is that without doubt your procuring the favor from Monsignor Archbishop will be greatly and universally appreciated, not only by the fathers, but by the brothers as well; but that it seems most fitting to delay the request until after Easter. Meanwhile, Sire, you will have been here and had the chance to speak of it directly with her, as she is truly a very judicious and discreet person, although quite timid.

Here she refers to the church governors and friars minor who bore responsibility for the Poor Clares.

I return your bleached collars which, for being so worn, cannot be done up with that perfection I would have wanted: if you need anything else remember that I have no greater pleasure in the world than busying myself taking care of whatever you would have me do, just as you, for your part, seem to have naught else to do but delight me and satisfy all my requests, since you provide for my every need with such solicitude.

lare dell'ultime c[he] per mano del nostro fattore ho ricevute, che furno due cartocci, uno di mandorle, l'altro di zibaldone, e 6 cantucci. Il tutto ci goderem in grazia sua. Et io gli fo un regalo da poveretta, ciò è questo barattolo di conserva, che sarà buona per confortar la testa; se bene miglior conforto credo che sarebbe l'affaticarla meno con lo studio e scrivere. Le bagattelle del panierino saranno per la Virginia.

Per carestia di tempo non dirò altro, se non che in nome delle solite la saluto affettuosamente, e prego N. S. che le conceda la Sua santa grazia. Di S. Matteo, li 17 di Marzo 1630.

Di V. S. molto Ill.re Fig.la Aff.ma

Suor Maria Cel.te

Amatiss.mo Sig.r Padre,

Le faccende della bottega mi hanno tenuta, et ancora mi tengono, così occupata, che non mi permettano il poterle dir altro per hora, se non che mi accuso della involontaria dilazione e tardanza in mandarla a visitare. Adesso, che mi è permesso, mando, per intender s'ella sta bene e se ha nuove di Vincenzio e della cognata, ciò è se crede che questa santissima Pasqua devino esser da lei, il che credo che a V. S. sarebbe di molto gusto, et a me ancora per amor suo.

Le paste che gli mando, son poche; con tutto ciò credo che gli basteranno, già che non ha con chi parteciparle, se non forse

I thank you for everything in general, and in particular for the most recent gifts that I received by hand from our steward, which were two little wrapped packets, one of almonds, the other of notebooks, and 6 *cantucci.* We enjoyed everything with thanks to you. And I have made you a poor man's present, namely this jar of conserve, which will be good for relieving your headache: although I think you might be better comforted by leaving off working yourself to exhaustion with study and writing. The trifles in the little basket are for our Virginia.

For want of time I will say no more. Except that in the name of all our friends I send you loving regards and pray Our Lord to grant you His holy grace. From San Matteo, the 17th of March 1630.

Sire's Most Affectionate Daughter,
Suor Maria Celeste

Most Beloved Lord Father,

The duties of the apothecary have kept me and still keep me so busy, that they prohibit me from saying anything else for now, if not that I acknowledge my involuntary delay and lateness in visiting with you by letter: now that I am allowed, I send to hear whether you feel well and if you have news of Vincenzio and my sister-in-law, namely if you think they will come to you this Most Holy Easter, which I think would thrill you, Sire, and me as well for loving you.

The cakes I send you are small ones; nevertheless I believe that they will suffice, now that you have no one to share them con Galileino, il quale si potrà trattenere con le pine che gli mandiamo, che sono tutta la porzione che ci ha distribuita la nostra ortolana, a Suor Arcangela et a me. Non rimando la pignattina delli spinaci, perchè non è ancora vota del tutto, chè, per esser stati così buoni, ne ho fatto a miccino. La saluto per parte di tutte le solite, e prego Dio benedetto che la feliciti sempre. Di S. Matteo, li 11 di Aprile 1631.

Sua Fig.^{la} Aff.^{ma}

Suor M.ª Celeste

Amatiss.^{mo} Sig.^{r} Padre,

Se la sua lettera non mi havessi assicurata che il suo male non è di gran considerazione, certo havrei havuto assai maggior disgusto di quello che provo al presente; e sentendo ch'ella va più presto migliorando, prendo speranza di doverla in breve rivedere del tutto sana, sì come mi promette.

Da Vincenzio ricevemmo due serque di uova e mezzo agnello, e la ringraziamo, sì come, e molto più, delle 4 piastre, le quali giungono in tempo di gran necessità.

La Piera fa instanza di partire, per ciò mi riserbo a scriver altra volta più a lungo. In tanto a lei di tutto cuore mi raccomando insieme con le solite. Nostro Signore sia sempre con lei. Di S. Matteo, li 22 di Aprile 1631.

Sua Fig.^{la} Aff.^{ma}

Suor M.ª Celeste

with except perhaps little Galileino, who will be able to amuse himself getting the nuts out of the pine cones we are sending him, which are all the ones the nun who tends our garden delivered here, to Suor Arcangela and me. I am not returning the little pot from the spinach because it is not completely empty; as the spinach is so tasty I am eating it slowly and sparingly. I greet you on behalf of all our usual friends, and I pray blessed God to keep you happy always. From San Matteo, the 11th of April 1631.

Your Most Affectionate Daughter,
Suor M. Celeste

Most Beloved Lord Father,

If your letter had not assured me that your illness is of no great concern, I would certainly have felt even more upset than I do: and hearing that you are improving quickly, I hold onto the hope of soon seeing you again in perfect health, as you promise me.

We received via Vincenzio two dozen eggs and half a lamb, and we thank you, indeed, and even more so, for the four *piastre* which arrive in a time of great monetary need.

*A **piastra** is a silver coin worth a little less than a **scudo**—five **lire** as opposed to seven.*

La Piera is prepared to leave this instant, wherefore I reserve my writing for another day at greater length. Meanwhile I send you love with all my heart together with our usual friends. May Our Lord be with you always. From San Matteo, the 22nd of April 1631.

Your Most Affectionate Daughter,
Suor M. Celeste

Molto Ill.re et Amatiss.mo Sig.r Padre,

Perchè dalla Piera intesi l'altro giorno che V. S. si ritrovava grandemente svogliata e senza appetito di mangiare, sono andata investigando quello ch'io havessi potuto mandarle che fossi buono per farle recuperar il gusto; et perchè per questo effetto ho sentito commendar dai medici la oxizacchara, ho fatta questa poca che gli mando, acciò ne faccia l'esperienza, essendo cosa che non dovrà nuocerli. Gl'ingredienti non sono altro, zucchero, vino di melagrane forti et un poco di aceto. È ben vero che la cottura mi è riuscita un poco più stretta del dovere, ma V. S. potrà pigliarne due o tre cucchiaiate per mattina, e, per mitigare la frigidità sua, aggiugnervi un poca di acqua di cannella, della quale, se non ne ha più, gliene manderò, pur che mi rimandi il fiaschetto ove altra volta glien'ho mandata.

I morselletti sono di tutto il cedro che mi mandò, e credo che siano buoni; et se altro sapessi indovinare che gli potessi gustare, non lascerei di far ogni diligenza per provvederlo, non solamente per dar gusto a lei, ma anco a me stessa, già che impiegandomi in suo servizio godo estremamente. La prego, se gl'occorre qualcosa, a non privarmi di questo contento, et anco a significarmi come stia di presente: con che, pregandole da Nostro Signore ogni bene, me le raccomando con tutto l'affetto insieme con le amiche. Di S. Matteo, li 25 di Aprile 1631.

Di V. S. molto Ill.re Fig.la Aff.ma

Suor M.a Celeste

Most Illustrious and Beloved Lord Father,

Because I heard from La Piera the other day that you had grown very listless again, Sire, and unable to eat anything, I went in search of whatever I might be able to send you to help you recover your appetite; and because I have heard the doctors recommend the Oxilacchara for this problem, I made a small amount for you to experiment with, as it is something that cannot do you any harm: the ingredients include nothing but sugar, strong pomegranate wine, and a little vinegar. It is very true that my preparation of it turned out a bit more concentrated than required, Sire, but you may take two or three teaspoons of it in the morning, and to mitigate its bitterness, add to it some cinnamon water, which, if you need more, I will send to you, provided you return the vial I used the last time.

The little candies are from all the citrons you sent me, and I believe they are very good; and if I knew of something else that would prove to be to your liking, I would not fail to make every effort to provide it, not only to please you, Sire, but also myself; since serving you makes me extremely happy. I beseech you, if you think of anything, to not deprive me of this contentment, and also to let me know how you feel now: with that, praying Our Lord for your every benefit, I send you regards with all my love together with our friends. From San Matteo, the 25th of April 1631.

Sire's Most Affectionate Daughter,

Suor M. Celeste

Amatiss.^{mo} Sig.^{r} Padre,

Per quanto ho potuto intendere, il prete di Monte Ripaldi non ha giuridizione sopra la villa della S.^{ra} Dianora Landi, se non in un campo solo. Intendo bene che su la casa vi è sodata la dote di una cappella della chiesa di Sta Maria del Fiore, e che per questa causa la sudetta S.^{ra} Dianora si ritrova in piato. V. S. potrà da l'apportatrice di questa, che è donna assai accorta et ha conoscenza quasi in tutto Firenze, intender chi sia quello che agiti la causa, già che essa lo conosce, e da esso haver poi informazione del negozio.

Ho anco inteso che il luogo del Mannelli non è ancora allogato, ma che si tratta bene di affittarlo. Questo è un luogo molto bello, e dicono che possiede la miglior aria di questo paese. Non credo che a V. S. mancherà entratura per tentar se potessi riuscir quanto lei et io molto desideriamo; e da questa medesima donna potrà forse haver qualche indirizzo.

Havevo accettato l'aceto per l'oximele, perchè il nostro non mi pareva di quella bontà che havrei desiderato; già che V. S. si è compiaciuta di mandarmi il vino in cambio, io ne la ringrazio, e sto aspettando d'intender s'Ella sarà sodisfatta della nostra manifattura, che sarà quando si servirà altre volte di noi, chè tanto mi vien detto da Suor Luisa et altre mie compagne in bottega, le quali, insieme con Sr Arcangela, la salutano affettuosamente. Et io da Nostro Signore gli prego ogni vera felicità. Di S. Matteo, li 18 Mag.^{o} 1631.

Sua Fig.^{la} Aff.^{ma}

Suor Maria Celeste

Most Illustrious Lord Father,

As far as I have been able to determine, the priest of Monteripaldi has no jurisdiction over the villa of Signora Dianora Landi save for a single field. I understand, however, that the house was assigned as a dowry to a chapel of the Church of Santa Maria del Fiore, and this is the reason that our same Signora Dianora finds herself in litigation. From the bearer of my letter, who is a very shrewd woman with acquaintances all over Florence, you will be able to discover, Sire, who is contesting this case, since she knows the man, and then from him you can find out more information about the sale.

Galileo has decided to move to Arcetri so he can visit his daughters more often, with less difficulty, and Suor Maria Celeste is actively seeking a new home for him.

Here Galileo wrote in the margin, "This is Mr. Curzio Sportelli."

I have also learned that Mannelli's villa is not yet taken, but is available for rent. This is a very beautiful property, and people say its air is the best in the whole region. I do not believe that you will lack the opportunity to secure it, Sire, if events turn out as well as you and I so strongly desire; and perhaps from this same woman you can receive some guidance.

I had accepted your vinegar for the oxymel because ours struck me as not being of the high quality I would have liked; now that you have been so kind as to send me the wine in exchange, Sire, I thank you for it and I am waiting to learn whether you are satisfied with the fruits of our labor, and when we will be allowed to do more for you, as this is the ardent wish of Suor Luisa and my other companions in the apothecary, all of whom, together with Suor Arcangela, send you their love. And I pray Our Lord for your every true happiness. From San Matteo, the 18th of May 1631.

Your Most Affectionate Daughter,

Suor Maria Celeste

Amatiss.mo Sig.r Padre,

Desidero in estremo, col mezzo di V. S., di dar segno di gratitudine e riconoscimento a'tanti oblighi che tengo con Suor Luisa, adesso che mi si porge buona occasione; poi che, ritrovandosi ella in necessità di cercar in presto la somma di ventiquattro scudi fino all'ultimo di Luglio, io vorrei ottener grazia che V. S. gli facessi lei questo servizio, se gli sia possibile, come credo. E se è vero, come so che è verissimo, che V. S. desideri di darmi ogni sodisfazione e gusto, si assicuri che questo sarà de i grandi che possa darmi; et la persona è tale che non dubito che corrisponderà pienamente, più presto avanti che doppo il prescritto termine di due mesi, havendo l'assegnamento sicuro di sua entrata; chè veramente, se fossi altrimenti, io non cercherei di metter V. S. in qualche intrigo, come per l'adietro è seguito con mio grandissimo disgusto. Non replicherò altro, supponendo che sia superfluo lo estendermi in più lunghe preghiere con persona la quale più desidera di farmi benefizio che non desidero io di riceverlo; solo starò aspettando di esser pienamente sodisfatta.

In tanto gli dico che ho sentito gusto particolare che sia caduta la elezione dell'Arcivescovo nella persona di Mons. Rinuccini, per l'interesse di V. S. o nostro ancora, come a suo tempo discorreremo.

Sto in dubbio se il primo et il secondo oximele, che gli mandai, sia stato di sua sodisfazione, già che non ne ha detto niente: et perchè V. S. non ha per ancora mandato lo aloè e rabarbaro per far le pillole papaline, gli mando due prese delle nostre, delle quali già altre volte ne ha prese, con riserbo di fargliene ogni volta che vorrà.

Most Beloved Lord Father,

I have the utmost desire to enlist your aid, Sire, in giving a sign of gratitude and recognition for all my indebtedness to Suor Luisa, now that an appropriate occasion has arisen; since, as she finds herself in need of borrowing the sum of twenty-four *scudi* until the end of July, I would like to entreat you to do her this favor, if you could, as I imagine you can, Sire. And if it is true, as I know it to be absolutely true, that you want to give me every satisfaction and enjoyment, Sire, I assure you that this will be one of the greatest joys you could possibly provide me: and her nature is such that I do not doubt she will repay you fully, most likely well before the end of the prescribed term of two months, as soon as she receives the guaranteed allowance from her income; for honestly, if matters stood otherwise, I would not even try to involve you in some imbroglio, as took place in the past to my everlasting regret. I will not dwell on this any longer, assuming that it would be superfluous to extend myself in lengthy entreaties to someone whose desire to shower me with goodness exceeds my own desire for any particular favor; I shall simply wait to be completely contented in this matter.

Meanwhile I tell you that I was extremely pleased that Monsignor Rinuccini was elected Archbishop, for your sake and ours, Sire, as we will discuss when the time is right.

Giovanni Battista Rinuccini, the archbishop of Fermo, is Grand Duke Ferdinando's choice as successor to Cosimo Bardi, who died in April. (Monsignor Rinuccini, however, refused the offer to come to Florence.)

I still do not know whether the first or the second oxymel I sent you was more to your liking, since you have not said anything about either: and because you have not yet sent the aloe and rhubarb for making your papal pills, here are two doses of ours, which you have taken previously, along with the promise to make you more of them whenever you like.

I cedrati sono bellissimi, et io, insieme con Suor Luisa, procurerò di far anco buoni i morselletti, acciò che a chi ha donato questi venga volontà di donarne de gl'altri. Ringrazio in tanto V. S. sì di questi come anco de i vasi di cristallo, che mi sono stati gratissimi; e pregandole da Nostro Signore ogni vero bene, me li raccomando insieme con le solite, e particolarmente Suor Arcangela, la quale se ne sta debolmente. Di S. Matteo, li 29 di Mag.º 1631.

Di V. S. molto Ill.re Fig.la Aff.ma

Suor M.a Celeste

Molto Ill.re et Amatiss.mo Sig.r Padre,

Da Suor Luisa mi vien imposto ch'io deva per sua parte render a V. S. quelle grazie ch'io posso maggiori per il comodo e servizio che ha da lei ricevuto con tanta prontezza e cortesia. Ma io, che per far questo mi conosco al tutto inhabile, me la passerò con silenzio, persuadendomi che a V. S. sarà di maggior gusto il sapere che io mi conosco e me le confesso obligata per una quasi infinita moltitudine di benefizii ottenuti da lei, e che tutto il mio desiderio è rivolto e tende solo a non essergliene ingrata, se bene veramente altro indizio di gratitudine non posso darle che di buona volontà. È ben vero che questa ultima grazia fattami, secondo il mio parere, supera le preterite, già che V. S. con questa mi dà segno di esser così pronta a beneficiarmi, che non solo per me stessa, ma anco per quelle persone alle quali io sono affezzionata et obligata, si dimostra liberale et amorevole; onde io la ricevo per grazia

The citrons are most beautiful and both Suor Luisa and I will try to make the candies taste as good as the fruit looks, so that he who gave them will be only too happy to give us more of them in the future. Meanwhile I thank you very much for these, Sire, as well as for the glass jars, for which I am so grateful; and praying Our Lord for your every true blessing, I greet you lovingly along with my usual companions, and especially Suor Arcangela, who is feeling rather weak. From San Matteo, the 23rd of May 1631.

Sire's Most Affectionate Daughter,

Suor M. Celeste

Most Illustrious and Beloved Lord Father,

Suor Luisa has enjoined me that I must, on her behalf, render to you those thanks she thinks I am better able to offer, for the comfort and attention she has received from you with such promptness and courtesy; but as I know myself to be utterly unfit for this task, I will pass over it in silence, persuaded as I am that you will be happier knowing that I understand myself, and confess myself indebted for an almost infinite multitude of blessings conferred by you: and for this reason all my desire is centered and focused solely upon not being ungrateful to you: although indeed I cannot give you a better indication of gratitude than my good will: it is surely true that this last kindness you have performed for me, Sire, to my mind, surpasses all the previous ones, since you thus signify your devotion to my well-being with expressions of generosity and love not only to me, but also to those who command my dupplicata, et alla mia Suor Luisa usurpo quell'obligazione che per ciò con V. S. potessi pretendere.

I morselletti, sì come sono riusciti de i più belli ch'io habbia mai fatti, così credo che saranno anco de i migliori; e non vorrei che V. S. gli distribuissi tutti, ma che ancor lei ne gustassi: sono n.º 8.

Sì come ella sa, Suor Arcangela si va purgando; et il medico giudica necessario il darle l'acqua del Tettuccio, ma in poca quantità, per esser ella assai debole e fiacca: et perchè questo medicamento ricerca bonissimo reggimento di vita, et io mi ritrovo molto scarsa di danari, havrei caro che V. S. mi mandassi un paio di polli, per poterli far buoni brodi anco il venerdì et sabato. Suor Chiara ancora se ne sta in letto malata; sì che con questo e con le faccende della bottega io ho dato bando all'ozio, anzi mi troverei soverchiamente aggravata, se Suor Luisa non volessi, per sua grazia, esser partecipe di tutte le mie fatiche. Saluto V. S. per sua parte e di Suor Arcangela, e prego Dio benedetto che la conservi lungamente per suo e nostro benefizio. Di S. Matteo, li 4 di Giug.º 1631.

Di V. S. molto Ill.re Aff.ma Fig.la

Suor M.a Celeste

devotion and obligation, whereby I am doubly rewarded; and to my Suor Luisa I begin to repay a debt that I can satisfy only with your help.

The candied citron morsels, since they turned out to be among the most beautiful ones that I have ever made, must also therefore taste the best; and I would not want you to give them all away, Sire, even if you took pleasure in doing so: there are 8 of them.

As you know, Suor Arcangela continues the purging; and the doctor deems it necessary to give her Tettuccio water, but in small quantities, on account of her being feeble and sluggish; and because this treatment requires very excellent care of the body, and I find myself quite short of funds, I would dearly hope that you could send me a couple of chickens, Sire, so I could make broth for her both Friday and Saturday. Suor Chiara is still sick in bed, so that with all of this and the duties of the apothecary, I have sent idleness into exile, on the contrary I would find myself overwhelmingly aggravated if Suor Luisa were not willing, by her goodness, to share in all my labors. I send you greetings from her and Suor Arcangela, and I pray blessed God to grant you long life for your sake and mine. From San Matteo, the 4th of June 1631.

Sire's Most Affectionate Daughter,

Suor M. Celeste

Vincenzio sent Galileo some of this Tettuccio water (a diuretic drawn from the Tettucio thermal spring near Pistoia) on May 21, along with a letter touting its effectiveness in treating hemorrhoids, "to wash the affected area," and also for use as an enema.

Amatiss.mo Sig.r Padre,

Fu qui domenica mattina Vincenzio, il quale mi disse esser venuto per veder il luogo de i Perini, se ben mi ricordo, il quale è in vendita, e, per quanto intendo, il comperatore c' haverà ogni vantaggio, sì come dal medesimo Vincenzio potrà V. S. esser informata. Io, perchè sento che è qui vicino a noi e perchè desidero la sodisfazione di V. S. (che so quanto desidera di esserne a presso) insieme con quella di Vincenzio e nostra ancora, vengo a pregarla che non si lasci scappar questa occasione delle mani, che Dio sa quando gli se ne porgerà una simile, già che si vede che quelli che posseggono luoghi in questi contorni non se ne vogliono privare altro che per estrema necessità, sì come adesso interviene a questi et al Mannelli, il quale mi è parso d'intendere che sia già allo gato. Se V. S. si risolve di venir a veder quest'altro, potrà con questa occasione esser qui da noi. In tanto gli dico che io sto bene, ma non già S.r Arcangela, la quale finalmente è ridotta a starsene del continuo in letto. Il suo male non è di gran considerazione, ma credo bene che s'ella non si fossi procurata, havrebbe havuto qualche gravissima malattia. Hebbi le galline per lei, e ne ringrazio V. S. infinitamente. Prego Nostro Signore che la conservi, e me li raccomando con tutto l'affetto, insieme con le solite. Di S. Matteo, li 10 Giug.o 1631.

Di V. S. molto Ill.re Fig.la Aff.ma

Suor M.a Celeste

Most Beloved Lord Father,

Sunday morning brought Vincenzio here, telling me he had come to see the Perini villa, as I recall, which is for sale, and, as far as I understand, the buyer will have every advantage, as you will no doubt be informed, Sire, by Vincenzio himself. For my part, because I hear that it is very close to us, and because I prize your satisfaction, Sire (knowing how much you want to be near us), along with that of Vincenzio and ours as well, I come to beg you not to let this opportunity slip through your fingers, for God knows when another such as this will present itself, now that we see how people who own properties in these parts cling to them, except in extreme necessity, as is now the case with these people and also Mannelli, whose villa I hear may have already been rented. If you decide to come and look yourself at this other one, you will be able to use the occasion to visit us as well. Meanwhile I assure you that I am fine, but not so Suor Arcangela, who is at last confined to bed: her illness is not one of grave concern, but I sincerely believe that, if she were not thus provided for, she would incur some far more serious malady. I received the hens for her and I thank you a thousandfold. I pray our Lord to bless you, and I send you regards with all my love, together with our usual friends. From San Matteo, the 10th of June 1631.

Sire's Most Affectionate Daughter,

Suor M. Celeste

Amatiss.mo Sig.r Padre,

Suor Luisa ha, per sua buona sorte, riscossa la sua entrata prima che non pensava, e subito viene a dar sodisfazione a V. S. delli scudi 24 che gli deve. Confessa bene di non volere nè poter sodisfarla quanto all'obligo che per ciò haverà perpetuo con lei, non le bastando l'animo di arrivar a contraccambiar la sua prontezza et amorevolezza altro che con la moneta di un buono e cordiale affetto in verso di V. S. e di noi ancora; e questo lo va manifestando giornalmente con gl'effetti in tutte le mie occorrenze, con maniera tale che più non potria fare se mi fosse madre. Ella ha aggiunto nel panierino queste paste, acciò V. S. le goda per suo amore.

Suor Arcangela se ne sta in letto, con poca febbre veramente, ma con gran debolezza e molti dolori; e se non m'inganno, credo che ci sarà da fare assai avanti ch'ella ritorni in sanità, se pur vi tornerà. Il medico, quando ultimamente la visitò, ordinò fra l'altre cose alcune untioni allo stomaco con olio da stomaco del G. D. e olio di noci moscade. Dell'uno e dell'altro ne siamo a carestia, e per ciò havrei caro che V. S. me ne provvedessi un poco.

Rimando due fiaschi voti; et veramente che se, in questa scesa che ho havuta, non fossi stato il vino bianco di V. S., l'havrei fatta male, perchè sono vivuta di pappe e zuppe, quali non mi hanno nociuto per esser fatte in vino così buono.

Havrò caro d'intender se sortirà la compra del luogo che V. S. venne a vedere, perchè io grandemente lo desidero, e mi parrebbe cosa molto ben fatta e utile per la lor casa. Non occor-

Most Beloved Lord Father,

Suor Luisa has by good fortune collected her income ahead of schedule, and she comes immediately to make good the loan of the 24 *scudi* that she owes you, Sire. She readily confesses being neither willing nor able to satisfy that other obligation she will always bear you, as her spirit is not appeased by offering only money in exchange for all your kindness and tenderness, but also seeks to repay you in the currency of a true and cordial affection for you as well as for us; and this she manifests daily by helping me in every contingency, in such a way that she could not do more for me if she were my own mother. She has added to the basket these little cakes, Sire, for you to enjoy with her love.

Suor Arcangela is in bed with a very slight fever, but great weakness and many pains, and, if I am not mistaken, I believe there will be much to do before she recovers her health, if she ever does. The doctor, when he last visited her, ordered among other things several stomach ointments made with stomach oil from the Grand Duke, and oil of nutmeg. We have neither of these, Sire, and therefore I would be most appreciative if you could get me some.

Nutmeg oil, a general stomach tonic, soothes nausea, vomiting, and miscellaneous stomach pain.

I am returning two empty flasks, and truly, in this slump I have had, were it not for your white wine, Sire, things would have gone much worse, since I sustain myself on pap and soup, which have not hurt me for being made with such good wine.

I will be eager to hear if you settle the purchase of the villa you came to see, Sire, because I want that so much: and the rendomi altro di presente, saluto caramente V. S. insieme con le solite, e prego Dio benedetto che la feliciti sempre. Di S. Matteo, li di *(sic)* Lug.° 1631.

Di V. S. Fig.la Aff.ma

Suor M. Celeste

Molto Ill.re et Amatiss.mo Sig.r Padre,

Perchè pur vorrei haver grazia che V. S. si avvicinassi a noi, vo continuamente procurando d'intendere quando qui all'intorno ci sia qualche luogo che si deva affittare; et hora di fresco sento esserci la villa del Sig.r Esaù Martellini, la quale è al Piano di Giullari, e confina con noi. Ho voluto avvisarglielo, acciò V. S. possa informarsi se per sorte fossi a suo gusto, il che havrei molto caro, sperando che con questa comodità non starei tanto senza saper qualcosa di lei, come di presente mi avviene, cosa che veramente io tollero malvolentieri; ma connumerando e ricevendo questo, insieme con qualche altro poco di disgusto, in vece di quelle mortificazioni ch'io per [. . .] negligenza tralascio, mi vo accomodando il meg[. . .] posso a quanto piace a Dio: oltre che mi persua[. . .] a V. S. non manchino intrighi e fastidii d'altro rilie[. . .] sono i miei, e con questo m'acquieto.

Suor Arcangela, che ta[. . .] mi ha dato da pensare, per grazia di Dio sta alquanto meglio, e se bene assai debole e fiacca si arrangement would seem to me a very good and helpful one for that household. Not having anything else to say at present, I send you loving greetings together with the others here, and I pray blessed God to keep you happy always. From San Matteo, the *(sic)* day of July 1631.

Sire's Most Affectionate Daughter,

Suor M. Celeste

Most Illustrious and Beloved Lord Father,

Because I do so desire the grace of your moving closer to us, Sire, I am continually trying to learn when places here in our vicinity are to be let. And now I hear anew of the availability of the villa of Signor Esaù Martellini, which lies on the Piano dei Giullari, and adjacent to us. I wanted to call it to your attention, Sire, so that you could make inquiries to see if by chance it might suit you, which I would love, hoping that with this proximity I would not be so deprived of news of you, as happens to me now, this being a situation I tolerate most unwillingly; but taking it into account and accepting it along with a few other trifling aversions, as opposed to those mortifications which I omit out of negligence, I bend myself as best I can to God's will. Beyond that I am convinced that you, too, Sire, do not lack for intrigues and troubles of an altogether different stamp from mine, and this silences me.

Galileo signed a contract the following month to rent this building, called ***Il Gioiello***—*"the jewel"—for thirty-five* ***scudi*** *per year.*

Suor Arcangela, who has preoccupied my thoughts, by the grace of God fares somewhat better, and although she still ritrova, comincia a sollevarsi; e perchè havrebbe gusto di mangiare qualche pesciuolo marinato, prega V. S. che gliene faccia provisione di qualcuno per questi prossimi giorni magri. In tanto V. S. procuri di mantenersi sana a questi gran caldi, e di grazia mi scriva un verso. La saluto affettuosamente per parte delle solite, e prego Nostro Signore che le conceda la Sua santa grazia. Di S. Matteo, li 12 di Agosto 1631.

Di V. S. molto Ill.re Fig.la Aff.ma

Suor M.a Celeste

Amatiss.mo Sig.r Padre,

Ci lamentiamo del tempo, invidioso del gusto che noi, insieme con V. S., in questo giorno havremmo potuto prendere con ritrovarci in compagnia. Ma, se piacerà a Dio, spero che potrà seguir presto un'altra volta; et in tanto godo con la speranza di dover haverla continuamente qua vicina, sì come per l'imbasciata fattami dalla Piera comprendo: e la prego a prosseguire l'impresa, acciò riesca il nostro disegno, chè, come V. S. vorrà, credo che si supererà ogni difficultà.

Stasera compartirò la buona provvisione mandata da lei con le amiche, ma della ricotta non ne prometto a troppe. La ringrazio per parte di tutte, e di cuore me le raccomando. Di S. Matteo, li 27 di Agosto 1631.

Sua Fig.la Aff.ma

Suor M.a Celeste

finds herself quite weak and listless, she is starting to sit up. And since she seems to have a taste for some salted fish, I entreat you, Sire, to try to provide her with some for these next fasting days. Meanwhile you must endeavor to keep yourself healthy in this terrible heat, and please write me a line. I send you loving greetings from all of us here, and I pray Our Lord to grant you His holy grace. From San Mattteo, the 12th of August 1631.

Sire's Most Affectionate Daughter,

Suor M. Celeste

Most Beloved Lord Father,

We lament the time away from you, Sire, covetous of the pleasure we would have drawn from this day, had we found ourselves all together in each other's company. But, if it please God, I expect that this will soon come to pass, and in the meanwhile I enjoy the hope of having you here always near us, as I understand from the message given me by La Piera; and I pray you to persist in this enterprise so that it succeeds according to our plan, because, if you will it so, Sire, I believe you can overcome every difficulty.

This evening I will share the bounty you sent me with my friends, but I will not promise them too much of the ricotta; I thank you on their behalf and I give you the loving greetings of my heart. From San Matteo, the 27th of August 1631.

Your Most Affectionate Daughter,

Suor M. Celeste

Amatiss.mo Sig.r Padre,

Se la misura o indizio dell'amore che si porta ad una persona è la confidenza che in lei si dimostra, V. S. non dovrà star in dubbio se io l'amo di tutte cuore, come è in verità; poi che tanta confidenza e sicurtà piglio con lei, che qualche volta temo che non ecceda il termine della modestia e reverenza filiale, e tanto più sapendo ch'ella da molti fastidii e spese si trova aggravata. Nondimeno la certezza che ho, che V. S. sovviene tanto volentieri alle mie necessità quanto a quelle di qualsivogl'altra persona, anzi alle sue proprie, mi somministra ardire di pregarla che si compiaccia di alleggerirmi di un pensiero che molto m'inquieta, mediante un debito che tengo di cinque scudi per la malattia d Suor Arcangela, essendomi convenuto in questi 4 mesi spender alla larga, in comparazione di quello che comportava la povertà del nostro stato; et hora, che mi trovo all'estremo et in necessità di sodisfare a chi devo, mi raccomando a chi so che può e vuole aiutarmi. Et anco desidero un fiasco del suo vino bianco, per farl[o] acciaiato per Suor Arcangela, alla quale credo che più gioverà la fede che ha in questo rimedio, che il rimedio istesso.

Scrivo con tanta scarsezza di tempo che non posso dirle altro, se non che vorrei che questi 6 calicioni fossino di suo gusto. E me le raccomando.   Di S. Matteo, li 30 Agosto 1631.

Sua ig.la Aff.ma

Suor M. Celeste

Most Beloved Lord Father,

If the measure or indication of the love one bears another person is the trust vested in the loved one, then you must never doubt, Sire, that I love you with all my heart, as in truth I do; since I draw such confidence and security from you that at times I fear I exceed the bounds of modesty and filial devotion, and all the more so as I know you to be beset by many worries and expenses. Nevertheless the certainty I have, that you will minister ever so much more willingly to my needs than to those of any other person, even including your own, lets me dare to ask you if you would be so kind as to relieve me of a worry that weighs heavily on my mind, regarding a debt I owe of five *scudi* incurred during Suor Arcangela's illness, as I was constrained during these four months to spend with largesse, compared to the economy that befits the poverty of our station: and now that I find myself desperate and pressed to repay the loan, I come to the one I know is willing and able to help me. And also I want a *fiasco* of your white wine to make a strengthening tonic for Suor Arcangela, who I think will be better served by her faith in this remedy than by the remedy itself.

This is the last of Suor Maria Celeste's letters addressed to Galileo at Bellosguardo. (Once he moves next door to her in Arcetri, she has no need to write to him again until the winter of 1632.)

I write with so little time that I cannot possibly say more, except that I hope you enjoy these six almond pastries, and I send you my love. From San Matteo, the 30th of August 1631.

Your Most Affectionate Daughter,

Suor M. Celeste

Molto Ill.re et Amatiss.mo Sig.r Padre,

I SSig.ri Bocchineri mi hanno trasmesse tutte le lettere che V. S. ha mandate, delle quali mi appago, sapendo quanto gli sia di fatica lo scrivere. Io non gl'ho scritto fin hora, perchè stavo aspettando l'avviso del suo arrivo a Roma; e quando per l'ultima sua intendo che deve trattenersi tanti giorni in abitazione così cattiva e priva di ogni comodità, ne ho preso grandissima afflizione. Non dimeno sentendo che ella, priva di consolazioni interne et esterne, si conserva sana, mi consolo, e rendo grazie a Dio beneddto, nel quale ho ferma speranza di ottener grazia che V. S. se ne torni qua da noi con quiete d'animo e sanità di corpo. In tanto la prego a star più allegramente che sia possibile; e si raccomandi a Dio, che non abbandona chi in Lui confida.

Suor Arcangela et io stiamo bene, ma non già Suor Luisa, che dal giorno che V. S. si partì in qua, è stata sempre in letto con dolori eccessivi, conforme al suo solito; et a me convenendo star in continuo moto et esercizio per applicargli rimedii e servirla, si porge occasione di sollevar l'animo da quel pensiero che forse troppo l'affliggerebbe per l'assenza di V. S.

Il Sig.r Rondinelli non è ancora venuto a goder la comodità che V. S. gl'ha largita della casa, dicendo che le sue lite non gliel'hanno permesso. Ma il nostro Padre confessore non lascia di darvi spesso volta: saluta V. S., et il simile fanno la Madre badessa e tutte le amiche. Suor Arcangela et io infinitamente e senza intermissione preghiamo Nostro Signore che la guardi e conservi.

Most Illustrious and Beloved Lord Father,

The Bocchineri family have managed to bring me all the letters that you sent Sire, and from their number I feel certain I know how tired you must be of writing. I have not written to you until now, because I was waiting to hear word of your arrival in Rome; and having learned from this last letter of yours that you are required to spend so many days in such poor lodgings, deprived of every comfort, I am extremely distressed. Nevertheless, hearing that while you lack all internal and external consolations, you still maintain your health, I console myself and give thanks to blessed God, steadfastly confident that by His grace you will return to us, Sire, with peace of mind and soundness of body. Meanwhile I entreat you to be as cheerful as you possibly can, and commend yourself to God, as He does not abandon those who put their trust in Him.

Galileo, summoned to Rome by the Inquisition, left home on January 20. Now he is detained in quarantine in Acquapendente because of the plague in Florence.

Suor Arcangela and I are well, but I cannot say as much for Suor Luisa, who, since the day of your departure has been confined to bed with the same terrible pains that have stricken her in the past; and I am content to stay continually active and take charge of applying her treatments and waiting on her, as this emergency relieves my mind of dwelling too disturbingly on your absence.

Signor Rondinelli has not yet arrived to enjoy the convenience you so graciously granted him of using your house, Sire, explaining that his litigations have prevented him. But our father confessor has gone there often to look it over; he

*Galileo has offered **Il Gioiello**, during his absence, to Francesco Rondinelli, the grand duke's librarian.*

L'inclusa che gli mando, fu trovata da Gioseppe lunedì, nel luogo dove hanno recapito ordinariamente le sue lettere. Di S. Matteo in Arcetri, li 5 di Febb.º 1633.

Di V. S. molto Ill.re Fig.la Aff.ma

Suor M.a Celeste

Molto Ill.re et Amatiss.mo Sig.r Padre,

La sua lettera scritta alli 10 di Febbraio mi fu resa alli 22 del medesimo, et in questo tempo credo sicuramente che V. S. haverà ricevuta un'altra mia, insieme con una del nostro R. Padre confessoro, per le quali haverà inteso qualche particolare circa a quello che desiderava; e vedendo io che ancora non compariscano lettere che ne diano avviso dell'arrivo suo a Roma (le quali può V. S. giudicare con quanto desiderio, da me in particolare, siano aspettate), torno a scriverle, sì perchè ella sappia con quanta ansietà io viva mentre le sto aspettando, et anco per mandarle la inclusa polizza, la quale da un giovane fu, 4 o 5 giorni sono, portata qui a casa di V. S. e pigliata dal Sig.r Francesco Rondinelli, et egli, dandomela, mi consigliò a dar sodisfazione senza aspettare qualche peggior affronto dal creditore, dicendomi non potersi trasgredire in alcuna maniera a questo comandamento, et offerendosi egli medesimo a trattar questo negozio. Io stamattina gl'ho consegnati li 6 scudi, quali non vuol altrimenti pagar a Vincenzio, ma de-sends his regards to you, and so do the Mother Abbess and all our friends; Suor Arcangela and I with all our hearts and without ceasing pray Our Lord constantly to protect you and bless you.

This enclosure I am sending you was found Monday by Giuseppe in the place where your letters are usually delivered. From San Matteo, the 5th of February 1632.

Giuseppe is Galileo's servant boy.

Sire's Most Affectionate Daughter,

Suor M. Celeste

Most Illustrious and Beloved Lord Father,

Your letter written on the 10th of February was delivered to me on the 22nd of the same month, and by now I assume you must have received another letter of mine, Sire, along with one from our father confessor, and through these you will have learned some of the details you wanted to know; and seeing that still no letters have come giving us definite news of your arrival in Rome (and you can imagine, Sire, with what eagerness I in particular anticipate those letters), I return to write to you again, so that you may know how anxiously I live, while awaiting word from you, and also to send you the enclosed legal notice, which was delivered to your house, 4 or 5 days ago, by a young man, and accepted by Signor Francesco Rondinelli, who, in giving it to me, advised me that it must be paid, without waiting for some more offensive insult from the creditor, telling me that one could not disobey such an order in any manner, and offering to handle the matter himself. This morning I gave him the 6 *scudi*, which he did not want positarli là in Magistrato, fino che da V. S. verrà avvisato quel tanto che si deva fare. È in vero il S.r Francesco persona molto grata e discreta, e non finisce mai di esagerare l'obligo che tiene a V. S. per questa habilità che ha della sua casa. Dalla Piera intendo che egli usa a lei et a Gioseppe molta amorevolezza pur di cose mangiative; et io nel resto supplisco a i loro bisogni, conforme all'ordine di V. S. Il ragazzo mi dice che questa Pasqua haverà bisogno di scarpe e calze, le quali fo disegno di fargli di filaticcio grosso o vero di stame. Dalla Piera intendo che V. S. più volte gl'ha detto che vuol far venire una balla di lino, onde per questo mi sono ritirata dal comprarne qualche poco e fargli principiar una tela di panno grosso per la cucina, sì come havevo dissegnato di fare; e non lo farò se da V. S. non mi verrà ordinato altro.

Le vite dell'orto si accomoderanno adesso che la luna è a proposito, per mano del padre di Gioseppe, il quale intendo che è suffiziente, et anco il S.r Rondinelli vi assisterà. La lattuga intendo che è assai bella, et ho commesso a Gioseppe che ne porti a vendere avanti che sia guasta da altri. Di 70 melangole che si venderono, se n'hebbe 4 lire, pago assai ragionevole, per quanto intendo, essendo un frutto di poca utilità. Le malarance si venderono 14 crazie il cento, e furono 200.

Di quella botte di vino che V. S. lasciò manomessa, il S.r Rondinelli ne piglia ogni sera un poco per sè, et in tanto fa anco benefizio al vino, il quale intendo che si mantiene bonissimo. Quel poco del vecchio l'ho fatto cavare ne i fiaschi, e detto alla Piera che se lo bevino quando haveranno finita la loro botticella, già che noi fino a qui, havendolo to pay to Vincenzio but chose to deposit the money with the magistrate until you have told him, Sire, what you want him to do. Signor Francesco is indeed a most pleasant and discreet person, and he never stops declaiming his gratefulness to you, Sire, for allowing him the use of your house. I heard from La Piera that he treats her and Giuseppe with great kindness, even in regard to their foods; and I provide for the rest of their needs, Sire, according to your directions. The boy tells me that this Easter he will need shoes and stockings, which I plan to knit for him out of thick, coarse cotton or else from fine wool. La Piera maintains that you have often spoken to her about ordering a bale of linen, on which account I refrained from buying the small amount I would need to begin weaving the thick cloth for your kitchen, as I had meant to do, Sire, and I will not make the purchase unless I hear otherwise from you.

Her cousin Vincenzio Landucci has sued Galileo for his living expenses.

The vines in the garden will take nicely now that the Moon is right, at the hands of Giuseppe's father, who they say is capable enough, and also Signor Rondinelli will lend his help. The lettuce I hear is quite lovely, and I have entrusted Giuseppe to take it to be sold at market before it spoils. From the sale of 70 bitter oranges came 4 lire, a very respectable price, from what I understand, as that fruit has few uses: Portuguese oranges are selling for 14 *crazie* per 100 and you had 200 that were sold.

As for that barrel of newly tapped wine you left, Sire, Signor Rondinelli takes a little for himself every evening, and meanwhile he makes improvements to the wine, which he says is coming along extremely well. What little of the old wine that havuto dal convento assai ragionevole et essendo sane, ne haviamo tolto poco.

Continuo a dar il giulio ogni sabato alla Brigida; e veramente che stimo questa una elemosina molto ben data, essendo ella oltremodo bisognosa e molto buona figliuola.

Suor Luisa, la Dio grazia, sta alquanto meglio, e si va ancora trattenendo in purga; et havendo, per l'ultima lettera di V. S., compreso quanto pensiero ella si pigli del suo male per l'affetto che gli porta, la ringrazia infinitamente, e già che V. S. si dichiara unita meco nell'amarla, ella all'incontro pretende di star al paragone, nè di un punto vuol cedergli, poi che l'affetto suo procede dall'istessa causa, che sono io; onde mi glorio e pregio di questa così graziosa contesa, e più chiaramente scorgo la grandezza dell'amore che ambe due mi portano, poi che è così soprabbondante che arriva a scambievolmente dilatarsi fra quelle due persone da me sopra ogn'altra cosa mortale amate e reverite.

Domani saranno 15 giorni che morà la nostra Suor Virginia Canigiani, la quale stava assai grave quando scrissi ultimamente a V. S.: et in questo tempo si è ammalata di febbre maligna Suor M.ª Grazia del Pace, che è la più antica di quelle tre monache che suonano l'organo e maestra delle Squarcialupe, monaca veramente pacifica e buona; et essendo stata fatta spacciata dal medico, siamo tutte sottosopra, dolendoci grandemente questa perdita.

Questo è quanto per adesso mi occorre dirgli, e subito che haverò sue lettere (che pur dovrebbono a quest'hora esser a Pisa, ove si ritrovano i SS.ri Bocchineri), scriverò di nuovo. In was left I had decanted into flasks, and told La Piera that she and Giuseppe could drink it when they had finished their small cask, since we of late have had reasonably good wine from the convent, and, being in good health, have hardly taken a drop.

I continue to give one *giulio* every Saturday to La Brigida, and I truly consider this an act of charity well deserved, as she is so exceedingly needy and such a very good girl.

*One **giulio** is a silver coin worth slightly more than half a **lira**.*

Suor Luisa, God bless her, fares somewhat better, and is still purging, and having understood from your last letter, Sire, how concerned you were over her illness out of your regard for her, she thanks you with all her heart; and while you declare yourself united with me in loving her, Sire, she on the other hand claims to be the paragon of this emotion, nor do I mind granting her that honor, since her affection stems from the same source as yours, and it is myself; wherefore I take pride in and prize this most delicious contest of love, and the more clearly I perceive the greatness of that love you both bear me, the more bountiful it grows for being mutually exchanged between the very two persons I love and revere above everyone and everything in this life.

Tomorrow will be 15 days since the death of our Suor Virginia Canigiani, who was already gravely ill when I last wrote to you, Sire, and since then a malevolent fever has stricken Suor Maria Grazia del Pace, the eldest of the three nuns who play the organ, and teacher of the Squarcialupis, a truly tranquil and good nun; and since the doctor has already given her up for dead, we are all beside ourselves, grieving over our loss.

tanto di tutto cuore a lei mi raccomando, insieme con le solite e nominatamente S.r Arcangela, il Sig.r Rondinelli et il Sig.r mesdico Ronconi, il quale ogni volta che vien qui mi fa grand'instanza di haver nuove di lei. Il Signor Iddio la conservi e feliciti sempre. Di S. Matteo, li 26 di Febb.° 1632.

Di V. S. molto Ill.re Fig.la Aff.ma

Suor M.a Celeste Galilei

In questo punto essendo tornato da Firenze il S.r Rondinelli, mi ha detto haver parlato al Cancelliere dei Consiglieri, et haver inteso esser necessario pagar li 6 scudi a Vincenzio Landucci e non altrimenti depositarli, e tanto si eseguirà; se bene io mi ci sono resa alquanto difficilmente, per non haver havuta commissione alcuna da V. S. di questo particolare.

Amatiss.mo Sig.r Padre,

Il Sig.r Mario Guiducci hiermattina mi mandò fin qui per un suo servitore le lettere di V. S. Lessi con mio particolar contento quella ch'ella scrive al medesimo S.r Mario, e subito gliela rimandai. L'altra ho consegnata al Padre confessore, il quale credo che senz'altro gli risponderà. Mi consolo, e sempre di nuovo ringrazio Dio benedetto, sentendo che il suo negozio fino a qui passi con tanta [. . .]te e silenzio, il quale in ultimo ne promette un felice e prospero successo, come ho

This is everything I need to tell you for the moment, and as soon as I receive your letters (which must surely have arrived at Pisa by now where the Bocchineri gentlemen are) I will write again. Meanwhile I send you the greetings of my heart together with our usual friends, and particularly Suor Arcangela, Signor Rondinelli and Doctor Ronconi, who begs me for news of you every time he comes here. May the Lord God bless you and keep you happy always. From San Matteo, the 26th of February 1633.

These men are the brothers of her sister-in-law, Sestilia.

Sire's Most Affectionate Daughter,

Suor M. Celeste Galilei

Signor Rondinelli, having this very moment returned from Florence, tells me he spoke to the Chancellor of the Advisors and learned that the 6 *scudi* must be paid to Vincenzio Landucci and not be deposited, and this will be done; I submitted to this decision reluctantly, not having had your instructions on the matter.

Most Beloved Lord Father,

Signor Mario Guiducci yesterday morning sent me, by one of his servants, all the way up here, the letters he had received from you. I read with especial delight the one you wrote to Signor Mario himself, and I sent it back to him right away. The other I gave to the Father Confessor, who I am certain will send a reply. I take comfort, and ever again I thank blessed God, hearing that your affairs thus far proceed with such tranquillity and silence, which bodes well for a happy

Mario Guiducci, a former student of Galileo's and an official of the Florentine Magistracy of Public Health, remains his devoted friend.

sempre sperato con l'aiuto divino e per l' intercessioni della Madonna Santissima.

Credo che a quest'hora V. S. haverà ricevuta l'ultima mia lettera; e da poi in qua le novità occorse sono: lo sborso delli 6 scudi, fatto dal S.r Francesco in nome di V. S. a Vincenzio Landucci, il quale venne in persona a pigliarli; il buon progresso in sanità che va facendo Suor Luisa, essendo stata parecchi giorni senza sentir travaglio; la indisposizione di Suor Arcangela da 10 giorni in qua, che travaglia con dolore eccessivo nella spalla e braccio sinistro, se bene con l'aiuto di alcune pillole e serviziali, è alquanto mitigato: et anco Gioseppe travaglia con il suo stomaco et enfiagione di milza, sì che è convenuto fargli guastar quaresima; et il S.r Rondinelli ne tiene cura particolare. Di più, la nostra Suor M.a Grazia organista, che avvisai a V. S. che stava grave, si morì, essendo di età di 58 o 60 anni; e tutte ne haviamo sentito gran travaglio. La Piera sta bene: le vite dell'orto sono accomodate: di lattuga venduta si è preso fino a qui un mezzo scudo.

Altro particolare non ho da dirle, se non che io tutto il giorno fo l'offizio di Marta, senza alcuna intermissione, e con questo me la passo assai bene di sanità; la quale participerei volentierissimo, anzi baratterei con l'indisposizione di V. S., acciò ella restasse libera da quei dolori che la molestano. Sto aspettando l'ordine suo circa il dar altri danari al Landucci questo mese presente, perchè non vorrei far errore, nè che incorressimo in spese, come questa volta, di 6. 13. 4. che importò la polizza che gli mandai. La lettera per la S.ra Ambasciatrice potrà sigillarla, quando l'haverà letta. E con questo di tutto and prosperous outcome, as I have always hoped would come with divine help and by the intercession of the most holy Blessed Virgin.

Although Galileo arrived in Rome on February 13, he has not yet been called for questioning.

I believe that by now you will have received my last letter, Sire, and since then new tidings are the disbursement of the 6 *scudi* by Signor Francesco in your name to Vincenzio Landucci, who came in person to collect them; the good progress in recovery being achieved by Suor Luisa, she having been free of pain for several days now; Suor Arcangela's illness of the past ten days, which afflicts her with terrible soreness in her left shoulder and arm, even though, with the help of various pills and enemas, the symptoms are somewhat mitigated: and even Giuseppe suffers from his stomach and swollen spleen, so that he is constrained to break Lent, and Signor Rondinelli is taking special care of him. More than that our Suor Maria Grazia, the organist who had been gravely ill, as I notified you, Sire, has died, at the age of 58 or 60 years, and all of us have felt grievously distressed. La Piera is well, the vines in the garden are staked; the sale of lettuce to date has brought in half a *scudo*.

Other details I have none to tell you, except that all day long I perform the office of Martha, without a single intermission, and thus I stay in reasonably good health, which condition I would most willingly share with you, Sire, or rather exchange my well-being for your indisposition, so that you could remain free of those ills that molest you. I am waiting for the order regarding other payments to the Landuccis for the present month, because I would not want to make any mistakes, nor have us incur expenses as we did this time in the lire

Saint Martha, the industrious sister of Mary Magdalene, is the patron saint of cooks and housekeepers.

cuore me le raccomando insieme con le solite. Di S. Matteo, li 5 di Marzo 1632.

Sua Fig.la Aff.ma

S.r M.a Celes[. .]

Molto Ill.re et Amatiss.mo Sig.r Padre,

L'ultima sua lettera, mandatami dal S.r Andrea Arrighetti, mi ha aportato gran consolazione, sì per sentire che ella si va mantenendo in buon grado di sanità, come anco perchè per quella vengo maggiormente certificata del felice esito del suo negozio, chè tale me l'hanno fatto prevedere il desiderio e l'amore: chè se ben veggo che, passando le cose in questa maniera, si andrà prolungando il tempo del suo ritorno, reputo non dimeno a gran ventura il restar priva delle mie proprie sodisfazioni per una occasione la quale habbia da ridondare in benefizio e reputazione della sua persona, amata da me più che me stessa; e tanto più m'acquieto, quanto che son certa che ella riceve ogni honore e comodità desiderabile da cotesti Ecc.mi Signori et in particolare dall'Ecc.ma mia Signora e Padrona, la visita della quale, se havessimo grazia Suor Arcangela et io di ricevere, certo che sarebbe favore segnalato et a noi tanto grato quanto V. S. può immaginarsi, chè io non lo so esplicare. Quanto al procurar che ella vedesse una comedia, non posso dir niente, perchè bisognerebbe governarsi secondo il tempo nel quale ella venissi, se bene io veramente crederei che stessimo più in salvo lasciandola in amounts of 6. 13. 4. which appears on the bill I sent you. The letter to her ladyship the Ambassadress can be sealed after you have read it. And ending here I give you all my loving greetings together with our usual friends. From San Matteo, the 5th of March 1632.

Your Most Affectionate Daughter,

S. M. Celes[. .]

Most Illustrious and Beloved Lord Father,

Your last letter, sent me from Signor Andrea Arrighetti, brought me great solace, as much for hearing that you are keeping up your good health, Sire, as for the good news that assures me of a happy ending to your affair, just as my longing and my love have led me to expect. Whereby even though I see that, with things progressing in this fashion, prolonging the time of your return, I consider it nonetheless a great destiny to be deprived of my own satisfaction for an occasion that has the potential to redound in the favorable recognition and reputation of your character, which I love more than my own. And I calm myself all the more by my certainty that you will receive every honor and desired comfort from those very excellent lords, and especially from my most excellent lady and patroness, whose visit, should Suor Arcangela and I be so fortunate as to receive one, would certainly be a noteworthy honor and as welcome to us as you will have to imagine yourself, Sire, for I know not how to express it. As for allowing her to view a play, I am speechless, because it would have to be rehearsed in time for her arrival, while I honestly believe, since she has evinced this desire to hear us perform, Sire,

Galileo's friend and fellow mathematician Andrea Arrighetti supervises the Tuscan fortifications.

Ambassador Francesco Niccolini and his wife, Caterina, are Galileo's warm-hearted hosts at the Tuscan Embassy in Rome.

quella buona credenza in ch'ella deve ritrovarsi mediante le parole di V. S., già che ella si mostra desiderosa di sentirci recitare. Similmente la venuta del P. D. Benedetto ci sarà gratissima, per esser egli persona insignie e tanto affezionata a V. S. Gli renderà dupplicate le salute per nostra parte, e mi farà anco grazia di darmi qualche nuova della Anna Maria, la quale V. S. esaltava tanto l'altra volta che tornò di costà, perchè io fino all'hora me gl'affezionai, sentendo il suo merito e valore.

S.r Arcangela sta alquanto meglio, ma non bene affatto, del suo braccio; e S.r Luisa sta ragionevolmente bene, ma però con grande osservanza di vita regolata. Io sto bene, perchè ho l'animo quieto e tranquillo; e sto in continuo moto, eccetto però le 7 hore della notte, le quali io mando male in un sonno solo, poi che questo mio capaccio così umido non ne vuol manco un tantino. Non lascio per questo di sodisfare il più ch'io posso al debito che ho con lei dell'orazione, pregando Dio benedetto che principalmente le conceda la salute dell'anima, et anco le altre grazie che ella maggiormente desidera.

Non dirò altro per ora, se non che habbia pazienza se troppo la tengo a tedio, pensando che io ristringo in questa carta tutto quello ch'io gli cicalerei in una settimana. La saluto con tutto l'affetto, insieme con le solite; et il simile fa il S.r Rondinelli. Di S. Matteo in Arcetri, li 12 di Marzo 1632.

Di V. S. molto Ill.re Fig.la Aff.ma

Suor M.a Celeste

that we would be safer leaving her believing in the talent she assumes us to have on your say-so. Similarly the arrival of the most reverend father Don Benedetto will be most appreciated here, on account of his being a renowned individual and so affectionate toward you, Sire, so please return his regards twofold from us, and also do me the favor of giving me some news of Anna Maria, whom you extolled so highly the last time you returned from Rome, because since then I find myself growing attached to her, having heard of her goodness and courage.

Don Benedetto Castelli, a Benedictine monk and one of Galileo's oldest friends and colleagues, now oversees water and drainage projects in Rome for Pope Urban VIII.

The work of Anna Maria Vajani, a painter of floral themes, finds favor with Galileo and the Tuscan ambassadress.

Suor Arcangela feels somewhat improved, but her arm is not altogether better yet, and Suor Luisa fares reasonably well, by virtue of her strict observance of her daily regimen. I feel all right because my mind is calm and clear, while my body stays in constant motion, except for the seven hours of the night, which I waste away by only sleeping, because this dull head of mine cannot survive with even a tiny bit less. I do not fail in any case to devote as much time as possible to my prayers, entreating blessed God to grant you first of all the health of your soul, and also the other favors that you most desire.

I will say no more for now, if not to beg your forbearance if I have bored you too much, thinking that I could compress into this paper all the things I would chatter to you about in a week's time. I send you all my love together with our usual friends; and Signor Rondinelli sends you his regards. From San Matteo, the 12th of March 1632.

Sire's Most Affectionate Daughter,

Suor M. Celeste

Molto Ill.re et Amatiss.mo Sig.r Padre,

Il Sig.r Mario con la solita sua gentilezza mi mandò iermattina le lettere di V. S. Ho recapitate le due incluse a chi andavano; e la ringrazio dell'avvertimento che mi dà dell'errore da me commesso nella lettera della Sig.ra Ambasciatrice, della qualle *(sic)* tengo una cortesissima lettera in risposta alla mia: e fra l'altre cose mi dice ch'io persuada V. S. a proceder con più libertà in cotesta essa, e con quella sicurtà che farebbe nella sua propria, e si dimostra molto ansiosa delle sue comodità e sodisfazioni. Io gli riscrivo, domandandole il favore che V. S. vedrà: se gli par ben fatto il presentarla, l'havrò caro; se no, me n'apporto al suo parere. Ma veramente, o per mezzo della medesima S.ra Ambasciatrice o di V. S., havr[. . .] caro di ottener questa grazia; sì come da V. S. desidererei un regalo al suo ritorno, il quale pur spero che non deva andar molto in lungo. Mi persuado che costà sia copia di buone pitture; onde io desidererei che V. S. mi portassi un quadretto di grandezza quanto questa carta qui inclusa, di questi che si serrano a uso di libriccino, con due figure una delle quali vorrei che fossi un Ecce Homo e l'altra una Madonna; ma vorrei che fossino pietosi e devoti al possibile. Non importerà già che vi sia altro adornamento che una semplice cornice, desiderandolo io per tenerlo sempre appresso di me.

Credo senz'altro che il S. Rondinelli scriva a V. S.; onde sarà bene ch'ella nella risposta gli dimostri gratitudine per le amorevolezze che ci ha usate di quando in quando in questa quaresima, e particolarmente perchè hieri fu qua a desinare e volse che ancor noi due v'intervenissimo, acciò si passassi

Most Illustrious and Beloved Lord Father,

Signor Mario, with his usual kindness, sent me your letters yesterday morning. I have forwarded the two enclosed ones to their intended recipients; and I thank you for your advice about the error I had committed in my letter to her ladyship the Ambassadress, from whom I have the most courteous letter in response to mine; and among other things she tells me that she encourages you, Sire, to come and go with greater freedom in their house, indeed with the same assurance as you would enter your own, and she shows herself very concerned about your comfort and satisfaction. I am writing to them again to ask her for a favor that you will see, Sire: if it seems proper to propose this to her, I will be only too happy to do so; if not, I will conform to your wish. But truly, whether by the help of her ladyship the Ambassadress, or from you, Sire, I would dearly love to obtain this good will, since I would like to have a gift from you upon your return, which event I surely hope will not have to be delayed much longer. I imagine there must be an abundance of good artwork available where you are, and so I would like you to bring me a small picture, about the size of the enclosed paper, in the form of a diptych that would stand open like a little prayer-book, with two figures, one of which I should want to be an Ecce Homo and the other a Madonna; but I would want each to be executed as piously and devoutly as possible. There is no need for any adornment other than a simple frame, as I intend to keep this always near me.

Mario Guiducci directs mail to and from Galileo, standing in for Geri Bocchineri, who has gone to Pisa with the court for Easter.

This enclosure has been lost.

Ecce Homo is the figure of Jesus crucified.

I believe without doubt that Signor Rondinelli must be writing to you, Sire, wherefore you would do well in your re-quel giorno allegramente, principalmente per amor di Suor Arcangela, la quale, per grazia di Dio, va migliorando del suo braccio. È ben vero che, per esser da parecchi giorni in qua sopraggiunto un catarro nelle reni a Suor Oretta, e non potendosi esercitare, tocca a me in gran parte il pensiero dell'offizio di Provveditora; e per questo e per altre mie faccende essendomi ridotta a scriver a mezza notte, et assalendomi il sonno, temo di non scriver qualche sproposito. Godo in estremo di sentir che V. S. si conservi in buona sanità, e prego Dio benedetto che la conservi. La saluto per parte di tutte le amiche et anco in nome del Sig.r Ronconi, il quale spesso con grande instanza mi domanda di V. S. Di S. Matteo in Arcetri, li 19 Marzo 1632.

Di V. S. molto Ill.re Fig.la Aff.ma

Suor M.a Celeste

Molto Ill.re et Amatiss.mo Sig.r Padre,

V. S. ha voluto che questi giorni santi io resti mortificata, privandomi di sue lettere; il che quanto io habbia sentito, non posso esprimerlo. Non voglio già io lasciar, se bene con molta strettezza di tempo, di salutarla con questi due versi, augurandoli felicissima questa Santissima Pasqua, colma di consolazioni spirituali a di buona salute e felicità temporale, chè tanto mi prometto e spero dalla liberalissima mano del Signor Iddio.

sponse to acknowledge the thoughtfulness he has shown us from time to time during this season of Lent, and especially because yesterday he was here to dine and he wished the two of us to join him, so that we might pass the halfway point of Lent happily, mostly for love of Suor Arcangela, who by the grace of God is finding her arm improved. The fact is, Sire, with Suor Oretta having been stricken several days ago by a catarrh in the small of her back, and thus unable to exert herself, I have had to assume most of the responsibilities of the Provider's office, and between this and my other duties, I am reduced to writing at midnight and assailing my sleep, so that I fear I may say something inappropriate. I take delight, however, in hearing that you guard your health, Sire, and I pray blessed God to keep you well. I send you regards from all our friends and also in the name of Doctor Ronconi, who often asks after you with great concern. From San Matteo, the 19th of March 1632.

March 18, the day before, marked the midpoint of the Lenten season.

Sire's Most Affectionate Daughter,
Suor M. Celeste

Most Illustrious and Beloved Lord Father,

You have wanted me to remain mortified through these holy days, Sire, depriving me of your letters, which, as much as I have felt about it, I cannot express in words. But still I do not want to neglect, despite the severe constraints on my time, to greet you with these two lines, wishing you joyfully a most holy Easter, replete with spiritual consolations and good health and temporal happiness, for all that I promise myself for you and hope from the most generous hand of the Lord God.

Qua di presente, la Dio grazia, siamo tutte sane, ma non già, il nostro Gioseppo, il quale, fatto le Feste, bisognerà che vadia a lo spedale, per curarsi della febbre e della milza che è assai gonfia; et io vo procurando, col mezzo della nostra Madre badessa, che egli sia ricevuto in Bonifazio, ove staraà meglio che in nessun altro luogo. La Piera sta bene a la saluta, sì come fo io di tutto cuore insieme con le solite, e gli ricordo che è in debito meco della risposta di 3 lettere. Di S. Matteo Arcetri, il Sabbato S.to del 1633.

Di V. S. molto Ill.re Fig.la Aff.ma

Suor M.a Celeste

Molto Ill.re et Amatiss.mo Sig.r Padre,

Sabato passato veddi la lettera che V. S. scrisse al S.r Andrea Arrighetti, e particolarmente mi dette gran contento quel sentire, che ella non solo si vada conservando in sanità, ma che più presto va guadagnando qualcosa con l'aiuto della quiete dell'animo che gode, mentre che spera placida e presta spedizione del suo negozio. Del tutto sia sempre lodato Dio benedetto, dal quale principalmente derivano queste grazie.

Hebbi anco molto caro di intender che V. S. presentò la mia lettera all'Ecc.ma Sig.ra Ambasciatrice, dal che fo conseguenza non esser stato sconvenevole, come temevo, il domandarle quella grazia, la quale con il suo favore spero di ottenere, promettendomi la sua incomparabil cortesia ogni possibile diligenza per impetrarla. Desidero che V. S. supplisca per me con far seco i dovuti complimenti: et oltre a questo da V. S.

Here for the present, God be praised, we are all well, but not so our Giuseppe, who, after the holidays, will need to go to the hospital to have his fever treated, and see to his spleen, which is greatly distended; wherefore I am trying, with the help of our Mother Abbess, to have him received in Bonifazio, where he will be better cared for than anywhere else. La Piera fares well and sends you her regards, as do I with all my heart together with our usual friends, and I remind you that you now owe me responses to three letters.   From San Matteo, Holy Saturday 1633.

Bonifazio is the city hospital in Florence.

Sire's Most Affectionate Daughter,

Suor M. Celeste

Most Illustrious and Beloved Lord Father,

Last Saturday I saw the letter you wrote to Signor Andrea Arrighetti, Sire, and it gave me especial pleasure to hear that you are not only keeping yourself well, but rather gaining something with the help of that peace of mind you enjoy, while you hope for a placid and rapid settlement of your affair; for all of this may blessed God be ever praised, as He is the principal source of these graces.

Although this letter has been lost, Geri Bocchineri took pains to share with "the dear sisters" and "Signor Vincenzio" many others that Galileo wrote to friends in Tuscany during this period.

I also had a great desire to know, Sire, if you gave my letter to Her Ladyship the Ambassadress, and if so whether it may have been improper, as I feared, to ask her that favor [procuring the diptych of Jesus and Mary], which with her help I hope to secure, as her incomparable courtesy assures me she will employ every diligence to obtain it. I want you to help me, Sire, by making the required ceremonial gestures for me; and beyond this I

Suor Maria Celeste refers to the diptych of Jesus and Mary.

desidero nuove grazie, non per me sola, ma per S.r Arcangela, la quale, per grazia di Dio, oggi a 3 settimane, che sarà l'ultimo del presente, deve lasciar l'offizio di Provveditora, nel quale fino a qui ha speso cento scudi e da vantaggio; et essendo in obligo di lasciarne 25 in conservo alle nuove Provveditore, nè havendo assegnamento di nessuno, io vorrei, con licenza di V. S., accomodarnela di quelli che tengo di suo, tanto che questa nave si conduca in porto, chè veramente senza l'aiuto di V. S. non arrivava nè meno alla metà del viaggio. Ma non occorre ch'io mi affatichi in esagerar questo, quando sarà dichiarato il tutto con dire che tutto il bene che haviamo, chè ne haviamo tanto, o quello che possiamo sperare e desiderare, l'haviamo e speriamo da lei, dalla sua più che ordinaria amorevolezza e carità, con la quale, oltre all'haver compitamente sodisfatto all'obligo di allogarne, continuamente ne sovviene tanto benignamente in tutti i nostri bisogni. Ma V. S. vede che la remunerazione gliene dà per noi Dio benedetto, al quale piaccia pure, con la sua conservazione e prosperità, di mantener lei e noi lungo tempo felici.

Il dolore eccessivo che sento in un dente m'impedisce il poter più lungamente scrivere, sì che non gli darò altra nuova se non che Gioseppo va migliorando e che noi tutte stiamo bene, insieme con la Piera, e tutte la salutiamo affettuosamente. Di S. Matteo in Arcetri, li 9 di Aprile 1633.

Di V. S. molto Ill.re Fig.la Aff.ma

Suor M.a Celeste

have another kindness to ask of you, not for myself, but for Suor Arcangela, who, by the grace of God, three weeks from today, which will be the last day of this month, must leave the office of Provider, in which capacity up till now she has spent one hundred *scudi* and fallen into debt; and being obliged to leave 25 *scudi* in reserve for the new Provider, not having anywhere else to turn, I beg your leave, with your permission, Sire, to help her out with the money of yours that I hold, so that this ship can bring itself safely to port, whereas truly, without your help, it would not complete so much as half its voyage. But there is no need for me to exhaust myself in exaggerating this situation, when it can all be explained by saying that every good thing we have, and we do have so much, or all that we may hope and desire, we have and we hope from you, Sire, from your extraordinary loving kindness and charity, with which, beyond having politely met your obligation as a parent to provide for us, you continuously assist us so graciously in all our needs: but you see, Sire, how blessed God rewards you on our behalf, as He deigns to grant you continued health and prosperity, keeping you and us happy all this time.

The office of Provider, charged with managing outside food purchases for the year, falls to each nun on a rotating basis.

The excessive pain in my tooth keeps me from being able to write at length, so that I will not give you other news, except that Giuseppe is getting better, and all of us are well: together with La Piera and everyone here we send you our loving regards. From San Matteo, the 9th of April 1633.

Sire's Most Affectionate Daughter,

Suor M. Celeste

Amatiss.mo Sig.r Padre,

Intendo per due lettere, che questa settimana tengo di suo, il buon progresso del suo negozio: me ne rallegro quanto ella può immaginarsi, e ne ringrazio Dio.

Hiersera qua fu un applauso et allegrezza grande, mediante la grazia impetrataci dall'Eco.ma S.ra Ambasciatrice, alla quale scrivo questi pochi versi, veramente di scarso ringraziamento a tanti benefizii che da essa ricevo: fo quel ch'io so, e non quel che dovrei. Scrissi al S.r Giovanni Rinuccini per conto del servizio che V. S. m'impone; e da esso tengo risposta che per adesso non bisogna trattarne, ma che quando verrà l'occasione, me ne farà avvisata.

Del mal cattivo intendo esserne in Firenze qualche poco, ma non già conforme a quello che si va dicendo e ragguagliando costà. Sento che ci sono dei carboncelli, ma che i più muoiano di petecchie e mal di punta. Quanto al suo ritorno, ancor che grandemente io lo desideri, la consiglierei a soprastare qualche poco, aspettando altri avvisi da gl'amici suoi, et anco a metter ad effetto il pensiero che haveva quando partì di qui, di visitare la Santa Casa di Loreto.

Vincenzio nostro c'ha scritto questa settimana, e mandatoci a donare un pezzo di prosciutto. Io haverei curiosità di sapere come egli visita spesso V. S. con lettere. Giuseppo è tanto migliorato che è partito da lo spedale, e per qualche giorno si trattiene in casa un suo zio in Firenze. La Piera sta bene, e attende a filare. De i limoni se ne son colti alcuni pochi che erano già bassi, avanti che fussero portati via da i malfattori; gl'altri intendo che sono molto belli, e similmente le fave, le

Most Beloved Lord Father,

Two letters from you this week inform me of the good progress of your affair: in this I rejoice as much as you can possibly imagine, Sire, and I thank God for it.

Yesterday evening here there was a great outburst of cheer and merriment, celebrating the successful intercession of Her Most Excellent Ladyship the Ambassadress, to whom I write the few lines enclosed herewith, which barely begin to thank her for all the many blessings I draw from her. I do as much as I can, though not nearly as much as I think I should. I wrote to Sig. Giovanni Rinuccini to request a bill for his services, as you asked me to do, Sire, and he answered that for now there is no need to speak of this business, but that, when the time comes, he will advise me.

I understand there are several cases of the evil pestilence in Florence, but not nearly as many as reports where you are would have you believe. I hear that there are buboes, but that more people die of rashes and lung disease. As for how this affects your return, as urgently as I desire it, I would advise you to leave it imminent for a while yet, awaiting other advice from your friends, and also to carry out the idea you had when you left here, of visiting the House of the Virgin Mary in Loreto.

Galileo visited this shrine on the Adriatic coast in 1618, after recovering from an illness.

Our Vincenzio wrote to us this week, and sent us as a gift a piece of ham; I would be curious to know how often he visits you, Sire, with his letters. Giuseppe is so greatly improved that he las left the hospital, and is staying for several days at the home of his uncle in Florence. La Piera fares well and

Vincenzio has moved his family to Poppi, where he has employment as head legal clerk.

quali cominciano ad allegare il frutto. Spero pure che V. S. sarà qua a corle da sè, quando saranno in perfezione.

La saluto caramente in nome di tutte e de i SS.[ri] Rondinelli et Orsi, e dal Signor Iddio gli prego ogni vero bene. Di S. Matt.° in Arcetri, li 16 Aprile 1633.

Sua Fig.[la] Aff.[ma]
Suor M.[a] Celeste

Suor Isabella nostra desidera che V. S. gli faccia grazia di mandar per il suo servitore l'inclusa in mano propria a chi va, perchè ne vorrebbe la risposta quanto prima.

Il nostro Sr Governatore, con occasione di venir a dar l'acqua benedetta; mi domandò instantemente di V. S., imponendomi ch'io gli facessi sue raccomandazioni.

Amatiss.[mo] Sig.[r] Padre,

Non hebbi tempo stamattina di poter risponder alla sua proposta, che fu che ella haveva intenzione di voler sollevare e far servizio solamente a noi due, e non a tutto il convento, come per aventura V. S. si persuade che sarà in effetto mentre mi accomoderà di danari per l'offizio di Sr Arcangela. Conosco veramente che V. S. non è interamente informata tends to her spinning. She picked a few small lemons that were hanging from the low branches, before they could be carried off by thieves. The rest I hear are coming along very beautifully, and the same may be said for the broad beans, which are beginning to produce a great yield. How I hope that you will be back in your garden to pick them yourself, Sire, when they are perfectly ripe.

I send you loving greetings on behalf of everyone here, as well as from their Lordships Rondinelli and Orsi; and from the Lord God I pray for every genuine goodness to be yours. From San Matteo, the 16th of April 1633.

Your Most Affectionate Daughter,

Suor M. Celeste

Our Suor Isabella wants you to do her the favor, Sire, of having your servant hand-deliver the enclosed letter to its addressee, because she would like an immediate response.

Our chaplain, who came to give the blessed water, asked after you the moment he arrived, Sire, urging me to pay you his respects.

Most Beloved Lord Father,

I did not have time this morning to be able to respond fully to your offer, which was that you intended to give comfort and come to the aid of just us two, and not the whole convent, as per chance you persuade yourself may be the case, Sire, when you help settle the debt for Suor Arcangela's office. I see verily that you are not entirely informed of our customs, or, to delle nostre usanze o, per meglio dire, ordini poco discreti; perchè, essendo ciascuna di noi obligata a spender in questo e in tutti gl'altri offizii, conviene a quella che di mano in mano si perviene secondo il grado, trovar quella somma di danari che fa di bisogno, e se non gl'ha, suo danno: onde molte volte avviene che per strade indirette et oblique (questo l'ho imparato da V. S.) si procurano simili servizii e si fanno molti imbrogli; et è impossibile il far altrimenti, convenendo a una povera monaca nell'offizio di Proveditora spender cento scudi. Per Suor Arcangela fino a qui ne ho provvisti vicino a 40, parte havuti in presto da Suor Luisa e parte della nostra entrata, della quale ci resta a riscuoter 16 scudi, decorsi per tutto Maggio: e Suor Oretta ne ha spesi 50. Adesso siamo in grande strettezza, e non so più dove voltarmi; e già che Nostro Signore la conserva in vita per nostro sollevamento, io, prevalendomi e facendo capitale di questa grazia, prego V. S. che per l'amor di Dio mi liberi dal pensiero che mi molesta, con prestarmi quella quantità di danari che può fino a l'anno prossimo futuro, chè all'hora si andrà riscotendo da quelle che dovranno pagare le spese, e se gli darà sodisfazione. Con che per fretta gli dico a Dio.

Sua Fig.^{la} Aff.^{ma}

Suor M.ª Celeste

say it more correctly, our indiscreet system of unofficial rules; for, as each one of us is compelled by turns to assume the expenditures of the Provider's office, and of all the other convent offices, it is incumbent upon every nun, as the various responsibilities devolve upon her, to find the requisite sum of money to meet the particular need in each case, and if she does not have it, the worse for her; wherefore many times it happens that by indirect and roundabout means (this I have learned from you, Sire) these sisters find ways to provide the required services by embroiling themselves in many predicaments: and it is impossible for them to manage it otherwise, when any poor nun in the office of Provider must spend one hundred *scudi*. For Suor Arcangela up till now I have paid close to 40, part of which I had received as a loan from Suor Luisa, and part from our allowance, of which there remains a balance of 16 *scudi* to draw upon for all of May. Suor Oretta spent 50 *scudi*: Now we are sorely pressed and I do not know where else to turn, and since the Lord God keeps you in this life for our support, I take advantage of this blessing and seize upon it to beseech you, Sire, that with God's love you free me from the worry that harasses me, by lending me whatever amount of money you can until next year comes around, at which time we will recover our losses by collecting from those who must pay the expenses then, and thereby repay you, with which thought, in haste, I commend you to God.

On the back of this letter, Galileo wrote, "Suor Maria Celeste needs money immediately."

Your Most Affectionate Daughter,

Suor M. Celeste

Amatiss.mo Sig.r Padre,

Dal Sig.r Geri mi vien avvisato in qual termine ella si ritrovi per causa del suo negozio, cioè ritenuto nelle stanze del S.to Offizio; il che per una parte mi dà molto disgusto, persuadendomi che ella si ritrovi con poca quiete dell'animo e forse anco non con tutte le comodità del corpo; dall'altra banda, considerando io la necessità del venir a questi particolari per la sua spedizione, la benignità con la quale fino a qui si è costà proceduto con la persona sua, e sopra a tutto la giustizia della causa e la sua innocenza in questo particolare, mi consolo e piglio speranza di felice e prospero successo, con l'aiuto di Dio benedetto, al quale il mio cuore non cessa mai di esclamare e raccomandarla con tutto quell'affetto e confidenza possibile. Resta solo che ella stia di buon animo, procurando di non progiudicare alla sanità con il soverchiamente affliggersi, rivolgendo il pensiero e la speranza sua in Dio, il quale, come padre amorevolissimo, non mai abbandona chi in Lui confida et a Lui ricorre.

Carissimo Sig.r padre, ho voluto scrivergli adesso, acciò ella sappia che io sono a parte de i suoi travagli, il che a lei dovrebbe esser di qualche alleggerimento: non ne ho già dato indizio ad alcun'altra, volendo che queste cose di poco gusto siano tutte mie, e quelle di contento e sodisfazione siano comuni a tutte; che però tutte stiamo aspettando il suo ritorno, con desiderio di goder la sua conversazione con allegrezza. E chi sa che mentre adesso sto scrivendo, V. S. non si ritrovi fuora d'ogni frangente e di ogni pensiero? Piaccia pur al Signore, il quale sia quello che la consoli e con il quale la

Most Beloved Lord Father,

Sestilia's brother Geri is secretary to the grand duke.

Signor Geri informed me of the conditions imposed on you on account of your affair, Sire, that alas you are detained in the chambers of the Holy Office; on the one hand this gives me great distress, convinced as I am that you find yourself with scant peace of mind, and perhaps also deprived of all bodily comforts: on the other hand, considering the need for events to reach this stage, in order for the authorities to dismiss you, as well as the kindliness with which everyone there has treated you up till now, and above all the justice of the cause and your innocence in this instance, I console myself and cling to the expectation of a happy and prosperous triumph, with the help of blessed God, to Whom my heart never ceases to cry out, commending you with all the love and trust it contains.

After months of waiting, Galileo gave his first deposition before the Inquisition on April 12.

The only thing for you to do now is to guard your good spirits, taking care not to jeopardize your health with excessive worry, but to direct your thoughts and hopes to God, Who, like a tender, loving father, never abandons those who confide in Him and appeal to Him for help in time of need. Dearest lord father, I wanted to write to you now, to tell you I partake in your torments, so as to make them lighter for you to bear: I have given no hint of these difficulties to anyone else, wanting to keep the unpleasant news to myself, and to speak to the others only of your pleasures and satisfactions. Thus we are all awaiting your return, eager to enjoy your conversation again with delight. And who knows, Sire, if while I sit writing, you may not already find yourself released from your predicament and free of all concerns? Thus may it lascio. Di S. Matteo in Arcetri, li 20 di Aprile 1633.

Di V. S. molto Ill.re Fig.la Aff.ma

Suor M.a Celeste

Molto Ill.re et Amatiss.mo Sig.r Padre,

Se bene V. S. nell'ultima sua lettera non mi scrive particolarità nessuna circa il suo negozio, forse per non mi far partecipe de i suoi travagli, io per altra strada ho penetrato qualcosa, sì come potrà comprender V. S. da una mia scrittali mercoledì passato. E veramente che questi giorni a dietro sono stata con l'animo molto travagliato e perplesso, fino che, comparendomi la sua, resto accertata della sua salute, e con questo respiro: e non lascerò di esseguire quanto in quella mi ordina, ringraziandola in tanto della habilità di danari che fa a Suor Arcangela, per sua parte e mia ancora, già che miei sono tutti i suoi pensieri.

Qua in monastero siamo tutte sane, la Dio grazia, ma sentiamo bene gran romori di mali cattivi che sono in Firenze, et anco fuora della città in qualche luogo. E per questo, di grazia, ancorchè V. S. fossi spedita presto, non si metta in viaggio per il ritorno, con tanto manifesto pericolo della vita, tanto più che l'infinita gentilezza di cotesti Signori suoi ospiti gli dà sicurtà di trattenersi quanto gli farà di bisogno.

S.r Luisa, insieme con gl'altri nominati, gli tornano dupplicate salute, et io dal Signor Iddio gli prego abbondanza di grazie. Desidero che faccia reverenza in mio nome all'Ecc.ma please the Lord, Who must be the One to console you, and in Whose care I leave you. From San Matteo, the 20th of April 1633.

Sire's Most Affectionate Daughter,

Suor M. Celeste

Most Illustrious and Beloved Lord Father,

Although in your last letter, Sire, you did not write me a single detail about your affair, perhaps to avoid making me a participant in your troubles, I, for my part, learned something, as you will be able to understand from my letter of last Wednesday. And truly I have passed these past few days with my mind greatly distressed and perplexed until, receiving this letter of yours, I am assured of your well-being, and with this comfort I can breathe again. Nor will I neglect to carry out all that you have ordered me to do, thanking you meanwhile for the assurance of money that you make to Suor Arcangela, on behalf of us both, since all her worries are also mine.

Here in the Monastery everyone is healthy, thank God, but we hear much talk of the evil pestilence in Florence and also outside the city in several locations. And for this reason, please, even if you were to be released immediately, do not set out on your return journey in the face of such a manifest threat to your life, especially when the limitless kindness of those gentle people serving as your hosts will surely extend to letting you stay with them as long as you have need to.

Suor Luisa, together with the others you mentioned by name, all return your greetings twice over, and I pray the Lord God mia Signora. Di S. Matteo in Arcetri, li 23 di Aprile 1633.

Di V. S. molto Ill.re Fig.la Aff.ma

S.r M.a Celeste

Amatiss.mo Sig.r Padre,

Ho vista l'ultima lettera che V. S. scrive al S.r Geri, il quale veramente è tutto cortese e molto sollecito in darmi nuove di lei; e se bene quando ella scrisse si ritrovava indisposta, spero che adesso ella stia bene, onde sto quieta, rallegrandomi di sentire che il suo negozio si vadia incaminando a buon fine et a presta spedizione. Tengo questa settimana lettere dell'Ecc.ma S.ra Ambasciatrice, la quale con la solita sua cortesia si è compiaciuta ragguagliarmi dello stato nel quale V. S. si ritrova, perchè, come ella mi dice, non crede che io tenga lettere di V. S. da poi che uscì di casa sua, et ella desidera che io stia con l'animo quieto; a questo mi è un indizio manifesto dell'amore che questi Signori portano a V. S., il quale è tanto che è bastante a participarsi tanto largamente ancora a me, sì come la medesima Signori me ne dà certissima caparra nella sua amorevolissima lettera. Io gl'ho risposto, indrizzando la lettera a lei assolutamente, parendomi che così convenga.

Del contagio ci son buone nuove, e si spera, per quanto dicono, che in brevi sia per cessar del tutto, sì che ella, se piacerà a Dio, non haverà questo impedimento per il suo ritorno.

to bless you with the fullness of His grace. I ask you to pay my respects to Her Excellency, My Ladyship. From San Matteo, the 23rd of April 1633.

Sire's Most Affectionate Daughter,

S. M. Celeste

Most Beloved Lord Father,

I saw the last letter you wrote to Signor Geri, Sire, which truly is pure politeness and very solicitous in giving all the news of you; and, if indeed when you wrote it you found yourself indisposed, I hope that now you are well again, wherefore I calm myself, rejoicing to hear that your affair is headed on the right path toward a good outcome and a swift dispatch. This week I have had letters from Her Excellent Ladyship the Ambassadress, who with her usual courtesy had the kindness to inform me of your circumstances, Sire, for, as she tells me, she does not believe I have had any letters from you since you left her house, and she knows you want to keep my mind at ease; and this gives me the clearest indication of the love these noble people feel for you, Sire, which is so abundant that it more than suffices to enfold me as well, as her Ladyship pledged to me most certainly in her ever so thoughtful letter. I have written back to them herewith, directing my letter to you, which seems the most appropriate thing to do.

There is good news regarding the plague, and we are hopeful, given what people say, that it will soon disappear altogether, and then, if it please God, you will not have this impediment preventing your return.

Sono occupata intorno al muratore, che ci accomoda, o per dir meglio fa, un fornello da stillare, e per questo scrivo brevemente. Stiamo tutte bene, eccetto Suor Luisa, la quale da 3 giorni in qua travaglia con il suo stomaco, ma non tanto malamente quanto l'altre volte. Giuseppo sta ragionevolmente, e la Piera bene. Il Sr Rondinelli la saluta, e ne farà grazia di pagar i danari per il fitto a Sr Lorenzo Bini. Il Padre confessore ancora se gli raccomanda, et il simile fanno tutte queste monache et in particolare Suor Arcangela. Nostro Signore la conservi. Di S. Matteo, l'ultimo di Aprile 1633.

Di V. S. molto Ill.^{re} Fig.^{la} Aff.^{ma}

Suor M.ª Celeste

Molto Ill.^{re} et Amatiss.^{mo} Sig.^{r} Padre,

L'allegrezza che mi apportò l'ultima sua amorevolissima lettera fu tale, a tale alterazione mi causò, che, con questo e con l'essermi convenuto più volte legger e rilegger la medesima lettera a queste monache, che tutte giubilavano sentendo i prosperi successi di V. S., fui soprapresa da gran dolor di testa, che mi durò dalle 14 hore della mattina fino a notte, cosa veramente fuori del mio solito. Ho voluto dirgli questo particolare, non per rimproverargli questo poco mio patimento, ma sì bene perchè ella maggiormente possa conoscere quanto mi siano a cuore e mi premino le cose sue, poi che causano in me tali effetti; effetti che, se bene, generalmente parlando, par che l'amor filiale possa e deva causar in tutti i figliuoli, in me ardiro di dire che habbino maggior forza, come quella che mi do vanto di avanzar di gran lunga la mag-

I am busy with the mason who is helping us, or, more precisely, is building for us a small stove for distilling, and on this account I must be brief. We are all feeling fine, except Suor Luisa, who for the past three days has been suffering on account of her stomach, although not as severely as at other times. Giuseppe fares reasonably well, and La Piera is fine. Signor Rondinelli sends you his regards and will do us the favor of paying the rent money to Signor Lorenzo Bini. The Father Confessor also sends you his good wishes, as do all of these nuns and Suor Arcangela most of all. May Our Lord bless you. From San Matteo, the last of April 1633.

*Lorenzo Bini is the son-in-law of Esaù Martellini, who rented **Il Gioiello** to Galileo.*

Sire's Most Affectionate Daughter,

Suor M. Celeste

Most Illustrious and Beloved Lord Father,

The delight delivered to me by your latest loving letter was so great, and the change it wrought in me so extensive, that, taking the impact of the emotion together with my being compelled many times to read and reread the same letter over and over to these nuns, until everyone could rejoice in the news of your triumphant successes, I was seized by a terrible headache that lasted from the fourteenth hour of the morning on into the night, something truly outside my usual experience. I wanted to tell you this detail, not to reproach you for my small suffering, but to enable you to understand all the more how heavily your affairs weigh on my heart and fill me with concern, by showing you what effects they produce in me; effects which, although, generally speaking, filial devotion can and should produce in all progeny, yet in me, I will

Galileo, having returned to the Tuscan Embassy after a second hearing in the chambers of the Holy Office, believes he has struck a deal with the Inquisitors that will help everyone save face.

gior parte degl'altri nell'amare e riverire il mio carissimo padre, sì come all' incontro chiaramente veggo che egli supera la maggior parte de i padri in amar me sua figliuola. E tanto basti.

Rendo infinite grazie a Dio benedetto per tutte le grazie e favori che fino a qui V. S. ha ricevuti e per l'avvenire spera di ricevere, poi che tutti principalmente derivano da quella pietosa mano, sì come V. S. molto giustamente riconosce. E se bene ella attribuisce in gran parte questi benefizii al merito delle mie orazioni, questo veramente è poco o nulla; ma è ben assai l'affetto con il quale io gli domando a S. D. M., la quale havendo riguardo a quello, tanto benignamente prosperando V. S., mi esaudisce, e noi tanto maggiormente Gli restiamo obligati: sì come anco grandemente siamo debitori a tutte quelle persone che a V. S. sono in favore et aiuto, e particolarmente a cotesti Ecc.mi SS.ri suoi ospiti; et io volevo scriver all'Ecc.ma Sig.ra Ambasciatrice, ma sono restata, per non la infastidire con replicarle sempre le medesime cose, cioè rendimenti di grazie a confessioni di oblighi infiniti. V. S. supplirà per me, con farle reverenza in mio nome. E veramente, carissimo S.r padre, che solamente la grazia che V. S. ha havuta del favore e della protezzione di questi Signori è tale, che è bastante a mitigare, anzi annullare, tutti i travagli che ha sofferti.

Mi è capitata alle mani una ricetta eccellentissima contro la peste, delta quale ho fatta una copia a gliela mando, non perchè io creda the costà vi sia sospezione alcuna di questo male, ma perchè è buona ad ogn'altra cattiva disposizione. Degl'ingredienti io ne sono tanto scarsa, anzi mendica, per me, che non dare to boast that they possess greater force, as does the power that places me far ahead of most other daughters in the love and reverence I bear my dearest Father, when I see clearly that he, for his part, surpasses the majority of fathers in loving me as his daughter: and that is all I have to say.

I offer endless thanks to blessed God for all the favors and graces that you have been granted up till now, Sire, and hope to receive in the future, since most of them issue from that merciful hand, as you most justly recognize. And even though you attribute the great share of these blessings to the merit of my prayers, this truly is little or nothing; what matters most is the sentiment with which I speak of you to His Divine Majesty, Who, respecting that love, rewarding you so beneficently, answers my prayers, and renders us ever more greatly obligated to Him, while we are also deeply indebted to all those people who have given you their goodwill and aid, and especially to those most preeminent nobles who are your hosts. And I did want to write to Her Most Excellent Ladyship the Ambassadress, but I stay my hand lest I vex her with my constant repetition of the same statements, these being expressions of thanks and confessions of my infinite indebtedness. You take my place, Sire, and pay respects to her in my name. And truly, dearest lord Father, the blessing that you have enjoyed from the favors and the protection of these dignitaries is so great that it suffices to assuage, or even annul all the aggravations you have endured.

Here is a copy I made you of a most excellent prescription against the plague that has fallen into my hands, not because I believe there is any suspicion of the malady where you are,

The "prescription" has been lost, but apparently called for faith and virtue.

gliene posso far parte di nessuno; ma bisogna che V. S. procuri di ottener quelli, che per avventura gli mancheranno, dalla fonderia della misericordia del Sig.r Iddio, con il quale la lascio: salutandola per fine in nome di tutte et in particolare di Suor Arcangela e Suor Luisa, la quale per adesso, quanto alla sanità, se la passa mediocremente. Di S. Matteo in Arcetri, li 7 di Maggio 1633.

Di V. S. molto Ill.re Fig.la Aff.ma

Suor M.a Celeste

Amatiss.mo Sig.r Padre,

Che la lettera scrittami da V. S. la settimana passata mi apportassi grandissimo gusto e contento, io già per altra mia glien'ho significato; et hora soggiungo, che essendomi convenuto rimandarla al S.r Geri, acciò anco Vincenzio la vedessi, ne feci una copia, la quale il S.r Rondinelli, doppo haverla letta, volse portar seco a Firenze per farla sentire ad alcuni amici suoi, a i quali sapeva egli che sarebbe stato di molta sodisfazione l'intender questi particolari di V. S., sì come è seguito, per quanto mi ha avvisato nel rimandarmela il medesimo Sig.r Rondinelli, il quale di quando in quando viene in casa di V. S., et altri non vi praticano. La Piera mi dice che non esce, se non quanto vien qua da noi, per sentir messa o per altre occorrenze; et il ragazzo qualche volta va but because this remedy also works well for all manner of ills. As to the ingredients, I am in such short supply that I must beg them for myself, on which account I cannot fill the prescription for anyone else; but you must try to procure those ingredients that perchance you may lack, Sire, from the heavenly foundry, from the depths of the compassion of the Lord God, with Whom I leave you. Closing with regards to you from everyone here, and in particular from Suor Arcangela and Suor Luisa, who for now, as far as her health is concerned, is getting along passing well. From San Matteo, the 7th of May 1633.

Sire's Most Affectionate Daughter,
Suor M. Celeste

Most Beloved Lord Father,

That the letter you wrote me last week brought me the greatest pleasure and joy, I have already indicated to you in a previous note of mine; and now I add that being compelled to send it to Signor Geri so that Vincenzio too could see it, I made a copy, which Signor Rondinelli, after having read it, wanted to take with him to Florence, to spread the news among several friends of his, whom he knew would derive great satisfaction from hearing these particulars about you, Sire, as indeed turned out to be the case, for so I was informed later on when Signor Rondinelli returned the letter to me. He is the one who from time to time comes to your house, Sire, and no others frequent it. La Piera tells me she does not go out at all, except when she comes here, to hear fino da i SS.ri Bocchineri a pigliar le lettere, nè si trasferisce altrove, perchè, oltre al fuggire i sospetti del male, è ancora deboluccio e di più pieno di rogna, aquistata nello ospedale, et hora si attende a medicarla con qualche untione che io gli vo facendo. Nel resto procuro che restino provvisti nella maniera che V. S. potrà vedere in questo scartafaccio che gli mando, ove fino a qui ho notate le spese fatte, et anco l'entrata havuta per questo effetto, la quale se bene è più che la spesa parecchie lire, io ho presa sicurtà di spenderla per bisogni mia e di Suor Arcangela; sì che si può dire che siamo del pari, et da qui avanti farò libro nuovo. L'altre spese che si son fatte doppo la partita di V. S. sono:

d. 17 1/2 al Sig.r Lorenzo Bini per il fitto della villa;

d. 24 in quattro paghe a Vincenzio Landucci, e lire 6. 13. 4 di spese fatte per la paga di Febbraio; e di tutti ne tengo le ricevute;

d. 25 presi io per accomodarne Suor Arcangela, come V. S. sa;

et altri d. 15 fui necessitata a pigliare, acciò ella potessi finir il suo benedetto uffizio, il quale è condotto con l'aiuto di Dio e di V. S., chè, senza questo gran sollevamento, non era possibile il tirarlo innanzi; et anco le monache si sono dimostrate assai sodisfatte, perchè, con le amorevolezze di V. S. e con l'havere supplito con danari, si sono ricoperte molte malefatte, o magagne che dir vogliamo. Questi ultimi 15 d. aspetto di rimettergli presto con l'entrata di ambe due noi, che a quest'hora doveremmo haver riscossa.

mass or for other needs, and the boy sometimes goes as far as the Bocchineris' house to pick up the letters, not daring to venture elsewhere, because, beyond shunning anyone suspected of plague, he is still a weakling and moreover covered with mange he acquired in the hospital; and now he needs to medicate the rash with some ointment that I am making for him. As for the rest I attempt to tend to everything in the manner you will be able to see, Sire, in this scribbling-pad that I am sending you, where thus far I have noted the expenditures paid out, and also the income gained on account. The income, although it exceeds the expenses by several *lire*, I took the liberty of spending on necessities for Suor Arcangela and myself, so that you could say the accounts are balanced now, and from this day forward I will make a new ledger. The other outlays after your departure, Sire, are,

This paper, too, has been lost.

Scudi 17 and a half to Signor Lorenzo Bini for the rent of the villa.

Scudi 24 in four payments to Vincenzio Landucci, and *lire* 6. 13. 4 in expenses for the February payment; and I have receipts for all of these.

Scudi 25 appropriated by me to care for Suor Arcangela, as you know, Sire, and others.

Scudi 15 it was necessary to take, so that she could finish her blessed office, which was conducted with the help of God and of you Sire, because, without this enormous relief, it would not have been possible to carry on; and also the nuns showed

Questo presente anno toccava a Suor Arcangela ad esser canovaia, uffizio che mi dava che pensare. Pur ho ottenuto grazia dalla Madre badessa che non gli sia dato, con allegar varie scuse, et in quel cambio è fatta pannaiuola, essendo obligata a imbiancare a tener conto delle tovaglie e bandinelle per asciugar le mani, del convento.

Sento gusto particolare nell'intender che V. S. stia bene di sanità, del che grandemente temevo mediante i travagli che ha passati; ma il Signor Iddio ha voluto concederne le grazie compite, liberandola da i travagli dell'animo e del corpo. Sia Egli sempre ringraziato!

Il male contagioso si sente che va per ancora perseverando; ma dicono che ne muor pochi e che si ha speranza che deva terminare, trattandosi di portar in processione a Firenze la Madonna dell'Impruneta per questa causa.

Al nostro già Padre confessore ho mandata la lettera a Firenze, già che egli non sta più qui al nostro convento, e ne haviamo havuto un altro, giovane di 35 anni, dalla Pieve a S.^{to} Stefano.

Mi maraviglio che Vincenzio non gl'habbia mai scritto, e mi glorio di averlo superato nell'esser fervente in visitarla con mie lettere, se bene qualche volta ho havuto ancor io gran strettezza di tempo, et oggi ho scritto questa in 4 volte, interrotta sempre da varii intrighi per amor della spezieria, e di più con dolor di denti, che mi causa il mio solito catarro, che già parecchi giorni sono che mi travaglia.

Finisco salutandola per parte delle nominate, e pregandola a ritornar centupplicati i saluti all' Ecc.^{ma} mia Signora, e pre-themselves entirely satisfied, because, with your loving attention, Sire, and your having provided money, they have covered up more bad deeds or secret vices than we wish to admit. These last 15 *scudi* I expect to repay you presently from our allowance, which we shall soon have to withdraw.

This current year was to bring Suor Arcangela's turn as Cellarer, an office that gave me much to ponder. Indeed I secured the Mother Abbess's pardon that it not be given to her by pleading various excuses; and instead she was made Draper, obliging her to bleach and keep count of the tablecloths and towels in the convent.

As Cellarer, Suor Arcangela would have had charge of the convent's wine cellar.

I feel particularly delighted to hear that your health is in good condition, Sire, as I was very worried about your well-being on account of the travails you have endured; but the Lord God wanted to grant you the combined graces of freeing you not only from the torments of the spirit but also those of the body. May He be ever praised!

The evil contagion still persists, but they say that only a few people die of it and the hope is that it must come to an end when the Madonna of Impruneta is carried in procession to Florence for this purpose.

This holy icon is carried in procession from Impruneta to Florence whenever disaster—flood, famine, war—threatens the city.

I sent your letter to our former Father Confessor in Florence, since he no longer comes to our convent, and we have had another confessor, a young man of 35 years, from the parish church of San Stefano.

I am stupefied to learn that Vincenzio has never written to you, and I revel in having outstripped him by my zeal in visiting you with my letters, although frequently I too had great

Vincenzio had finally written to Galileo on May 2.

gando Nostro Signore che la conservi e feliciti sempre. Di S. Matteo in Arcetri, li 14 di Maggio 1633.

Sua Fig.la Aff.ma

Suor M.a Celeste

Da S. Casciano sono venute in due volte 8 staia di farina per la Piera, ma io non ho cercato di pagarla, sapendo che Fra V. S. e il Ninci sono altri conti.

Amatiss.mo Padre,

Io non ho mai lasciato passar ordinario nessuno senza scrivergli, e mandate le lettere al Sig.r Geri, il quale mi avvisa che a quest'hora V. S. dovrà haverle ricevute. Quanto al tornarsene ella in qua, con questo ordinario non posso darle risoluzione nè sicurtà alcuna per conto del male contagioso, atteso che tutta la speranza della città di Firenze è riposta nella Madonna Santissima, et a questo effetto questa mattina con gran solennità si è portata la sua miracolosa immagine dell'Impruneta a Firenze, ove si sente che dimorerà 3 giorni, e nel ritornarsene haviamo speranza di haver grazia di vederla ancor noi. Sentiremo pertanto quello che seguirà, e strictures on my time, and today I have written this one in four installments, interrupted constantly by various complications for the sake of the apothecary; and further by toothache that brings on my typical catarrh, which has already troubled me for several days.

I end by greeting you on behalf of everyone mentioned herein, and entreating you to return the regards of my Most Excellent Ladyship multiplied a hundredfold, and praying Our Lord to bless you and keep you happy always. From San Matteo, the 14th of May 1633.

Your Most Affectionate Daughter,
Suor M. Celeste

From S. Casciano have come two deliveries totaling 8 *staia* of flour for La Piera, but I did not try to pay for it, knowing there are other bills outstanding between you and Ninci.

A ***staio*** *is a grain measure roughly the equivalent of a bushel.*

Most Beloved Lord Father,

I have never let a courier pass this way without writing to you, Sire, and sending the letters to Signor Geri, who assures me that you must have received them by now. As for your returning here under these prevailing conditions, I can guarantee you neither resolution nor assurance on account of the contagious pestilence, whose end is so urgently desired that all the faith of the city of Florence is now vested in the Most Holy Madonna, and to this effect this morning with great solemnity her miraculous image was carried from Impruneta to Florence, where it is expected to stay for 3 days, and we cherish the hope that during its return journey we will enjoy the privquest'altro sabato gliene darò ragguaglio. In tanto, sentendo che la dilazione giova a i suoi interessi, andiamo più facilmente tolerando la mortificazione che proviamo per la sua assenzia.

In questi contorni sono state due case di contadini infette dal mal cattivo, ma di presente non si sente altro; e già che tutti i gentiluomini che c'hanno le ville, ci si sono ritirati, è segno che non ci sono sospetti.

Mi sarà molto grato, per amor di Suor Luisa, che V. S. vegga se può favorir il nostro vecchino nel suo negozio; ma sarà di necessità che V. S. vegga di parlarne con il Sig.r Giovanni Mancini, al quale si mandorno le scritture un pezzo fa, nè mai da lui nè da altri, a i quali si è raccomandata questa causa, si è potuto haver risposta nessuna.

Mi sono fatta portare un poco di saggio del vino delle due botte piene, e mi par che sia molto buono. La Piera mi dice haverle ripiene più volte, ma che da un pezzo in qua non ne hanno più bisogno.

Giuseppo mi aspetta per portar le lettere, sì che non posso dir altro, se non che la prego a non disordinar col bere, come sento che va facendo. La saluto in nome di tutte, e dal Signor Iddio gli prego vera felicità. Di S. Matteo, li 21 di Magg.o 1633.

Sua Fig.la Aff.ma
Suor M.a Celeste

ilege of seeing her. We will hear what happens in any case, and next Saturday I shall give you a full report. Meanwhile, learning how the delay of your departure favors your interests, we more easily tolerate the sorrow that tries us during your absence.

Geri Bocchineri and his brothers moved into Vincenzio's vacated house in Florence, which stood along the procession route, and decorated the grounds for the occasion with an elaborate display including an altar and fountain. Their efforts were judged the most beautiful in the neighborhood, and passersby said the fountain's mechanism must be a Galilean secret.

In this neighborhood there have been two peasants infected by the evil pestilence, but at present no others are known, and now that all the gentlemen who own villas in the area have retreated to these parts, we take it as a sign that they suspect no sickness here.

I will be most grateful, for the love of Suor Luisa, if you would be so kind as to assist our dear old Confessor with his cause; but you will have to see, Sire, if you can talk about it to Signor Giovanni Mancini, who was sent the documents some time ago, though there has never been a response from him or from any of the others to whom this affair was referred.

I asked to have a little sample of the wine sent to me from your two recently filled casks, and it seems to me to be very good. La Piera tells me to have them refilled more often, but for quite a long time now they have not needed it.

Giuseppe is waiting to deliver these letters, so that I cannot add anything else, except that I implore you not to confuse yourself with drink, as I hear you have been doing. I greet you on everyone's behalf, and from the Lord God I pray your true happiness. From San Matteo, the 21st of May 1633.

Your Most Affectionate Daughter,

Suor M. Celeste

Molto Ill.re et Amatiss.mo Sig.r Padre,

Da l'inclusa scrittami hoggi dal S.r Rondinelli V. S. potrà venir in cognizione dello stato nel quale, circa il male, si ritrova Firenze e questi contorni; che per esser assai buono, et V. S. quasi del tutto spedita da i suoi negozii, spero pure che non dovrà indugiar molto a ritornarsene da noi, che con tanto desiderio la stiamo aspettando: sì che la prego a non lasciarsi tanto legare dalla gentilezza indicibile di cotesti Ecc.mi Signori, che noi doviamo restar prive di lei per tutta l'estate. Pur assai ha ricevuto fin qui, nè mai sarà possibile il poter ricompensar tante grazie e favori, ricevuti da lei e partecipati da noi.

Desidero che V. S., in particolare all'Ecc.ma Sig.ra Ambasciatrice, faccia per nostra parte la solita reverenza. Di più havrò caro che nel suo ritorno mi porti un poco di amido, conforme a che ha fatto l'altre volte; e gli ricordo le due figurine che gli domandai è già un pezzo.

Quanto all'orto, per quanto dalla Piera intendo, le fave hanno fatta bellissima verzura, essendo alte quanto lei, ma il frutto è stato poco e non molto bello, e similmente i carciofi, i quali intendo che fecion meglio l'anno passato; non dimeno ve ne sono stati per la casa, per noi, et anco qualcuno se n'è mandato a Vincenzio e al Sig.r Geri. Gl'aranci ancora non hanno gran quantità di fiori, atteso che il freddo e vento, che questi giorni passati ha dominato, gl'ha fatto gran danno: quelli che cascano, La Piera gli va raquistando e gli stilla. I limoni sono tanto maturi, che hanno necessità che V. S. venga a corgli; e di quando in quando ne casca qualcuno, che sono veramente belli e bonissimi.

Most Illustrious and Beloved Lord Father,

From the enclosure written to me today by Signor Rondinelli you will be able to gain full comprehension, Sire, of the conditions in Florence and its environs concerning the plague; and seeing as they are fairly good just now, and you almost fully released from your affairs, I truly hope that you will not have to delay your return to us much longer, as we are awaiting you with such longing; therefore I pray you not to let the ineffable kindness of those most Excellent Lords bind you to them so tightly that we must be deprived of you for the whole summer. Great indeed has been their generosity up until now, nor will it ever be possible to repay all the favors and kindnesses bestowed on you and shared by us.

Signor Rondinelli knows more about the course of the plague than anyone, as he is writing the official account of the epidemic for the grand duke. (The letter of his that Suor Maria Celeste mentions here has not survived, but his book, ***Relazione del Contagio stato in Firenze l'anno 1630 e 1633****, was published in 1634.)*

I want you to pay our usual respects to your hosts, Sire, especially to Her Most Excellent Ladyship the Ambassadress. Moreover I will be most appreciative if upon your return you will bring me a little starch, as you did the last time; and I remind you of the two portraits that I asked you for, a while ago.

As for the garden, according to what I hear from La Piera, the beans have formed the most beautiful verdure, climbing as tall as she is, but the fruit has been small and not very good, and the same for the artichokes, which I understand were much better last year: nonetheless there were enough for the house, for us, and also some went to Vincenzio and to Signor Geri. The orange trees still do not have a great quantity of flowers, and I expect the cold and wind that have dominated these past few days have done them considerable damage; those that fall, La Piera gathers and makes into juice. The

Questo è quanto le faccende della bottega mi permettono che io gli possi dire, poi che Suor Luisa et un'altra delle mie compagne sono in purga, et io, per conseguenza, sola a lavorare. La saluto caramente per parte di tutte le solite, e di più di Suor Barbera e Suor Prudenza, e prego il Signor Iddio che la conservi. Di S. Matteo, li 28 di Mag.º 1633.

Sua Fig.la Aff.ma

Suor M.a Celeste

Amatiss.mo Sig.r Padre,

Nell'ultima mia detti buone nuove a V. S. circa il male, et adesso (Dio lodato e la Madonna Santissima, dalla quale si riconosce la grazia) gliene do migliori, già che intendo hieri non esserne morti nessuno e due soli andati al lazaretto, ammalati di altro male che di contagio, mandati là perchè gl'ospedali non ne pigliano o pochi. Si sente bene ancora non so che là in verso Rovezzano, ma poca cosa; e con il buon governo e con il caldo, che adesso si fa sentire assai gagliardo, si spera in breve la intiera liberazione.

In questi contorni non è sospetto alcuno: le case che nel principio del male hanno patito detrimento, sono quella de i Grazini, lavoratori del Lanfredini, e quella de i Farcigli, che stavano a Mezzo Monte: era una gran famiglia, divisa in 2 o 3 case; non so già di chi fossero lavoratori, so bene che son finiti tutti. Queste sono le nuove che con ogni diligenza ho lemons are so ripe that they require you, Sire, to come and harvest them, and from time to time, whenever one of them drops, it proves to be truly beautiful and most delicious.

This is as much as the duties of the apothecary will permit me to tell you, since Suor Luisa and another of my companions are purging themselves, and I am consequently alone at work. I send you loving regards from all our usual friends, and also from Suor Barbara and Suor Prudenza, and I pray the Lord God to keep you. From San Matteo, the 28th of May 1633.

Your Most Affectionate Daughter,

Suor M. Celeste

Most Beloved Lord Father,

In my last letter I gave you good news regarding the plague, Sire, and now (God be praised and the Most Holy Madonna, from Whom this grace is acknowledged) I give you even better news, having learned that yesterday no one died of it and only two went to the *lazaretto*, sick with illnesses other than the contagion, sent there because the hospitals do not take in such cases, or very few. I am not certain whether people are still feeling well in the direction of Rovezzano; but this is a small thing, and with good management and the help of the warm weather, which now makes its presence felt intensely, we hope in short for a complete liberation.

*The **lazaretto** is the plague hospital.*

In these regions no one is suspected of infection; the families that suffered the greatest losses at the beginning of the outbreak are those of the Grazzini who are the workers of the Lanfredini, and the Farcigli, who lived halfway up the hill:

procurato di haver certe, per potergliene partecipare e con questo inanimirla al ritorno, caso che sia spedita costà del tutto: chè pur troppo è stato lungo questo tempo della sua assenzia fino a qui, nè vorrei in alcuna maniera che ella indugiassi fino all'autunno, come temo se ella tarda troppo a partirsi; tanto più che sento che ella adesso si ritrova più libera e con tante recreazioni, del che godo e mi rallegro grandemente, sì come all'incontro mi dispiace che le sue doglie non la lascino: se bene par quasi necessario che il gusto ch'ella sente nel bere cotesti vini così eccellenti, sia contrapesato da qualche dolore, acciò, astenendosi dal berne maggior quantità, venga ad ovviare a qualche altro maggior nocumento che potrebbe riceverne.

Ultimamente non hebbi tempo a dirgli, come nel ritorno, che fece da Firenze l'immagine della Santissima Madonna dell'Impruneta, venne nella nostra chiesa; grazia veramente segnalata, perchè passava dal Piano, si che venne qui a posta, havendo a ritornar in dietro tutta quella strada, che V. S. sa, et essendo il peso di più di 700 lib., quello del tabernacolo et adornamenti; mediante i quali non potendo entrare nelle nostre porte, bisognò rompere il muro della corte et alzare la porta della chiesa, il che da noi si è fatto con molta prontezza per tale occasione.

Suor Arcangela di S. Giorgio, doppo l'havermi più volte mandato a domandare di V. S. con molta instanza, mi scrive adesso facendomi un lungo cordoglio per la morte della sua Suor Sibilla, e mi prega che io preghi V. S., come fo, che gli faccia carità di far dir una messa per quell'anima all'altare di there was a large family divided among two or three houses, and though I do not yet know whose workers they were, well I know they are all dead. These are the confirmed reports that I have diligently gathered so as to be able to keep you informed, and thus encourage you to return, should you be dispatched from all your affairs there. For indeed this period of your absence has worn on much too long, nor would I want you by any means, Sire, to tarry until autumn, as I fear may happen, if you wait too long to take your leave; all the more so since I hear that you now find yourself free to pursue many recreations, which gladdens and delights me greatly, while on the other hand I am sorry that your pains give you no respite, although it seems almost requisite for the pleasure you take in drinking those excellent wines to be counterbalanced by some pain, so that, if you refrain from imbibing large quantities, you may avoid some greater injury that could be incurred by drinking.

Galileo may suffer from gout, which can be aggravated by drinking large quantities of red wine.

In my last letter I did not have time to tell you how, during its return from Florence, the image of the Most Holy Madonna of Impruneta came into our Church; a grace truly worthy of note, because she was passing from the Plain, so that she had to come here, going back along the whole length of that road you know so well, Sire, and weighing in excess of 700 *libbre* with the tabernacle and adornments; its size rendering it unable to fit through our gate, it became necessary to break the wall of the courtyard, and raise the doorway of the Church, which we accomplished with great readiness for such an occasion.

The Madonna weighs about a quarter of a ton.

Suor Arcangela Landucci di San Giorgio, after having sent several times to demand two *scudi* from me with great

Suor Arcangela of San Giorgio, another first cousin, is the sister of Suor Chiara and Vincenzio Landucci.

S. Gregorio, del che vorrebbe la certezza per poter star quieta, promettendo di non lasciar di pregar per V. S.

Adesso che ho ricordato S. Gregorio, mi è sovvenuto che V. S. non mi ha mai detto niente di haver ricevuto una ricetta che gli mandai per la peste. Mi è paruto strano, perchè mi pareva di havergli mandata una bells cosa, e dubito che non sia andata male. E qui, facendo fine con salutarla caramente per parte delle solite, prego Nostro Signore che gli conceda la Sua santa grazia. Di S. Matteo in Arcetri, li 4 Giug.º 1633.

Di V. S. molto Ill.re Fig.la Aff.ma

Suor M.a Celeste

Amatiss.mo Sig.r Padre,

Ultimamente scrissi a V. S., le cose del contagio esser ridotte in assai buon termine; ma adesso non posso con verità replicar il simile, già che da alcuni giorni in qua, essendo variata la stagione con un fresco più che ordinario in questo tempo, il male ha ripreso forze, et ogni giorno si sente serrarsi nuove case, se bene il numero di quelli che muoiono non è grande, non passando, per quanto dicono, i sette o gl'otto il giorno, et altrettanti se ne ammalano. Standо per tanto le cose in questo termine, giudicherei che ad ogni modo ella se ne potessi venire alla volta di Siena, come già ha dissegnato, quando però siano terminati del tutto i suoi negozii, per tutto entreaty, now writes me a long lament for the death of her Suor Sibilla, and implores me to beg you, Sire, as I am, that you do her the kindness of having a mass said for that soul at the altar of San Gregorio, as she needs such assurance to feel at peace, promising not to neglect you with her prayers.

Now that I have remembered San Gregorio, I am reminded that you never said anything to me, Sire, of having received a prescription I sent you for the plague. That struck me as strange, because it seemed to me I had offered you something useful, and I sincerely doubt that it has failed to do you good. And here, coming to an end by giving you loving greetings on behalf of our usual friends, I pray Our Lord to grant you His holy grace. From San Matteo, the 4th of June 1633.

Sire's Most Affectionate Daughter,

Suor M. Celeste

Most Beloved Lord Father,

In my last letter, Sire, I said the situation regarding the contagion seemed well under control, but now I cannot in all honesty give a similar report, since for the past several days, the weather having turned unusually cool for this time of year, the plague has regathered its strength, and every day one hears of more houses being shut up, although the death toll is not that large, not exceeding seven or eight per day, as far as we can tell, with an equal number of people falling ill. Consequently, things having reached this pass, I would judge that you may still be able to travel in the direction of Siena, as you had intended, provided that your affairs can be con-il presente mese: già che poi fino all'autunno non si può batter la campagna di Roma, per quanto intendo dal Sr Rondinelli; et io non vorrei già che V. S. fossi astretta a far costà tanto lunga dimora. Sì che di grazia procuri, per quanto può, la sua spedizione, la quale spero puro che sia per ottener quanto prima, con l'aiuto di Dio benedetto e del S.r Ambasciatore, il quale si vede chiaramente non essersi mai straccato nell'aiutare e favorir V. S. con tutte le sue forze. E veramente, carissimo S.r Padre, che se da una parte il Signor Iddio l'ha travagliata e mortificata, dall'altra poi l'ha sollevata et aiutata grandemente. Solo l'haverla conservata sana, con i disagi che patì per il viaggio e di poi con i travagli che ha passati, è stata una grazia molto particolare. Piaccia a S. D. M. di concederci che non siamo ingrati a tanti benefizii e di conservarla e protegerla fino all'ultimo, del che Lo prego con tutto il cuore; et a V. S. mi raccomando per mille volte insieme con le solite.   Di S. Matteo in Arcetri, li 11 di Giugno 1633.

Di V. S. molto Ill.re Fig.la Aff.ma
Suor M.a Celeste

Amatiss.mo Sig.r Padre,

Quando io scrissi a V. S. dandolgli conto del male che era stato in questi contorni, già era cessato quasi del tutto ogni sospetto, essendo scorsi molti giorni, anzi settimane, senza sentirsi niente; e, come all'hora gli soggiunsi, me ne dava intiera sicurtà il vedere che tutti questi gentiluomini nostri cluded this month, because from then on till autumn no one will be allowed to frequent the open country around Rome, according to Signor Rondinelli; and I surely would not want to see you forced, Sire, to make such a long sojourn so far away. Therefore please do everything you can to expedite your dispatch, which I still hope can be obtained as soon as possible with the help of blessed God and his Lordship the Ambassador, who clearly feels he can never do enough to aid and protect you, Sire, with all the forces at his command. And truly, dearest Lord Father, if on the one hand the Lord God has afflicted and mortified you, He has then on the other relieved and assisted you greatly. Only to have conserved your health against the hardships you suffered through the journey, and since that time despite the torments you have endured, was in itself a most singular grace. May it please the Lord God to realize that we are not ungrateful for so many blessings, and to keep you and protect you till the very last, for which I pray Him with all my heart, and to you, Sire, I send a thousand loving greetings together with our dear ones.

Although the hearings concluded on May 10, Galileo is still awaiting the outcome of his trial, at which time he expects to be able to leave Rome.

From San Matteo, the 11th of June 1633.

Sire's Most Affectionate Daughter,

Suor M. Celeste

Most Beloved Lord Father,

When I wrote to you, Sire, giving you an account of the contagion's spread in this region, it had already very nearly ceased, for many days had run their course, weeks even, without anyone's hearing word of any new cases; and, as I suggested to you then, I felt entirely reassured by the knowledge that all vicini se ne stavano qui in villa, come seguitano ancora di starci tutti; e, che è piu, nella medesima città di Firenze si sentiva che il male andava tanto diminuendo, che si sperava che presto dovessi restar libera del tutto: onde, con questa sicurtà, mi mossi ad esortarla e sollecitarla per il suo ritorno, se bene nell'ultima che gli scrissi, sentendo che le cose erano peggiorate, mutai linguaggio, come si suol dire. Perchè, se bene è verissimo che desidero grandemente di rivederla, desidero non dimeno molto più la sua conservazione e salute; e riconosco per grazia speciale del Signor Iddio l'occasione che V. S. ha havuta di trattenersi costà più lungamente di quello che lei et noi havremmo voluto; perchè, se bene credo che gli dia travaglio il trattenersi così irresoluta, maggiore gliene darebbe forse il ritrovarsi in questi pericoli, i quali tuttavia vanno continuando, e forse aumentando: e ne fo conseguenza da una ordinazione venuta al nostro monastero, come ad altri ancora, da parte dei SS.ri della Sanità, et è che per spazio di 40 giorni doviamo, due monache per volta, star continuamente giorno e notte in orazione, a pregar S. D. M. per la liberazione di questo flagello. Havemmo da i sudetti Signori d. 25 di elemosina; e oggi è il quarto giorno che demmo principio.

A S.r Arcangela Landucci ho fatto intendere che V. S. gli farà il servizio che desiderava, et ella la ringrazia infinitamente.

Per dargli avviso di tutte le cose di casa, mi farò dalla colombaia, ove fino di quaresima cominciorno a covare i colombi; et il primo paio che naque, fu mangiato una notte da qualche animale, et il colombo che gli covava fu trovato dalla Piera sopra una trave, mezzo mangiato e cavatone tutte l'interiora, those gentlemen neighbors of ours were staying here in their villas, as they still continue to do; and moreover, in the city of Florence itself, one heard that the pestilence was abating so appreciably that people were expecting they must soon be liberated from the whole misery. Wherefore, with this security, I moved to exhort you and implore you to return, although in my last letter, hearing that things were taking a turn for the worse, I held my tongue, so to speak. Because, although it is very true that I have a strong desire to see you again, what I want much more is the preservation of your health and safety; and I recognize the special grace of the Lord God in the opportunity you have had, Sire, to remain where you are much longer than you and I would have wished. For even though I believe it must grieve you to stay on there so irresolutely, it would perhaps give you far more grief for us to be reunited among these perils, which in spite of everything continue on and may even be multiplying; and in consequence an order has come to our Monastery, and to others as well, from the Commissioners of Health, stating that for a period of 40 days we must, two nuns at a time, pray continuously day and night beseeching His Divine Majesty for freedom from this scourge. We received alms of 25 *scudi* from the commissioners for our prayers, and today marks the fourth day since our vigil began.

I have let Suor Arcangela Landucci know that you will perform the service she desires, Sire, and she thanks you profusely.

To give you news of everything about the house, I will start from the dovecote, where since Lent the pigeons have been brooding; the first pair to be hatched were devoured one che per questo si giudicò che fossi stato qualche uccello di rapina. Gl'altri colombi spauriti non vi tornavano; ma seguitando la Piera a dargli da mangiare, si sono ravviati, et adesso ve ne covano due.

Gl'aranci hanno havuti pochi fiori, i quali la Piera ha stillati, e mi dice haverne cavato una metadella d'acqua. I capperi, quando sarà tempo, si accomoderanno. La lattuga che si seminò, secondo che V. S. haveva ordinato, non è mai nata, e in quel luogo la Piera vi ha messo de i fagiuoli, che dice esser assai belli, e similmente de i ceci, de i quali la lepre ne vorrà la maggior parte, havendo già cominciato a levargli via. Delle fave ve ne sono da seccare, et i gambi si danno per colazione alla muletta, la quale è diventata così altiera, che non vuol portar nessuno, et alcune volte ha fatto far de i salti mortali al povero Geppo, ma con gentilezza, poi che non si è fatto male. Ascanio, fratello della cognata, la domandò una volta per andar di fuora, ma quando fu vicino alla Porta al Prato, gli convenne tornar in dietro, non havendo mai hauto forza di scaponire l'ostinata mula acciò andassi innanzi; la quale forse sdegna di esser cavalcata da altri, trovandosi senza il suo vero padrone.

Ma ritornando all'orto, gli dico che le vite mostrano assai bene; non so poi se prosseguiranno così, mediante il torto che ricevano di esser custodite dalle mani della Piera, in cambio di quelle di V. S. De i carciofi non ve ne sono stati molti; con tutto ciò se ne seccherà qualcuno.

In cantina le cose passano bene, andandosi il vino conservando buono. In cucina non manco di somministrare quel night by some animal, and the pigeon who had been setting them was found draped over a rafter half eaten, and completely eviscerated, on which account La Piera assumed the culprit to be some bird of prey; and the other frightened pigeons would not go back there, but, as La Piera kept on feeding them they have since recovered themselves, and now two more are brooding.

The orange trees bore few flowers, which La Piera pressed, and she tells me she has drawn a whole pitcherful of orange water. The capers, when the time comes, will be sufficient to suit you, Sire. The lettuce that was sown according to your instructions never came up, and in its place La Piera planted beans that she claims are quite beautiful, and coming lastly to the chickpeas, it seems the hare will win the largest share, he having already begun to make off with them. The broad beans are set out to dry, and their stalks fed for breakfast to the little mule, who has become so haughty that she refuses to carry anyone, and has several times thrown poor Geppo so as to make him turn somersaults, but gently, since he was not hurt. Sestilia's brother Ascanio once asked to ride her out, though when he approached the gate to Prato he decided to turn back, never having gained the upper hand over the obstinate creature to make her proceed, as she perhaps disdains to be ridden by others, finding herself without her true master.

Geppo is a nickname for Giuseppe, Galileo's servant boy.

But returning to the garden, I tell you that although the grapevines appear very well, I do not know whether they will continue so, considering the abuse they take in being cared for at the hands of La Piera, instead of by yours, Sire. Only a poco che fa bisogno per la servitù, eccetto che nel tempo che ci viene il Sig.^{r} Rondinelli, chè all' hora ci vuol pensar lui; anzi che in questa settimana volse che una mattina noi stessimo in parlatorio a desinar da lui. Queste *(sic)* sono tutti gl'avvisi che mi par di potergli dare.

L'Archilea desidera che V. S., di costì dove è abbondanza di buoni maestri di musica gli provvegga qualche bella cosa da sonar su l'organo. Suor Luisa havrebbe caro di sapere se V. S. ha poi visto il Sig.^{r} Giovanni Mancini, che è mercante, per conto del negozio del nostro vecchino; e similmente Suor Isabella desidera di sapere se la lettera che gli mandò per il Sig.^{r} Francesco Cavalcanti habbia havuto ricapito, desiderando pur di sapere da cotesto gentiluomo se un fratello che ha costì sia morto o vivo.

Finisco, per riserbar qualcosa da dirgli quest'altra volta che gli scriverò; ma mi sovviene che devo salutarla per parte di Suor Barbera, e dirgli così che ella non va più fuora, se non tanto quanto entra in chiesa dal primo usciolino per parare e sparare. Tutte l'altre amiche la salutano, et io da Dio benedetto gli prego ogni vero bene. Di S. Matteo, li 18 di Giug.^{o} 1633.

Di V. S. molto Ill.^{re} Fig.^{la} Aff.^{ma}

Suor M.ª Celeste

few artichokes have shown themselves, yet surely we will dry one or two.

In the cellar everything is going well, the wine staying in good condition. In the kitchen I have no trouble providing what little the servants need, except when Signor Rondinelli comes, because then he wants to take care of everything, as for example this week he graciously arranged for us to dine one morning in the convent parlor with him. These are all the reports that I seem to be able to think of to share with you.

L'Archilea wants you to bring her, since there is such an abundance of good music teachers where you are, something beautiful to play on the organ. Suor Luisa is most eager to know if you have yet visited Signor Giovanni Mancini, the merchant, to settle the business for our dear old friend, and by the same token Suor Isabella would like to know if the letter that she sent you for Signor Francesco Cavalcanti has been delivered, as she wanted to learn from that gentleman if a brother of hers in those parts is dead or alive.

I close in order to keep something in reserve to tell you the next time I write, but I recall that I must give you greetings from Suor Barbera, and tell you, therefore, that she no longer ventures out except to enter the church by the first doorway to put up or and take down the hangings. All our other friends send you their regards, and I from blessed God pray for your every true good. From San Matteo, the 18th of June 1633.

Sire's Most Affectionate Daughter,

Suor M. Celeste

The church's cloths and candles are normally changed for the various liturgical seasons, such as red for Christmas and white for Easter, but now black ones must be hung often for the many funerals caused by the plague.

Amatiss.mo Sig.r Padre,

Ringraziato sia Dio, che pur sento che V. S. comincia a trattar di mettersi in viaggio per il suo ritorno, il quale io ho grandemente desiderato, non solo per rivederla, quanto anco perchè, con la totale spedizione del suo negozio, dovrà ella restar con l'animo quieto e tranquillo, il che sono molti mesi che non ha potuto provare. Ma si potranno benedire tutti i travagli sofferti, se saranno terminati con tanto buon esito, quanto ella mi accenna di sperare.

Ho caro che V. S. se ne vadia a Siena, sì perchè ella non venga in questi sospetti di contagio, il quale s'intende però che questa settimana è assai alleggerito, sì anco perchè, sentendo che quell'Arcivescovo l'invita con tanta instanza e gentilezza, mi prometto che quivi havrà molto gusto e sodisfazione. La prego bene a venirsene a suo bell'agio, e pigliarsi tutte quelle comodità che gli saranno possibili, poi che è stata necessitata a viaggiare in due estremi di freddo o di caldo; et anco a darmi nuove di sè ogni volta che gli sarà possibile, sì come ha fatto in tutto il tempo che è stata assente, del che devo ringraziarla, essendo stato questo il maggior contento ch'io potessi ricevere.

Volevo con questa mandarle una lettera per la S.ra Ambasciatrice (alla quale per amor di V. S. mi conosco tanto obligata); ma perchè sto in dubbio se all'arrivo di questa V. S. sarà già partita, mi risolvo a indugiar a quest'altra settimana o, per dir meglio, a quando V. S. mi avviserà ch'io deva farlo. Del servizio del vecchino ne tratteremo in voce, se piacerà a Dio, il

Most Beloved Lord Father,

Thanks be to God that at last I hear you begin to speak of setting out on your journey home, which I have greatly desired for so long, not solely to see you again, but also for the final settlement of your affair, which must set your mind at ease and peace. Surely you have not been able to feel such calm for many months. But all the hardships you suffered may ultimately confer blessings if they come to as good a conclusion as you lead me to hope.

Unbeknownst to Suor Maria Celeste, Galileo faced his sentencing by the Inquisition on June 22, at which time his ***Dialogue*** *was banned and he was censured and humiliated.*

I am very pleased that you are going to Siena, Sire, partly because you will avoid contact with the contagion of the plague, which we understand, however, is somewhat alleviated this week, and also because, hearing how that archbishop invited you with such insistence and kindess, I feel certain that you will enjoy much pleasure and contentment there. Well I pray you to proceed at your own convenience, and to afford yourself every possible comfort, since you have now had to travel in two extremes of temperature, and also to give me news of yourself whenever you can, just as you have done the entire time you have been absent, for which I must thank you, this being the greatest happiness I could have received under the circumstances.

Monsignor Ascanio Piccolomini, the archbishop of Siena, has invited Galileo to be his guest at the archiepiscopal palace.

I wanted to send along a letter for Her Ladyship the Ambassadress (to whom, for love of you, Sire, I know myself much obliged), but because I suspect that, when this one arrives, you will already have left, I am resolved to wait until next week, or better, until you advise me when I should do it.

quale prego che la guardi e conservi in questo viaggio; e la saluto caramente, insieme con le solite. Di S. Matteo in Arcetri, li 25 Giugno 1633.

Sua Fig.^{la} Aff.^{ma}

Suor M.ª Celeste

Molto Ill.^{re} et Amatiss.^{mo} Sig.^{r} Padre,

Tanto quanto mi è arrivato improvviso et inaspettato il nuovo travaglio di V. S., tanto maggiormente mi ha trafitta l'anima di estremo dolore il sentire la risoluzione che finalmente si è presa, tanto sopra il libro quanto nella persona di V. S.: il che dal Sig.^{r} Geri mi è stato significato per la mia importunità, perchè, non tenendo sue lettere questa settimana, non potevo quietarmi, quasi presaga di quanto era accaduto.

Carissimo Sr Padre, adesso è il tempo di prevalersi più che mai di quella prudenza che gl'ha concessa il Signor Iddio, sostenendo questi colpi con quella fortezza di animo, che la religione, proffessione et età sua ricercano. E già che ella per molte esperienze può haver piena cognizione della fallacia e instabilità di tutte le cose di questo mondaccio, non dovrà far molto caso di queste burasche, anzi sperar che presto siano per quietarsi, e cangiarsi in altrettanta sua sodisfazione.

Dico quel tanto che mi somministra il desiderio, e che mi pare che ne prometta la clemenza che S. Santità ha dimostrata in verso di V. S., in haver destinato per la sua carcere luogo così delizioso; onde mi pare che si possa sperare anco com-

Of the service you performed for our dear old friend, Sire, we will speak in person, if it pleases God, Whom I pray to watch over you and protect you on this journey; and I greet you lovingly with our usual friends. From San Matteo, the 25th of June 1633.

Your Most Affectionate Daughter,

Suor M. Celeste

Most Illustrious and Beloved Lord Father,

Just as suddenly and unexpectedly as word of your new torment reached me, Sire, so intensely did it pierce my soul with pain to hear the judgment that has finally been passed, denouncing your person as harshly as your book. I learned all this by importuning Signor Geri, because, not having any letters from you this week, I could not calm myself, as though I already knew all that had happened.

My dearest lord father, now is the time to avail yourself more than ever of that prudence which the Lord God has granted you, bearing these blows with that strength of spirit which your religion, your profession, and your age require. And since you, by virtue of your vast experience, can lay claim to full cognizance of the fallacy and instability of everything in this miserable world, you must not make too much of these storms, but rather take hope that they will soon subside and transform themselves from troubles into as many satisfactions.

In saying all that I am speaking what my own desires dictate, and also what seems a promise of leniency demonstrated toward you, Sire, by His Holiness, who has destined for your mutazione più conforme al suo e nostro desiderio, il che piaccia a Dio che sortisca, se è per il meglio. In tanto la prego a non lasciar di consolarmi con sue lettere, dandomi ragguaglio dell'esser suo quanto al corpo e molto più quanto all'animo; et io finisco di scrivere, ma non già mai di accompagnarla con il pensiero e con le orazioni, pregando S. D. M. che gli conceda vera quiete e consolazione. Di S. Matteo in Arcetri, li 2 di Luglio 1633.

Di V. S. molto Ill.re Fig.la Aff.ma

Suor M.a Celeste

Molto Ill.re et Amatiss.mo Sig.r Padre,

Che la lettera che V. S. mi scrive di Siena (ove dice di ritrovarsi con buona salute) mi habbia apportato contento grandissimo, e similmente a Suor Arcangela, non occorre che io mi affatichi in persuadernela, perchè ella saprà meglio penetrarlo che non saprei io esplicarlo; ma ben vorrei sapergli descriver il giubilo et allegrezza che queste Madri e Sorelle hanno dimostrato nel sentire il felice ritorno di V. S. (che è veramente stato straordinario), poi che la Madre badessa, con molte altre, sentendo questo avviso, mi corsono incontro con le braccia aperte e lacrimando per tenerezza et allegrezza; cosa veramente che mi ha legata per schiava di tutte, per haver da questo compreso quanto affetto esse portino a V. S. et a noi. Il sentir poi ch'ella se ne stia in casa di ospite tanto cortese e benigno quanto è Mons.r Arcivescovo, raddoppia il contento e sodisfazione, ancorchè ciò potessi prison a place so delightful, whereby it appears we may anticipate another commutation of your sentence conforming even more closely with all your and our wishes; may it please God to see things turn out that way, if it be for the best. Meanwhile I pray you not to leave me without the consolation of your letters, giving me reports of your condition, physically and especially spiritually: though I conclude my writing here, I never cease to accompany you with my thoughts and prayers, calling on His Divine Majesty to grant you true peace and consolation. From San Matteo, the 2nd of July 1633.

Sire's Most Affectionate Daughter,

Suor M. Celeste

Although Galileo's sentence consigned him to the dungeons of the Holy Office, his friend Francesco Cardinal Barberini, the pope's nephew, immediately intervened and changed the place of his imprisonment to the Tuscan Embassy. Within days, again thanks to Cardinal Barberini, Galileo was remanded to the palace of the archbishop of Siena.

Most Illustrious and Beloved Lord Father,

That the letter you wrote me from Siena (where you say you find yourself in good health) brought me the greatest pleasure, and the same to Suor Arcangela, is needless for me to weary myself in convincing you, Sire, since you will well know how to fathom what I could not begin to express; but I should love to describe to you the show of jubilation and merriment that these mothers and sisters made upon learning of your happy return, for it was truly extraordinary; since the Mother Abbess, with many others, hearing the news, ran to me with open arms, and crying with tenderness and happiness; truly I am bound as a slave to all of them, for having understood from this display how much love they feel for you, Sire, and for us. Hearing furthermore that you are staying in the home of a host as kind and courteous as Monsignor Archbishop multiplies the pleasure and satisfaction, despite the potential

This is the first of Suor Maria Celeste's letters addressed to Galileo in Siena.

esser con qualche progiudizio del nostro proprio interesse, poi che facilmente potrà essere che quella così dolce conversatione la trattenga costì più lungamente di quello che havremmo voluto. Ma già che qua per ancora non terminano i sospetti del contagio, lodo che ella si trattenga et aspetti (come dice di voler fare) la sicurezza da gl'amici più cari, li quali, se non con maggior affetto, almeno con più sicurezza di noi potranno accertarla della verità.

Ma fra tanto stimerei che fossi bene il pigliar compensa del vino che si ritrova nella sua cantina, almanco di una botte, perchè, se bene per ancora si va mantenendo buono, dubito che a questi caldi non faccia qualche stravaganza; e già quella botte che V. S. lasciò manomessa, del quale beano la serva e il servitore, ha cominciato a entrar in fortezza. V. S. potrà dar ordine di quello che vorrà che si faccia, perchè io non ho troppa scienzia in questo negozio; ma vo facendo il conto, che essendosi V. S. provvista per tutto l'anno, et essendo stata fuora 6 mesi, di ragione dovrà avanzarne, ancorchè ella tornasse fra pochi giorni.

Ma lasciando questo da parte e venendo a quello che più mi preme, io veramente haverei desiderio di sapere in che maniera sia terminato il suo negozio con sodisfazione sua e dei suoi aversarii, sì come mi accennò nella penultima che mi scrisse di Roma. Faccilo con suo comodo e quando sarà ben riposata, che haverò pazienza un altro poco, aspettando di restar capace di questa contradizione.

Il Sig.r Geri fu qui una mattina, mentre si dubitava che V. S. si trovasse in travagli, et insieme con il S.r Aggiunti fece in casa di V. S. l'opera che poi mi avvisa che gli ha fatto intenprejudicial effect this may have on our own interests, because it could well prove to be the case that his extremely enjoyable conversation may engage and detain you much longer than we would like. However, since here for now the suspicions of contagion continue, I commend your remaining there and awaiting (as you say you wish to do) the safety assurance from your closest friends, who, if not with greater love, at least with more certainty than we possess, will be able to apprise you of the facts.

But meanwhile I should judge that it would be wise to draw a profit from the wine in your cellar, at least one cask's worth; because although for now it is keeping well, I fear this heat may precipitate some peculiar effect: and already the cask that you had tapped before you left, Sire, from which the housemaid and the servant drink, has begun to spoil. You will need to give orders as to what you want done, because I have so little knowledge of this business; but I am coming to the conclusion that since you produced enough to last the entire year, and as you have been away for six of those months, you will still have plenty left, even if you should return in a few days.

Leaving this aside, however, and turning to that which concerns me more, I am longing to know in what manner your affair was terminated to the satisfaction of both you and your adversaries, as you intimated in the next to last letter you wrote me from Rome: tell me the details at your convenience, and only after you have rested, because I can be patient awhile longer awaiting enlightenment on this contradiction.

Signor Geri was here one morning, during the time we susdere; la quale ancora a me parve ben fatta e necessaria per ovviare a tutti gl'accidenti che fossero potuti avvenire, onde non seppi negargli le chiavi e l'habilità di farlo, vedendo massime la premura che egli haveva ne gl'interessi di V. S.

Alla Sig.ra Ambasciatrice scrissi sabato passato con quel maggior affetto ch'io seppi, e, se ne haverò risposta, V. S. ne sarà consapevole. Finisco perchè il sonno mi assale, essendo 3 hore di notte, sì che V. S. mi haverà per scusata se haverò detto qualche sproposito. Gli ritorno dupplicate le salute per parte di tutte le nominate e particolarmente la Piera e Geppo, li quali per il suo ritorno son tutti allegri, e prego Dio benedetto che gli doni la Sua santa grazia. Di S. Matteo in Arcetri, li 13 di Luglio 1633.

Di V. S. molto Ill.re Fig.la Aff.ma

Suor M.a Celeste

Molto Ill.re et Amatiss.mo Sig.r Padre,

Ho visto la lettera del Sig.r Mario con mia grandissima consolazione, havendo per mezzo di essa compreso in quale stato V. S. si ritrovi quanto all'interna, quiete dell'animo; e con questo anco il mio si sollieva e tranquilla in gran parte, ma non in tutto, mediante questa lontananza e la incertezza del quando io deva rivederla: et ecco quanto è pur vero che in cosa alcuna di questo mondo non può trovarsi vera quiete e pected you to be in the greatest danger, Sire, and he and Signor Aggiunti went to your house and did what had to be done, which you later told me was your idea, seeming to me at the time well conceived and essential, to avoid some worse disaster that might yet befall you, wherefore I knew not how to refuse him the keys and the freedom to do what he intended, seeing his tremendous zeal in serving your interests, Sire.

Geri Bocchineri and the young mathematician Niccolò Aggiunti came to Arcetri to remove possibly incriminating papers from Galileo's house.

Last Saturday I wrote to her ladyship the Ambassadress with all the great love that I felt, and if I receive an answer, I shall share it with you. I close here because sleep assails me now at the third hour of the night, on which account you will excuse me, Sire, in the event I have said anything inappropriate. I return to you doubled all the regards you offered to those named in your letter and especially La Piera and Geppo, who are thoroughly cheered by your return; and I pray blessed God to give you His holy grace. From San Matteo, the 13th of July 1633.

The hour approaches 11 P.M.

Sire's Most Affectionate Daughter,
Suor M. Celeste

Most Illustrious and Beloved Lord Father,

I saw the letter from Signor Mario with greatest pleasure, having thus understood your condition, Sire, regarding your inner peace of mind, and with this my soul is also soothed and calmed to a large extent, but not entirely, given the vast distance between us and the uncertainty of when I will see you again: and here we observe a certain truth, that one cannot find genuine tranquility and contentment in any worldly thing. When you

Mario Guiducci, like Geri Bocchineri, shares the letters he receives from Galileo with Suor Maria Celeste.

contento. Quando V. S. era a Roma, dicevo nel mio pensiero: Se ho grazia che egli si parta di là e se ne venghi a Siena, mi basta, potrò quasi dire che sia in casa sua; et hora non mi contento, ma sto bramando di riaverla qua più vicina. Horsù, benedetto sia il Signore che fino a qui c'ha fatto grazia così grande. Resta che procuriamo di esser grati di questa, per maggiormente disporlo e commuoverlo a concedercene dell'altre per l'avvenire, come spero che farà per Sua misericordia. In tanto io principalmente fo grande stima di quest'una più che di tutte l'altre, la quale è la conservazione di V. S. con buona sanità, in mezzo a i travagli che ha passati.

Non ho nè tempo nè occasione di scriver più a lungo per hora. Con l'occasione di un'altra sua, che pur presto doverà comparirmi, scriverò più a lungo, e gli darò ragguaglio minuto della casa.

La saluto in nome di tutte le solite e del Sig.r Rondinelli, tutto amorevole inverso di noi, e dal Signor Iddio gli prego consolazione. Di S. Matteo in Arcetri, li 16 di Luglio 1633.

Di V. S. molto Ill.re Fig.la Aff.ma

Suor M.a Celeste

Molto Ill.re et Amatiss.mo Sig.r Padre,

Il Sig.r Geri non mi ha per ancora potuto mandar la lettera che V. S. gl'ha scritto, essendole bisognato lasciarla al G. Duca: mi promette bene di procurar che io l'habbia quanto prima. In tanto io resto molto sodisfatta con questa che V. S.

were in Rome, Sire, I said to myself: if I have the grace of your leaving that place and coming as far as Siena I will be satisfied, for then I can almost say that you are in your own house. And now I am not content, but find myself longing to again have you here even closer. Be that as it may, blessed be the Lord for having granted us His grace so magnanimously until now. It falls to us to try to be truly grateful for this much, so that He may be the more favorably disposed and compassionately moved to bless us in other ways in the future, as I hope He will do by His mercy. Meanwhile I pray most fervently for one thing above all others, Sire, which is the preservation of your health in the face of all the torments you have survived.

Although Siena lies within the Grand Duchy of Tuscany, the distance between Suor Maria Celeste and her father still exceeds forty miles of rough terrain.

Neither the time nor the occasion permits me to write at greater length just now. Upon receipt of another letter from you, which indeed must soon reach me, I will write longer and give you a detailed report about the house.

I send you regards on behalf of all our usual friends and Signor Rondinelli who treats us so tenderly; and from the Lord God I pray for your consolation. From San Matteo in Arcetri, the 16th of July 1633.

Sire's Most Affectionate Daughter,

Suor M. Celeste

Most Illustrious and Beloved Lord Father,

Signor Geri has not thus far been able to send me the letter that you wrote him, Sire, as he was required to leave it with the Grand Duke: he promised me he will try to let me have it before long. Meanwhile I am quite pleased with this one that

Geri Bocchineri reads certain letters of Galileo's to Ferdinando, who has always favored and protected his court philosopher and mathematician.

scrive a me, per la quale comprendo che ella sta bene di sanità e con ogni comodità e sodisfazione; e ne ringrazio Dio, dal quale (come altre volte gl'ho detto) riconosco la sua sanità per grazia speciale.

Iermattina mi feci portar un porn di saggio del vino delle 2 botti, delle quali una è bonissima, l'altra ha cattivo colore, et anco il sapore non mi sodisfà, parendomi che voglia guastarsi. Stasera lo farò sentire al S.r Rondinelli, che, conforme al solito de gl'altri sabati, dovrà venirsene alla villa; et egli meglio saprà, conoscere se sia cattivo per la sanità, chè quanto al gusto non sarebbe dispiacevole, et io ne darò parte a V. S., acciò ordini quello che se ne deva fare, caso che non sia buono. Quel bianco che è nei fiaschi è forte, e farà un aceto esquisito, eccetto che quello della fiasca, che, per haver solamente un porn il fuoco, ce lo andiamo bevendo avanti che egli peggiori. Il difetto non è già stato della Piera, perchè gl'ha spesso riguardati e visto che si mantenevano pieni. De i capperi se ne sono acconci una buona quantità, ciò è tutti quelli che sono stati nell'orto, perchè la Piera mi dice che a V. S. gli gustano assai.

Son parecchi giorni che in casa non è più farina; ma perchè a questi gran caldi non si può far quantità di pane, chè indurisce subito e muffa, e per il poco non torna il conto a scaldar il forno, fo che il ragazzo lo compri qui alla bottega.

Con quest'altra gli darò più minuto ragguaglio delle spese fatte alla giornata, perchè adesso non me ne basta l'animo, sentendomi (conforme al mio solito in questa stagione) con una estrema debolezza, tanto che non ho forza di muover la penna, per così dire. La saluto caramente per parte di tutte you wrote to me, from which I understand that you are in good health, and enjoying every comfort and satisfaction, and for that I thank God, from Whom (as I have told you many times) I acknowledge your well-being as a special grace.

Yesterday morning I had some small samples taken of the wine from your casks, one of which is extremely good, the other has a bad color, and also the flavor does not seem right to me, almost as though it has spoiled. This evening I will tell Signor Rondinelli, who, following his usual Saturday custom, will be sure to come to the villa; and he will know better how to recognize whether drinking it may be bad for one's health, for the taste alone would not be all that unpleasant, and I will give you his opinion, Sire, so you can dictate what you want done, in the event it is not good. That white wine in the *fiaschi* is strong and will make an exquisite vinegar, except for the one in the small flask, which, on account of being only just beginning to spoil, we are drinking before it turns any worse: the defect was no fault of La Piera's, because she examined the bottles often and made sure to keep them filled. Quite a large quantity of capers was harvested and preserved, Sire, namely all those that were in the garden, for La Piera tells me you are especially fond of them.

There has not been any flour in your house for several days, but because this terrible heat makes it impossible to bake much bread, seeing as it hardens quickly and turns moldy, and it is not worth the effort of heating the oven to bake only a little bit, I have the boy buy it here in our shop.

With the next letter I will give you a more specific account of the daily expenditures, because now I lack the energy, sucqueste Madri, alle quali par ogn'hora mille anni per il desiderio che hanno di rivederla, e prego il Signore che la conservi. Di S. Matteo in Arcetri, li 23 di Luglio 1633.

Sua Fig.la Aff.ma

Suor M.a Celeste

Molto Ill.re et Amatiss.mo Sig.r Padre,

Ho letto la lettera che V. S. scrive al Sig.r Geri con mio particolar gusto e consolazione per le cose che nel primo capitolo di essa si contengono. Nel terzo capitolo ancora io m'intrometterò, per esser esso attenente al negozio di non so che casetta, la quale ho penetrato che il Sig.r Geri ha gran desiderio che Vincenzio compri, ma con l'aiuto di V. S. Io veramente non vorrei esser prosontuosa, entrando in quelle cose che non mi appartengono; non dimeno, perchè assai mi preme qualsivoglia minimo interesse di V. S., la pregherei et esorterei (caso che ella si trovi in stato di poterlo fare) a dar loro, non dirò in tutto, ma qualche parte di sodisfazione, non solo per amor di Vincenzio, quanto per mantener il Sig.r Geri in quella buona disposizione che ha in verso di lei, havendo egli, nell'occasioni che son passate, mostrato grande affetto a V. S. e, per quanto mi pare, procurato di aiutarlo in quel poco che ha potuto: sì che, se senza suo molto scomodo V. S. potesse darle qualche segno di gratitudine, non lo stimerei se non per ben fatto. So che da per sè medesima può infinitamente meglio di me discorrere e penetrar queste cose, et io forse non so quel cumbing (as is typical for me in this season) to extreme weakness, so that you might say I barely have the strength to move my pen. I greet you lovingly on behalf of all these reverend mothers, to whom every hour feels like a thousand years, on account of their strong desire to see you again, and I pray the Lord to bless you. From San Matteo, the 23rd of July 1633.

Your Most Affectionate Daughter,

Suor M. Celeste

Most Illustrious and Beloved Lord Father,

I read the letter you wrote to Signor Geri with particular pleasure and consolation, Sire, on account of the things contained in its first section. I will be so bold as to venture on into the third section as well, although it pertains to the purchase of some little house I do not know about, which I have inferred that Signor Geri very much wants Vincenzio to buy, albeit with your help. I certainly would not want to be presumptuous, interfering in matters that do not concern me. Nonetheless, because I care a great deal about whatsoever is of even minimal interest to you, Sire, I would implore you and exhort you (assuming you are in a position to be able to do this) to give them, if not the full amount, then some appreciable part of it, not only for love of Vincenzio, but just as much to keep Signor Geri favorably disposed toward you, as he has, on past occasions, shown great fondness for you, Sire, and, from all I have seen, tried to help you in any way he could: therefore, if, without too much trouble on your part, you could give him some sign of gratitude, I should judge that a deed well done. I know that you yourself can perceive and arrange such matters

Assuming Vincenzio moves back to Florence from Poppi, he may need a bigger house than the one he left on the Costa San Giorgio, which is currently occupied by Sestilia's brothers. The availability of the property immediately next door strikes Geri as an irresistible opportunity to enlarge the first house by joining it to the second.

che mi dica; ma so ben che dico quello che mi detta un puro affetto in verso di lei.

Il servitore che è stato a Roma con V. S., venne qui hiermattina, esortato a ciò fare da Mess.r Giulio Ninci. Mi parve strano di non veder lettere di V. S.; pur restai appagata della scusa che per lei fece il medesimo huomo, dicendo the V. S. non sapeva the egli passasse di qua. Adesso che V. S. è senza servitore, il nostro Geppo non può star alle mosse, e vorrebbe in ogni maniera, se gli fossi concesso il passo, venir da lei, et io l'havrei caro. V. S. potrà dir il suo pensiero, chè vedrei di mandarlo con buona accompagnatura, e credo che il Sig.r Geri gli potrebbe far haver il passaporto.

Desidero anco di sapere quanta paglia si deva comprare per la muletta, perchè la Piera ha paura che non si muoia di fame, e la biada non è troppo per lei, che è bizzarra d'avanzo.

Da poi in qua che gli mandai la nota delle spese fatte per la sua casa, son corse queste che gli mando notate, oltre a i danari che ogni mese ho fatto pagare a Vincenzio Landucci, che di tutti tengo le ricevute, eccetto che di questi ultimi; nel qual tempo, sì come anco segue di presento, egli si ritrovava serrato in casa con i due figliolini, per essergli morta la moglie, per quanto si dice, di mal cattivo; che veramente si può dire che sia uscita di stento e andata a riposarsi la poverella. Egli mandò a domandarmi li 6 d. per l'amor di Dio, dicendo che si moriva di fame, et essendo anco compito il mese glieli mandai; e lui promisse la ricevuta quando fossi fuor di sospetto, e tanto procurerò the mantenga, se non altro, avanti lo sborso di quest'altri, caso che V. S. non sia qua da infinitely better than I, and perhaps I do not even know what I am saying, but well I know how anything I say is dictated by pure love toward you.

The servant who was in Rome with you came here yesterday morning, urged to do so by Signor Giulio Nunci. It seemed strange to me not to see letters from you, Sire. Yet I was appeased by the excuse this same man made, explaining that you had not known whether he would pass this way. Now that you are without a servant, Sire, our Geppo, who cannot move freely about here, desires nothing more, if only he were granted permission, than to come to you, and I should very much like that, too. If your thoughts concur, Sire, I could see to sending him well escorted, and I believe Signor Geri can secure him a permit to travel.

I also want to know how much straw to buy for the little mule, because La Piera fears she will die of hunger, and the fodder is not good enough for her, as she is a most original animal.

Since I sent you the list of expenses paid out for your house, we have incurred these others that I give you account of now, besides the money that every month I have made sure was paid to Vincenzio Landucci, for which I keep all the receipts, except the last two payments; for at those times he was, as he continues to be now, locked up in his house with the two little children because the plague killed his wife; whereby truly one may say she is released from her toil and gone to her rest, the poor woman. He sent early to ask me for the 6 *scudi* for the love of God, saying they were dying of hunger, and as the month was almost at its end I sent him the money; he per sè, come dubito mediante questi eccessivi caldi che si fanno sentire.

I limoni dell'orto cadevano tutti, onde quei pochi restati si sono venduti, e delle 2 lire che se ne sono havute ne ho fatto dir tre messe per V. S. secondo la mia intenzione.

Scrissi alla Sig.ra Ambasciatrice, come V. S. ordinò, e mandai la lettera al Sig.r Geri, ma non ne tengo risposta, onde non so se sarà bene tornar a riscrivergli con dimostrar dubbio se forse o la mia o la sua lettera siano andate male. E qui, salutando V. S. di tutto cuore, prego Nostro Signore che la conservi. Di S. Matteo in Arcetri, li 24 di Luglio 1633.

Sua Fig.la Aff.ma

Suor Maria Celeste

Amatiss.mo Sig.r Padre,

Mi maraviglio che V. S. sia stato un ordinario senza mie lettere, non havendo io lasciato di scriverle e mandarle al Sig.r Geri; e quest'ultima settimana ne ho scritte due, una sabato et una il lunedì. Ma forse a quest'hora gli saranno pervenute tutte, e V. S. resterà minutamente informata di ogni particolarità di casa, come desidera. Restava solo imperfetta la relazione del vino, il quale sentito dal Sig.r Rondinelli, con il suo consiglio si è travasato in un'altra botte per levarlo di sopra quel letto. Si starà a veder qualche giorno, e se non migliorerà, bisognerà vedere di contrattarlo avanti che si promised the receipt when he is beyond suspicion of contagion, and I will endeavor to hold him to that; if nothing else I will first see to these other disbursements, in the event you are not here to take care of them yourself, Sire, which I suspect on account of the excessive heat that is upon us.

The lemons that hung in the garden all dropped, the last few remaining ones were sold, and from the 2 *lire* they brought I had three masses said for you, Sire, on my own initiative.

I wrote to her ladyship the Ambassadress, as you told me to, and sent the letter to Signor Geri, but I do not have a reply, wherefore I suppose I might be wise to write again suggesting the possibility that either my letter or hers has gone astray. And here, sending you love with all my heart, I pray Our Lord to bless you. From San Matteo, the 24th of July 1633.

Your Most Affectionate Daughter,
Suor Maria Celeste

Most Beloved Lord Father,

I am astonished that a courier has left you without any letters from me, as I have not failed to write them and forward them to Signor Geri, and this past week I wrote you two, Sire, one Saturday and one Monday: but perhaps by this time they have both reached you, and you are scrupulously informed of every household detail, as you wish. The sole unfinished business involves the wine, which, tasted by Signor Rondinelli, was decanted on his advice into another cask in order to remove it from the sediment: it will sit under watch for a few days, and, if it does not improve, then something else guasti affatto. Questo e quanto alla botte che già gl'havevo avvisato che cominciava a patire: l'altra, per ancora si mantiene molto buono.

Non ho mancato di preparar l'aloè per V. S., e fino a qui vi ho ritornato sopra il sugo di rose sette volte; e perchè di presente non è tanto asciutto che si possi metter in opera nelle pillole, gli mando per hora un girelletto di quelle che facciamo per la nostra bottega, nelle quali è lo aloè pur lavato con sugo di rose, ma una sol volta. Non dimeno non credo che per una presa sola siano per fargli danno, havendo havuto qualche correzione.

Quanto il Landucci si dolga per la morte di sua moglie, io non posso saperlo, nè haverne altra relazione che quella che mi dette Giuseppo il giorno che andò, insieme con il Sr Rondinelli, a portargli li 6 d., che fu li 18 stanti; e mi disse che posò i danari su la soglia dell'uscio, e che vedde Vincenzio, là in casa lontano dalla porta assai, che mostrava di esser molto afflitto, con una cera di morto più che di vivo, e con lui erano li due figliolini, un maschio e una femmina, che tanti e non gliene sono restati.

Godo di sentire che V. S. si vadia conservando in sanità, e la prego a procurare di conservarsi col regolarsi particolarmente nel bere, che tanto gl'è nocivo, perchè dubito che il gran caldo e la conversazione non gli siano occasione di disordinare, con pericolo di ammalarsi e per conseguenza di differire ancora il suo ritorno, tanto da noi desiderato.

La nostra Suor Giulia, maestra di Sr Luisa e sorella del Sig.^r^ Corso, ha in questi giorni fatto alle braccia con la morte, et, must be done before it spoils altogether: this concerns only the cask I had already warned you was beginning to suffer, as the other for the time being maintains its good condition.

I have not neglected to prepare the aloe for you, Sire, and thus far I have poured the rose essence over it seven times; but because it is not yet dry enough to begin working into pill form, I send you for now a sample of those pills we produce for our apothecary shop, which contain the pure aloe washed only once with rose juice; nonetheless I do not believe that taking a single dose will do you any harm, even though the recipe has been altered somewhat.

Aloe, an esteemed purgative, has a foul odor and bitter taste than can be softened by rose water.

As for how sorrowfully poor Landucci grieves over the death of his wife, I have no way of knowing, nor do I have any word of him except for what Giuseppe told me the day he went with Signor Rondinelli to deliver the 6 *scudi*, which was the 18th of this month; and he said that he set the money on the front steps and that he had only a glimpse of Vincenzio there inside the house quite far from the doorway, and that he looked sorely afflicted with an expression more of the grave than of life, and with him were the two little children, a boy and a girl, who are all that he has left of his family.

I am happy to hear that you keep your good health, Sire, and I pray you to endeavor to continue this way, by governing yourself well particularly with regard to the drinking that is so hurtful to you, for I fear that the intense heat and your social obligations to your host afford you ample opportunity for indulging with great risk of getting sick, which would only further postpone your ever so eagerly awaited return to us.

ancor che vecchia di 85 anni, l' ha superata, contro ogni nostra credenza, essendo stata tanto male che si trattava di darle l'Olio Santo. Adesso è tanto fuor di pericolo che non ha più febbre, e si raccomanda a V. S. per mille volte, et il simile fanno tutte le amiche. Il Signor Iddio gli conceda la Sua santa grazia. Di S. Matteo in Arcetri, li 28 di Luglio 1633.

Di V. S. molto Ill. Fig.la Aff.ma

Suor M.a Celeste

Amatiss.mo Sig.r Padre,

Scrivo questi pochi versi molto in fretta, per non trasgredire al precetto di V. S., che mi impone ch'io non lasci passar settimana senza scrivere.

Quanto al vino che si travasò, par che più tosto sia alquanto migliorato di colore, e alla Piera non gli dispiace e no va bevendo. Si è trovato da darne a vin per vino 3 barili: 2 ne piglierà il fabbro, mezzo il lavoratore dell'Ambra, e mezzo Domenico che lavora qui il podere de i SS.i Bini; si cercherà di darne ancora un altro barile, perchè finalmente non vorrei che ne gettassimo via punto, e il resto, che sarà un altro barile o poco più, se lo beveranno, perchè così si contentano, et anco Suor Arcangela non si fa pregare a dar loro aiuto.

In colombaia sono 2 para di piccioncini, che aspettanoc che V. S. venga in persona a dar loro l'ultima sentenza. I limoni mostra ragionevole, se andranno innanzi; ma le melangole e

Our Lady Giulia, teacher of Suor Luisa and sister of Signor Corso, has in recent days locked arms with death, and although she is an old woman of 85 years, she has won out against all expectations, having been so seriously ill that we were on the verge of administering the last rites: now she is so far out of danger that she has not a trace of fever, and she sends a thousand regards to you, Sire, and all our friends do the same. May the Lord grant you His holy grace. From San Matteo, the 28th of July 1633.

Sire's Most Affectionate Daughter,

Suor M. Celeste

Most Beloved Lord Father,

I write these few lines in great haste so as not to disobey your precept that I never let a week go by without writing.

As for the wine that was decanted, it seems to be quite improved in color, and La Piera finds it not at all unpleasant so she continues drinking it: we have finally found willing takers for the 3 barrels worth that we must give away; 2 the smith will take, a half to Ambra's employee, and half for Domenico who works nearby on the Bini family's farm: we are looking to give away one more, because in the end I would not want to discard any of it, and the rest, which will be another barrel or a little more, will be consumed by the servants, because it does please them so, and also Suor Arcangela will not have to be begged to help them along.

In the dovecote there are two pairs of pigeon chicks waiting for you to come in person, Sire, to pronounce their final senmelarance fecion pochi fiori, e di quei pochi ne sono andati innanzi pochissimi: pur ve no è qualcuna.

Il pane che si compra per 8 quattrini è grande a bianco. La paglia per la mula si provvederà. Dello strame non bisogna farne disegno, perchè quest'anno è stato carestia d'erba, oltre dice la Piera che alla signora mula non gli sodisfà molto, e che V. S. si ricordi che l'anno passato ella se ne faceva letto per star più soffice. Adesso ha havuto un poco di male in bocca, perchè ha lo stomaco tanto gentile che dicono che il ber fresco gl'habbia fatto male, d[. .] che la Piera è stata tribolata. Adesso sta meglio.

V. S. fece bene ad aprire la lettera della cortesissima Sig.^ra^ Ambasciatrice, alla quale vorrei in ogni maniera mandar a presentare qualche galanteria insieme con il cristallo, quando si apriranno i passi. Il Sig.^r^ Geri non è ancora venuto qui, sì che per hora non posso dir altro a V. S. se non che di molto gusto mi sono stati gl'altri avvisi che mi dà nell'ultima s[ua] circa gl'honori e sodisfazioni che riceve costì. E caramente la saluto, e prego Nostro Signore che la conservi. Di S. Matteo, li 3 d'Agosto 1633.

Sua Fig.^la^ Aff.^ma^

Suor M.ª Celeste G.

tence. The harvest of lemons will prove fully satisfactory if the crop continues on like this, but the Seville oranges and the Portuguese oranges put out few flowers, and from those few only a tiny number matured; indeed there is not a single survivor from the whole grove.

The bread that can be bought for 8 *quattrini* is large and white. The straw for the mule will be provided: as for fodder, there is no point in thinking of it, because of the scarcity of grass this year, besides which, La Piera says, Madame Mule does not care for it much, but you may recall, Sire, how last year she used it to make her bed softer. Recently she has had some soreness in her mouth, because her stomach is so sensitive, they say, that drinking something cold may have made her sick, which has been a trial for La Piera. Now she is better.

You did well to open the letter from her most gracious ladyship the Ambassadress, to whom I should like to be able to send for a present some delicacy together with the crystal, whenever the roads reopen. Signor Geri has not yet come by. For now I can say no more to you Sire, except that I was most pleased with all the news you gave me in your last letter, concerning the tributes and satisfactions you are receiving over there. And I greet you lovingly, and I pray Our Lord to bless you. From San Matteo, the 3rd of August 1633.

Your Most Affectionate Daughter,

Suor M. Celeste G.

The archbishop is trying everything to make Galileo comfortable, even hosting elaborate dinners in his honor, although he is technically under house arrest in the palace.

Amatiss.mo Sig.r Padre,

Il Sig.r Geri fu hiermattina a parlamento meco per conto del negozio della casetta; e per quanto potetti comprendere, egli non ha altra pretensione che l'utile a benefizio di Vincenzio, il quale sarebbe assai con l'occasione di questa compra, potendo bonificare et accrescere la casa grande, che pur gli pare angusta, niente niente che Vincenzio cresca in famiglia; tanto più che dice, esservi una stanza sopra la citerna, che non si può habitare per esser malsana, et al quesito ch'io gli feci, se haveva pensiero di habitarvi insieme con Vincenzio, mi rispose che, quando egli havessi voluto starvi, non poteva, e che è di necessità che egli ne pigli una più comoda e vicina a Palazzo, perchè, tanto per lui quanto per quelli che tutto il giorno vanno a trovarlo, questa su la Costa è troppo disadatta e fuor di mano. Stando saldo questo punto, concludo che il Sig.r Geri havrebbe desiderato che V. S. havessi interamente comprata la casetta, la quale non passerà i 300 d. in modo alcuno, per quanto egli dice. Gli replicai che non mi pareva nè possibile nè dovere che V. S. fossi aggravata di tanto, essendo verisimile che ella si trovi scarsa di danari, havendo havuto oocasioni di far spese più che ordinarie; e gli soggiunsi che si poteva proporre e pregar V. S. a concorrere alla metà della spesa, caso che si trovi in comodo e già che dice anco che si sforzerà a dar loro ogni possibil sodisfazione, e che l'altra metà de i danari havrebbe potuto il medesimo Sig.r Geri accomodar a Vincenzio, fino che egli habbia comodità di renderglieli: al che il S.r Geri condescese con molta prontezza e cortesia, dicendomi che, se bene nel tempo che V. S. è stata fuora ha accomodati altri danari a Vincenzio, non di meno havrebbe preso ogni scomodo, prestandoli anco

Most Beloved Lord Father,

Signor Geri was here yesterday morning for a parley with me to settle the business of the little house; and, as far as I was able to understand, he has no other interest beyond Vincenzio's advantage and benefit, which would be considerably advanced by this purchase, enabling him to increase the value and size of his own house, which may well seem to be closing in on him, in the event Vincenzio enlarges his family; moreover he says no one can live in the room over the cistern because it is unhealthy: and as for the question I raised as to whether Signor Geri had any thought of living there with Vincenzio, he answered that, while he might like to do so, he could not, as he needs to find more convenient lodgings closer to the Palace, for his sake as well as for those who come looking for him all day long, because this one on the Costa is too unsuitable and out of the way. As he stood firm on this point, I conclude that Signor Geri had wanted you to pay the full cost of the little house, which should not exceed 300 *scudi*, by his estimation: I repeated to him that it seemed neither possible nor appropriate for you, Sire, to take on this entire expense, as you understandably were short of money, having been confronted with expenses far beyond the ordinary, so I suggested to him that one might propose and pray you to contribute half the cost, if this were convenient for you, and then too, since he also says he will do his utmost to give the couple every possible advantage, providing the other half of the money would enable Signor Geri to help establish Vincenzio, until such time as he is able to repay the loan; to which Signor Geri yielded very promptly and politely, telling me that, although during your absence he has advanced questi 150 d., purchè questa buona occasione non gli fuggissi delle mani. Questo è quello che si concluse che si dovesse propor a V. S., come fo di presente: a lei sta lo eleggere, poi che molto meglio di me può sapere quanto si possa distendere. Solamente soggiugnerò che l'essermi convenuto interessarmi in questo negozio, non mi è stato di poca mortificazione: prima, perchè non vorrei in minima cosa disturbar la sua quiete, da lei raccomandatami, il che temo che non segua, già che mi pare che ella non inclini troppo a questa spesa; dall'altra banda, l'escluder affatto il Sig.r Geri, che domanda a V. S. per un suo figliuolo e che dimostra tanto affetto a lei e a tutta la casa nostra, non mi par cosa lodevole. Di grazia, V. S., col darmi risposta quanto prima, mi liberi da questa sollevazione d'animo; et anco potrà avvisarmi che effetto habbiano fatto le pillole e se vorrà ch'io gliene mandi dell'altre di queste medesime, non potendosi per ancora metter in opera l'aloè che ho preparato per formarne di nuovo.

Suor Giulia gli ritorna le salute, e sta con desiderio aspettando, non il fiasco del vino bianco che V. S. gli promette, ma ben lei medesima; et il Sig.r Rondinelli fa l'istesso, al quale non lascio di partecipare le lettere che V. S. mi scrive, quando mi par di poterlo fare. E qui a lei mi raccomando, e dal Signor Iddio prego felicità. Di S. Matteo in Arcetri, li 6 di Agosto 1633.

Di V. S. Fig.la Aff.ma

Suor M.a Celeste

other sums to Vincenzio, nevertheless he would have deprived himself if need be in order to lend him also these 150 *scudi*, to prevent this excellent opportunity from slipping through his fingers. This is how it transpired that a proposal comes before you, Sire, in the form I present to you now: it is up to you to decide, since you know far better than I how much you can afford to pay; I will only add that it has seemed incumbent upon me to involve myself in this business, which has been quite mortifiying for me, primarily because I would not want in the slightest way to disturb the peace that you tell me you are enjoying; which I fear may follow in any case, as you do not seem enthusiastically inclined to make this purchase. On the other hand, to entirely reject Signor Geri, who was appealing to you on behalf of your own son, and who shows such affection for you and for all our family, does not seem to me a laudable act. Please, Sire, by giving me an answer as soon as possible, free me from my uneasy state; and also let me know what effect the pills may have had, and whether you would like me to send you some more of the same type, as I have not yet been able to work with the aloe I prepared for formulating the new ones.

Suor Giulia returns your good wishes, and is eagerly awaiting, not the flask of white wine which you promised her, Sire, but rather you yourself; and the same for Signor Rondinelli, with whom I never fail to share the letters you write me, Sire, when I deem it permissible to do so; and here I give you my love, and pray your happiness from the Lord God. From San Matteo, the 6th of August 1633.

Sire's Most Affectionate Daughter,

Suor M. Celeste

Amatiss.mo Sig.r Padre,

Se le mie lettere (come ella mi dice in una sua) gli sono rese spesse volte in coppia, et io gli dico, per non replicar il medesimo, che questa ultima volta le sue sono venute come i frati zoccolanti, non solamente accoppiate, ma con gran strepito, facendo in me una commozione più che ordinaria di gusto e contento, che ho preso in sentire che la supplica che per Vincenzio e per il Sig.r Geri ho presentata a V. S. o raccomandata per dir meglio, sia da lei stata segnata con tanta prontezza e con più larghezza di quella che io domandavo: e da questo fo conseguenza che non sia altrimenti, con la mia importunità, restata disturbata la sua quiete, ch'è quello che mi premeva; e per questo mi allegro e la ringrazio.

Quanto al suo ritorno, Dio sa quanto io lo desidero; non dimeno, quando V. S. potessi penetrare che, partendosi di cotesta città, gli convenissi per qualche tempo fermarsi in luogo, se ben vicino, fuori di casa sua, crederei che fossi meglio per la sua sanità e per la sua reputazione il trattenersi qualche settimana d'avantaggio dove di presente si ritrova, in un paradiso di delizie, principalmente mediante la dolcissima conversazione di cotesto Ill.mo Mons.r Arcivescovo, e poter poi a dirittura venirsene al suo tugurio, il quale veramente si lamenta di questa sua lunga assenzia; e particolarmente le botti, le quali, invidiando le lodi che V. S. dà a i vini di cotesti paesi, per vendetta una di loro ha guastato il vino, o pure il vino ha cercato di guastar lei, come già gl'ho avvisato; e l'altra havrebbe fatto il simile, se non fossi stata prevenuta dall'accortezza e diligenza del Sig.r Rondinelli, il quale, conoscendo il male, ha procurato il rimedio, con-

Most Beloved Lord Father,

If my letters, as you told me in one of yours, often reach you coupled in pairs, then I can tell you, not to repeat your exact words, that in this last post your letters arrived like the Franciscan friars wearing their wooden clogs, not only yoked together, but with a resounding clatter, creating in me a much greater than usual commotion of pleasure and happiness, Sire, especially when I learned that my supplication on behalf of Vincenzio and Signor Geri, which I submitted to you, or rather urged upon you, to speak more accurately, has been agreed to and settled so promptly and with even more generosity than I had requested: and consequently I conclude that my importuning in no way posed a disturbance to your peace, for indeed that possibility had worried me greatly, and now I feel cheered and relieved and I thank you.

As for your return, God knows how much I desire it; nonetheless, Sire, when you consider taking your leave from that city, where it has suited you for some time to remain in a place quite nearby, yet outside your own house, I should deem it better for both your health and your reputation, to stay on for several more advantageous weeks where for now you inhabit a veritable paradise of delights, especially considering the enchanting conversation of that most illustrious Monsignor Archbishop; rather than to have to return right away to your hovel, which has truly lamented your long absence; and particularly the wine casks, which, envying the praise you have lavished on the vintages of those other regions, have taken their revenge, for one of them has spoiled its contents, or indeed the wine has contrived to spoil itself, as I have already sigliando et operando acciò il vino si venda, come si è fatto per mezzo di Mattio bottegaio, ad un oste. Oggi appunto s'infiasca e se ne manda via 2 some, et il Sig.[r] Rondinelli assiste, delle quali senza fallo credo che se ne haveranno 8 d.: quello che sopravanzerà alle due some, si metterà ne i fiaschi per la famiglia e per noi, che ne piglieremo volentieri qualche pocherello. Si è sollecitato a pigliar questo spediente avanti che il vino facessi altra novità maggiore; per non l'haver a buttar via. Il Sig.[r] Rondinelli attribuisce questa disgrazia al non essersi levato il vino di sopra quel letto che fa nella botte, avanti che venissero i caldi; cosa che io non sapevo, perchè non son pratica in questi maneggi.

La mostra dell'uva dell'orto era assai scarsa, e due furie di gragniuola, che l'ha percossa, ha finito di rovinarla: se ne è colta un poca di quells lugliola, avanti che vi arrivino i malandrini, quali, non havendo trovato altro da dissipare, hanno colte alcune mele. Il giorno di S. Lorenzo fu qui all'intorno un tempo cattivissimo, con vento tanto terribile che fece molto danno, et alla casa di V. S. ne toccò qualche poco, essendo andato via un buon pezzo di tetto dalla banda del Sr Chellini, et anco fece cadere un di quei vasi ne i quali sono i melaranci: il frutto si è trapiantato in terra, fino che V. S. dirà se si deva comprar altro vaso per rimettervelo; e del tetto si è fatto sapere a i SS.[ri] Bini, che hanno promesso di farlo rassettare. Di altre frutte non vi è quasi niente; e particolarmente delle susine, nessuna; e quelle poche pere che vi erano, il vento le ha vendemiate. Molto bene son riuscite le fave, che, per quanto dice la Piera, saranno intorno a 5 staia, e molto belle. Adesso vi sono de i fagiuoli.

warned you might happen. And the other would have done the same, had it not been prevented by the shrewdness and diligence of Signor Rondinelli, who by recognizing the malady has prescribed the remedy, advising and working to bring about the sale of the wine, which has been accomplished, through Matteo the merchant, to an innkeeper. Just today two mule loads are being decanted and sent off, with Signor Rondinelli's assistance. These sales, I believe, must bring in 8 *scudi*: any surplus left over after the two loads will be bottled for the family and the convent as we will gladly take this little bit: it seemed imperative to seize such an expedient before the wine sprang any other surprise on us that would have necessitated throwing it away. Signor Rondinelli atttributes the whole misfortune to our not having separated the liquid from the sediment in the casks before the onset of the hot weather; something I did not know about, because I am inexperienced in this enterprise.

The grapes in the vineyard already looked frightfully scarce before two violent hailstorms struck and completed their ruination. A few grapes were gathered in the heat of July before the arrival here of the highwaymen, who, not finding anything else to steal, helped themselves to some apples. On the feast day of San Lorenzo there came a terribly destructive storm that raged all around these parts with winds so fierce that they wreaked great havoc, and touched your house as well, Sire, carrying away quite a large piece of the roof on the side facing Signor Chellini's property, and also knocking over one of those terra-cotta flower pots that held an orange tree. The tree is transplanted in the ground for the time being,

August 10 marks the feast day of San Lorenzo, martyred in Rome in the year 258.

Mi resterebbe da rispondergli qualcosa circa quel particolare che ella mi dice del stare o non star in ozio; ma lo riserbo a quando haverò manco sonno che adesso, che sono 3 hore di notte. La saluto per parte di tutti i nominati, e di più del Sig.r medico Ronconi, il quale non vien mai qui che con grand'instanza non mi domandi di lei. Il Signor Iddio la conservi. Di S. Matteo, li 13 d'Agosto 1633.

Di V. S. molto Ill.re Fig.la Aff.ma

Suor M.a Celeste

Amatiss.mo Sig.r Padre,

Quando scrissi a V. S. circa il suo avvicinarsi qua o vero trattenersi costì ancora qualche poco, sapevo l'instanza che si era fatta al Sig.r Ambasciatore, ma non già la sua risposta, la quale intesi dal Sig.r Geri, che fu qui martedì passato quando già havevo scritto a V. S. un'altra lettera et inclusovi la ricetta delle pillole, che a quest'hora doverà esserle pervenuta. Il motivo adunque che m'indusse a scriverle in quella maniera until we have word from you as to whether you want another pot purchased to hold it, and we reported the roof damage to the Bini family, who promised to have it repaired. The other fruit trees have borne practically nothing; particularly the plums, of which we had not a single specimen; and as for those few pears that were there, they have been harvested by the wind. However the broad beans gave a very good yield, which, according to La Piera, will amount to 5 *staia* and all of them beautiful: now come the beans.

*The Binis, the in-laws of the now-deceased Esaù Martellini, own **Il Gioiello**.*

It would behoove me to give you an answer concerning your inquiry about whether or not I sit idle; but I am saving that until some time when I cannot sleep, as it is now the third hour of the night. I send you greetings on behalf of everyone I have mentioned, and even more from Doctor Ronconi who never comes here without pressing me for news of you, Sire. May the Lord God bless you. From San Matteo, the 13th of August 1633.

Sire's Most Affectionate Daughter,

Suor M. Celeste

Most Beloved Lord Father,

When I wrote to you about your coming home soon, Sire, or your otherwise remaining where you are for a while longer, I knew of the petition you had made to his lordship the Ambassador, but was not yet aware of his answer, which I since learned from Signor Geri when he came here last Tuesday, just after I had written yet another letter to you, enclosing the recipe for the pills that by now must surely have reached you.

fu, che essendomi io trovata più volte a discorrer con il Sig.r Rondinelli, il quale in questo tempo è stato il mio refugio, perchè, come pratico et esperimentato nelle cose del mondo, molte volte mi ha alleggerito il travaglio pronosticandomi per appunto come le cose di V. S. potevon passare, le quali io mi figuravo più precipitose di quello che poi sono state, fra l'altre una volta mi disse che in Firenze si diceva che quando V. S. partiva di Siena doveva andare alla Certosa, cosa che a nessuno de gl'amici era di gusto; e vi aggiunse buone ragioni, ma in particolare alcune di quelle che intendo che ha poi addotte il medesimo S.r Ambasciatore, e quella massimamente che, se con troppo sollecitar il ritorno di V. S., si haveva una negativa, bisognava poi necessariamente lasciar scorrer più lunghezza di tempo avanti che si ritornasse a supplicare: onde io, che temevo di questo successo che facilmente saria seguito, sentendo che V. S. sollecitava, mi mossi a scriverle in quella maniera; chè se a lei non fo gran dimostrazione del desiderio che ho del suo ritorno, resto per non accrescergli lo stimolo e inquietarla maggiormente. Anzi che in questi giorni sono andata fabbricando castelli in aria, pensando fra me medesima se, doppo questi due mesi di dilazione non si ottenendo la grazia, io havessi potuto ricorrere alla S.ra Ambasciatrice, acciò, col mezzo della cognata di S. S.tà, havessi ella procurato di impetrarla. So, come gli dico, che questi son disegni poco fondati; con tutto ciò non stimerei per impossibile che le preghiere di pietosa figliuola superassero il favore di gran personaggi. Mentre adunque mi ritrovo in questi pensieri, e veggo che V. S. nella sua lettera mi soggiugne che una delle cause che gli fanno desiderare il suo ritorno è per vedermi rallegrare di certo presente, o gli so

My motive for addressing you in that seemingly distant fashion had grown out of my frequent discussions with Signor Rondinelli, who all through this period has been my refuge (because, as practical and experienced as he is in the ways of the world, he has many times alleviated my anxiety, prognosticating for me the outcome of situations concerning your affairs, especially in cases that seemed more precipitous to me than they later turned out to be); once during those discussions he told me how people in Florence were saying that when you departed from Siena, Sire, you would have to go to the Certosa, a condition that displeased every one of your friends; yet he saw some good in going along with those orders, as I understand the Ambassador himself did, too, for they both suspected that soliciting too urgently for your direct return here, Sire, might bring about some negative consequence, and therefore they wanted to allow more time to elapse before entreating again. Whereupon I, fearing the worst could all too easily come to pass, and hearing you were preparing to petition yet again, set myself to write to you as I did. If ever I fail to make a great demonstration of the desire I harbor for your return, I refrain only to avoid goading you too much or disquieting you excessively. Rather than take that risk, all through these days I have been building castles in the air, thinking to myself, if, after these two months of delay in not obtaining the favor of your release, I had been able to appeal to her Ladyship the Ambassadress, then she, working through the sister-in-law of His Holiness, might have successfully implored the Pope on your behalf. I know, as I freely admit to you, that these are poorly drawn plans, yet still I would not rule out the possibility that the prayers of a pious daughter could outweigh

Ambassador Niccolini has informed Galileo that he may be sent from Siena to the Certosa of Florence—a vast hilltop monastery south of the city—for further rehabilitation before being allowed to go home.

The pope's sister-in-law is Costanza Barberini, the mother of Francesco Cardinal Barberini.

dire che mi sono alterata da ver da vero, ma però di quella adirazione alla quale ci esorta il santo re David in quel salmo ove dice *Irascimini a nolite peccare*; perchè mi par quasi quasi che V. S. inclini a creder che più sia per rallegrarmi la vista del presente che di lei medesima: il che è tanto differente dal mio pensiero, quanto sono le tenebre dalla luce. Può esser che io non habbia inteso bene il senso delle sue parole, e per questo mi acqueto, chè altrimenti non so quel ch'io dicessi o facessi. Basta: V. S. vegga pure se può venirsene al suo tugurio, che non può star più così derelitto, a massimamente adesso che si approssima il tempo di riempier le botti, le quali, per gastigo del male che hanno lo commesso in lasciar guastare il vino, si sono tirate su nella loggia e quivi sfondate, per sentenza de i più periti bevitori di questo paese, i quali notano per difetto assai rilevante quella usanza che ha V. S. di non le far mai sfondare, e dicono che adesso non posson patire e non hanno il sole addosso.

Hebbi li 8 d. del vino venduto, che ne ho spesi 3 in 6 staia di grano, acciò che, come rinfresca, la Piera possa tornare a far il pane; la qual Piera si raccomanda a V. S., e dice che se si potesse metter in bilancia il desiderio che ha V. S. del suo ritorno e quello che prova lei, sarebbe sicura che la bilancia di lei andrebbe nel profondo e quella di V. S. se n'andrebbe al cielo: di Geppo poi non bisogna ragionare. Il Sig.r Rondinelli ha questa settimana pagati li 6 d. a Vincenzio Landucci, et havuto due ricevute, una per il mese passato, l'altra del presente. Intendo che stanno bene lui et i figliuoli; quanto al lor governo, non so come si vadia, non l'havendo potuto spiare da nessuna banda. Mando altra pasta delle medesime pillole, e la saluto di tutto cuore insieme con le even the protection of great personages. While I was wandering lost in these schemes, and I saw in your letter, Sire, how you imply that one of the things that fans my desire for your return is the anticipation of seeing myself delighted by a certain present you are bringing, oh! I can tell you that I turned truly angry; but enraged in the way that blessed King David exhorts us in his psalm where he says, *Irascimini a nolite peccare.* Because it seems almost as though you are inclined to believe, Sire, that the sight of the gift might mean more to me than that of you yourself: which differs as greatly from my true feelings as the darkness from the light. It could be that I mistook the sense of your words, and with this likelihood I calm myself, because if you questioned my love I would not know what to say or do. Enough, Sire, but do realize that if you are allowed to come back here to your hovel, you could not possibly find it more derelict than it is, especially now that the time approaches to refill the casks, which, as punishment for the evil they committed in allowing the wine to spoil, have been hauled up onto the porch and there staved according to the sentence pronounced by the most expert wine drinkers in these parts, who point out as the primary problem your practice, Sire, of never having broken them open before, and these same experts claim the casks cannot suffer now for having had some sunshine upon their planks.

I received 8 *scudi* from the sale of the wine, of which I spent 3 on 6 *staia* of wheat, so that, as the weather turns cooler, La Piera may return to her bread baking; La Piera sends her best regards to you, and says that if she were able to weigh your desire to return against her longing to see you, she feels certain her side of the scale would plummet to the depths solite e il Sr Rondinelli. Nostro Signore la conservi. Di S. Matt.^{o} in Arcetri, li 20 di Agosto 1633.

Di V. S. molto Ill.^{re} Fig.^{la} Aff.^{ma}

Suor Maria Celeste

Amatiss.^{mo} Sig.^{r} Padre,

Sto con speranza che la grazia che V. S. (con quelle condizioni che mi scrive) ricerca di ottenere, gl'habbia a esser concessa, e mi par mill'anni di sentir la risposta che V. S. ne ritrarrà; sì che, di grazia, me lo avvisi presto, quando anco sortisse in contrario, il che pur non voglio credere.

Gli do nuova come, mediante la morte del Sig.^{r} Benedetto Parenti, che seguì mercoledì passato, il nostro monasterio ha ereditato un podere all'Ambrogiana, et il nostro proccuratore andò l'istessa notte a pigliarne il possesso. Da più persone haviamo inteso che è stimato di valuta di più di 5 mila scudi; e dicono che quest'anno vi si sono ricolte 16 moggia di grano, e vi saranno 50 barili di vino e 70 sacchi di miglio a altre biade, sì che il nostro convento resterà assai sollevato.

while yours would fly up to the sky: of Geppo there is no news worthy of mention. Signor Rondinelli this week has paid the 6 *scudi* to Vincenzio Landucci and has retained two receipts, one for last month, one for this: I hear that Vincenzio and the children are healthy, but as for their welfare I do not know how they are getting along, not having been able to inquire after them from a single person. I am sending you another batch of the same pills, and I greet you with all my heart together with our usual friends and Signor Rondinelli. May Our Lord bless you. From San Matteo in Arcetri, the 20th of August 1633.

Sire's Daughter,
Suor Maria Celeste

Most Beloved Lord Father,

I live with the hope that the favor you are seeking to obtain, Sire (under those conditions you wrote about) will be granted to you; and it seems to me to be taking a thousand years to hear what answer will be handed down, so that I beseech you to notify me immediately of the outcome even if it runs contrary to our wishes; though I surely do not want to believe anything else could go wrong.

I have news for you of how, through the death of Signor Benedetto Parenti, which occurred last Wednesday, our Monastery has inherited a farm at Ambrogiana, and our procurator went that very same night to take possession of it. Several people have estimated its value at more than five thousand scudi, and they also say that this year's harvest will

Benedetto Parenti, a cousin of Suor Clarice Burci, had inherited the farm from Suor Clarice's brother, Giannozzo, whose will stated that upon Benedetto's death, the property must go to Suor Clarice or, in the event of her death, to all the sisters of San Matteo.

Il giorno avanti che io ricevessi la lettera di V. S., Mess.r Ceseri s'era servito della muletta per andar a Fiesole, et Geppo mi disse che la sera la rimenò a casa tutta sferrata e mal condotta, sì che gl'ho imposto, che quando M.r Ceseri tornasse a domandarla, gli risponda con creanza, allegandoli la impossibilità della bestiuola e la volontà di V. S., che è che essa non si scortichi.

Sono parecchie settimane che la Piera non ha da lavorare per la casa; e perchè intendo che costà vi è abbondanza di lino buono, se è vero, V. S. potrebbe veder di comprarne qualche poco, che, se bene è sottile, sarà migliore per far pezzuole, federe e simil cose: et io desidero che V. S. mi provvegga un poco di zafferano per la bottega, del quale ne entra anco nelle pillole papaline, come havrà potuto vedere.

Non mi sento interamente bene, e per questo scrivo così a caso: mi scusi e mi voglia bene. A Dio, il quale sia quello che gli doni ogni consolazione. Di S. Matteo in Arcetri, li 27 di Agosto 1633.

Sua Fig.la Aff.ma
Suor M.a Celeste

yield 16 *moggia* of wheat along with 50 barrels of wine and 70 sacks of millet and other grains, so that my convent will be greatly relieved.

The day before I received the letter from you, Sire, Master Ceseri borrowed the little mule to go to Fiesole, and Geppo told me how that evening he brought her back to the house completely unshod and badly handled, so that I have enjoined Geppo, in the event Master Ceseri may return to request her again, to refuse him politely, alleging the orneriness of the little beast along with your desire, Sire, that she not be flayed alive.

Cesare Galletti is the father-in-law of Galileo's sister Livia.

For the past several weeks La Piera has had no needlework to do in the house, and if it is true what I hear that very good quality linen can be had where you are, Sire, you might see about buying a small quantity of it; for if it is indeed fine, it will be the best thing for making handkerchiefs, pillowcases and similar items: and I want you to procure me a bit of saffron for the apothecary, since it is called for in the formulation of the papal pills, as you will have noticed.

Saffron works as a cordial to stimulate the heart and also induces therapeutic sweating.

I am not feeling entirely well, and this accounts for my writing so disjointedly. I commend you to God, may He be the One to give you every consolation. From San Matteo, the 27th of August 1633.

Your Most Affectionate Daughter,

Suor M. Celeste

Amatiss.mo Sig.r Padre,

Il sentir ragionar di andar in campagna mi piace per la parte di V. S., sapendo quanto quell'abitazione gli sia utile e gustosa, ma mi dispiace per la parte nostra, vedendo che andrà in lungo il suo ritorno. Ma sia pur come si voglia; mentre che ella, per grazia di Dio benedetto, si conserva sana e lieta, tutti gl'altri accidenti son tolerabili, anzi si fanno soavi e gustosi con la speranza che tengo che da queste sue e nostre mortificazioni il Signor Iddio, come sapientissimo, sia per cavarne gran bene, per Sua pietà.

La disgrazia del vino è stata grande per V. S., e sto per dire maggiore per noi, che, perchè lei trovassi le botti ben condizionate, non ne haviamo mai bevuto un pocolino, e di quella che V. S. lasciò manomessa ne pigliammo poco, perchè presto prese il fuoco e non ci piaceva più, e quel poco di bianco, per aspettar troppo lungamente V. S., diventò aceto. Ve ne sono in casa 6 fiaschi dell'ultimo che si è venduto, che è ragionevole per la servitù: ve n'erano alcuni di quel primo che si levò via, che era diventato cattivo affatto, e non ho voluto che lo bevino; fino al nuovo bisognerà che lo comprino a fiaschi, e pre gherò il S.r Rondinelli che indrizzi Geppo ove possa andar a trovarne di quella sorte che sarà proporzionata per loro.

Per la muletta si è fatto provvisione di 3 migliaia di paglia bonissima, e si è pagata sette lire e quattro crazie il migliaio. Strame quest'anno non ce n'è stato, oltre che non sodisfà alla bestiolina.

Most Beloved Lord Father,

Hearing the discussion of your going into the countryside brings me pleasure for your sake, Sire, knowing as I do how much the rural lifestyle both suits and delights you, though I am sorry for us, seeing that your return will be further delayed: but may it all turn out as you wish, for as long as the grace of blessed God keeps you healthy and happy, all the other problems are tolerable, rather they become gentle and enjoyable with the hope I cherish that on account of these mortifications sent to you and to us by the Lord God, in His supreme wisdom, you stand ready to draw great good from them through His mercy.

The disgrace of the wine was a blow for you, Sire, and I am prepared to call it an even worse one for us, because, had you come upon well conditioned casks, we would never have come to drink a drop of their contents, and even from the one you left newly tapped we took very little, since it quickly grew too fiery to suit us, and that little of the white, after waiting too long for you, Sire, became vinegar: there are six flasks in the house left over from the wine we sold, and this is good enough for the servants: the remainder from the first cask was discarded because that wine had gone completely sour, and I did not want them to drink it: until your new vintage is ready they will need to buy wine by the flask, and I will implore Signor Rondinelli to direct Geppo where to go to find the variety most appropriate for them.

The little mule has been provided with three loads of extremely good straw, for which we paid seven *lire* and four

È un gran pezzo che havevo mandato il ragazzo a pigliar l'orivolo, ma il maestro non glielo volse dare, dicendo che voleva aspettare che V. S. tornasse. Hieri mandai di nuovo a dirgli che lo rimandassi in ogni maniera, e disse che bisognava prima rivederlo, che tornassi un altro giorno, e così si farà; e se per sorte non lo dessi, ordinerò al ragazzo che sia con il Sr Rondinelli.

Sig.^{r} padre, vi fo sapere che io sono una bufola assai maggiore di quelle che sono in coteste maremme, perchè, vedendo che V. S. mi scrive di mandar 7 uova di cotesto animale, mi credevo che veramente fussino vuova, e facevo disegno di far una grossa frittata, persuadendomi che fossero grandissime, e ne havevo fatta allegrezza con Sr Luisa, la quale non ha havuto poco da ridere della mia goffaggine. Domattina, che sarà domenica, il ragazzo andrà a S. Casciano a pigliar le bisacce, come V. S. ordina; in tanto gli rendo grazie per tutte le cose che ella dice di mandare.

Quando V. S. tornerà qua, non ci ritroverà il Sr Donato Gherardini, rettore di Sta Margherita a Montici e fratello della nostra Sr Lisabetta, perchè è morto due giorni sono, e ancora non si sa chi deva essergli successore.

Suor Polisena Vinta havrebbe desiderio di sapere se in alcuni sollevamenti che è fama che siano seguiti costà, vi interviene il Sr Cav.^{r} Emilio Piccolomini, figliuolo del capitan Carlo, che fu marito di una nipote della medesima Sr Polisena; la quale, per poter maggiormente raccomandarlo al Signore, desidera di saper da V. S. qualche verità, poi che molte cose che si dicono non si posson credere, nè stimar che sieno altro che bugie e favole del vulgo.

crazie each; fodder this year was simply unavailable, not to mention that it does not satisfy the dear creature.

A long time ago I sent the boy to retrieve the clock, but the maestro would not give it to him, saying that he wanted to wait until you came back, Sire; yesterday I sent word again to tell him to return it in any case, and he said that first he needed to look it over again, and so he will, and if perchance he should still not release it, I will order the boy to stop in with Signor Rondinelli.

Lord Father, I must inform you that I am a blockhead, indeed the biggest one in this part of Italy, because seeing how you wrote of sending me seven "buffalo eggs" I believed them truly to be eggs, and planned to make a huge omelette, convinced that such eggs would be very grand indeed, and in so doing I made a merry time for Suor Luisa, who laughed long and hard at my foolishness. Tomorrow morning, which will be Sunday, the boy will go to San Casciano to pick up the packages, as you ordered, Sire; meanwhile I offer my thanks for all the things that you say are in them.

"Buffalo eggs" are the egg-shaped lumps of mozzarella cheese made from water buffalo milk.

When you return here, Sire, you will not find Signor Donato Gherardini, rector of Santa Margherita and brother of our Suor Lisabetta, because he died two days ago, and as yet we do not know who will succeed him.

Suor Polissena Vinta had wanted to know if, among the several well-known relief efforts being undertaken where you are, any help has been forthcoming from Signor Cavalier Emilio Piccolomini, the son of Captain Carlo who was married to the neice of our same Suor Polissena; who, in order to

Procurai che le due lettere che mi mandò incluse fossero subito recapitate.

Altro non posso dirle, se non che quando ricevo sue lettere, subito lette torno a desiderare che giunga l'altro ordinario per haverne dell'altre, e particolarmente adesso che aspetto qualche avviso di Roma.

La Madre badessa, il Sr Rondinelli e tutte l'altre gli tornano dupplicate salute, et io da Dio benedetto gli prego abbondanza di grazie celesti. Di S. Matteo in Arcetri, li 3 di 7mbre 1633.

Sua Fig.^la Aff.^ma
Suor Mar. Celeste

Amatiss.^mo Sig.^r Padre,

Giovedì passato, et anco venerdì fino a notte, stetti con l'animo assai sospeso, vedendo che non comparivano sue lettere, non sapendo a che attribuirmi la causa di quel silenzio. Quando poi le ricevei, e che intesi che Monsr Arcivescovo era stato consapevole della mia goffaggine, non potei non arrossire, se bene dall'altra banda ho caro di haver dato a V. S. materia di ridere e rallegrarsi, chè per questo molte volte gli scrivo delle scioccherie.

be able to commend this man to the Lord in her prayers, wants to discover several facts through your help, Sire, since many things that are said of him are simply incredible; nor can one believe them to be aught but lies and fables spawned by rumor.

I made sure that the two letters you enclosed were forwarded immediately to their rightful recipients; more I cannot tell you if not that, when I receive your letters, I no sooner read them than I begin looking for another courier to come bearing still more of them, and especially now that I await certain words from Rome.

The Mother Abbess, Signor Rondinelli, and all the others return your regards doubled, Sire, and from Blessed God I pray that you receive an abundance of Heavenly grace. From San Matteo, the 3rd of September 1633.

Your Most Affectionate Daughter,
Suor Mar. Celeste

Most Illustrious Lord Father,

Last Thursday, and also Friday until nightfall, I stood with my soul in suspense, seeing that your letters were not going to arrive, not knowing to what cause I could arrogate that silence. When later I received them, and thus learned that Monsignor Archbishop was well aware of my gaffe regarding the buffalo eggs, I could not help but blush for shame, although on the other hand I am happy to have given you grounds for laughter and gladness, as it is with this motive I so often write to you of foolish things.

Ho consolata la Madre Vinta con la sicura nuova che V. S. dà del suo nipote; e quando ella intese il particolare soggiunto dal medesimo Monsignore circa l'haver delle carità, si risentì gagliardamente, dicendo che non solamente il Sr Emilio, ma l'istessa Sig.^{ra} Elisabetta sua madre, non la ricordano mai, e che ella crede che essi si persuadino che sia morta: e pure se sia bisognosa, V. S. lo sa, standο ella quasi del continuo in letto malata.

Hebbi le bisaccie, con tutte le robe che V. S. scriveva di mandare: dell'uova bufaline ne ho fatto parte all'amiche et al Sig.^{r} Rondinelli; il zafferano è bonissimo e più che a bastanza per le pillole, per le quali ho corretto intorno a 4 o 5 on. di aloè, che doverà esser assai buono, havendovi io tornato sopra sette volte il sugo di rose. La prima volta che torno a scrivere, che procurerò che sia avanti martedì, gli manderò della pasta che voglio far di nuovo oggi o domani, se il dolore di testa e di denti, che provo di presente, si mitigherà alquanto, chè per questo lascio di scrivere, e seguo di tenerla raccomandata al Signor Iddio, il quale sia quello che gli conceda vera consolazione. Di S. Matteo, li 10 di 7mbre 1633.

Di V. S. molto Ill.Fig.^{la} Aff.^{ma}

Suor Mar. Celeste

I have consoled Mother Vinta with the reassuring news you gave me of her great-nephew, Sire, and when she learned the details of that self-same magnanimous man's charitable acts, she became sorely resentful, saying that not only Signor Emilio but also his mother Elisabetta never give a thought or a penny to her, so that she believes they assume she must be dead: and yet you know how needy she is, Sire, being almost continuously sick in bed.

I received the bags with all the things that you wrote you were sending: the buffalo eggs I have shared with our friends here and also with Signor Rondinelli; the saffron was excellent and more than enough to make the pills, for which I have purified about 4 or 5 ounces of aloe, sure to be of the best quality for my having run it over the rose water seven times. The very next opportunity I have to write, which I will find before Tuesday, I will send you some of the preparation I want to make fresh today or tomorrow, provided that the headache and toothaches, which I endure at the moment, will ease enough, for now they force me to leave off writing, while I continue always to commend you to the Lord God as the One to grant you true consolation. From San Matteo, the 10th of September 1633.

Sire's Most Affectionate Daughter,

Suor Mar. Celeste

Amatiss.^{mo} Sig.^{r} Padre,

Pensavo pure di far una burla a V. S., facendole comparir costì il nostro Geppo all'improvviso; ma, per quanto intendo, il Sr Geri mi haverà prevenuta con avvisarglielo. Ho havuto questo desiderio da poi in qua che ella si trova in Siena; hier l'altro finalmente mi risolvei, e hieri, per mia buona sorte, andò un bando che contiene la libertà de i passi quasi per tutto lo Stato, che così mi avvisa il Sr Rondinelli, dicendo che nella sua non ne dà parte a V. S., perchè non si era ancora publicato quando egli la scrisse. Credo che ella vedrà volentieri il ragazzo, sì per haver sicure nuove di noi, come anco minuto ragguaglio della casa; e noi all'incontro havremo gusto particolare d'intendere il suo ben essere da persona che l'haverà veduta. Intanto V. S. potrà vedere se ha bisogno di qualcosa, ciò è di biancherie o altro, et avvisarlo, perchè haverò comodità di mandarle sicure.

Quanto alle botti, che è il principal capitolo della sua lettera al quale devo rispondere, avanti questa sera ne parlerò con Luca nostro lavoratore, e lo pregherò che vada a vederle e le procuri secondo che sarà di bisogno, perchè in questo negozio egli mi pare assai intendente.

Il zafferano, a Suor Luisa et a me ci par perfettissimo, e per conseguenza a buon mercato a 2 lire l'oncia, stante la sua bontà; e noi non l'haviamo mai havuto a così buona derrata, ma si bene a 4 giulii o 50 soldi.

Il lino di 20 crazie la lib. è buono, ma non credo che metta conto a pigliarne a questo prezzo per far tele dozzinali per la casa. Ne ho consegnato un mazzo alla Piera, dicendoli che lo

Most Beloved Lord Father,

I was thinking of playing a wonderful prank on you, Sire, which was to have our Geppo arrive unexpectedly on that distant doorstep; but, from what I understand, Signor Geri has foiled my plan by warning you all about it. I have had this wish ever since you got to Siena. Recently I resolved at last to carry it out, and yesterday by my good fortune a proclamation went into effect including the freeing of roadways all around the region, for so I am advised by Signor Rondinelli, who also told me he did not give away this fact in his letter, Sire, because the ruling had not yet been made public when he wrote to you. I believe that you will be happy to see the boy, to have trustworthy news of us, with an equally detailed report of the house, and we on the other hand shall be especially pleased to hear of your welfare from someone who will actually have seen you. Meanwhile you can take some time to determine your needs, be they linens or other items, and let him know, since I now have the means to send them safely.

Geri Bocchineri told Galileo, in a letter dated 16 September, that he had secured the health passes for Geppo and his father, Simone, to travel to Siena.

As for the wine casks, the main subject of your letter to which I must respond, I will speak of them with Luca our worker before this evening, and implore him to go see them and take care of whatever may need to be done, because he strikes me as quite well informed in these matters.

The saffron seems perfection itself to Suor Luisa and me, and quite a bargain at 2 *lire* per ounce, owing of course to your kindness; and we have never before had any of such good quality, even at 4 *giuli* and 50 *soldi.*

The linen at 20 *crazie* per pound is a good value, although I do not believe it pays to buy it at that price for making plain fili sottile; vedremo come riuscirà. È ben stupendo quell'altro di 4 giulii, e qua ci sono delle monache che l'hanno pagato fino a mezzo scudo la lib., di questa sorte. Se V. S. ce ne mandassi un altro poco, faremmo una tela di soggoli molto bella.

La Sig.ra Maria T. fu qui la settimana passata con la sua figliuola restata vedova, e mi disse che adesso più che mai desiderava il ritorno di V. S., ritrovandosi bisognosa del suo favore nell'occasione del rimaritar quella giovanetta, havendo la mira e il desiderio di darla ad un tale de i Talenti, con il quale non ha altro miglior mezzo che quello di V. S.; e se per lettere V. S. credessi di poterli dar qualche aiuto, ella lo desidererebbe. Tanto m'impose ella ch'io dovessi dirgli, e tanto le dico.

Gli mando buona quantità di pillole, quelle dorate, acciò le possi donare, e quelle in rotelle per pigliarne per sè quando ne ha bisogno.

Havrò caro di sapere se quelle poche paste che gli mando gli saranno gustate, non essendo riuscite a mia intiera sodisfazione, forse per il desiderio che ho che le cose che fo per lei siano di tutta quella esquisitezza che sia possibile, il che mai mi riesce. I morselletti di cedro (che son quelli che sono in fondo della scatola) per lo manco saranno troppo duri per lei, havendogli io fatti subito che V. S. venne a Siena, sperando di poterglieli mandar molto prima che adesso. Gli raccomando la scatola, perchè non è mia.

La nota delle spese che gli mando, questa volta importa più dell'altre; ma non si è potuto andar più ritirato. Almeno V. S. vedrà che Geppo ci fa honore con la sua buona cera, et ha cloths for the house; I gave a bundle to La Piera, telling her to spin it very fine; we will see how it turns out: that other for 4 *giuli* is indeed splendid, and several nuns here say they have paid up to half a *scudo* per pound for this type; if you could send us a little bit more of it, Sire, we will make some beautiful wimples.

Her Signora Maria Tedaldi was here last week with her widowed daughter, and she told me that now more than ever she longed for your return, Sire, finding herself in need of your help in the matter of remarrying that young woman, having the aim and desire to betrothe her to a certain member of the Talenti family with whom she has no better contact than through you, Sire, and if via a letter you thought you might be able to give her some assistance, she would like that a great deal; all this did she press me that I must convey to you, Sire, and thus do I tell you.

This is Maria Tedaldi, member of a family related to the Galilei by marriage.

I am sending you a large quantity of the golden pills so you can give some away, and the round ones for you to take yourself as you need them.

I will be very happy to know if these few cakes I send along conform to your liking, though they have not turned out to my entire satisfaction, perhaps because of my wish to have everything I make for you succeed to the highest possible standards of excellence, which rarely happens for me: the candied citron morsels (which are at the bottom of the box) will perhaps by now be too hard for you, as I made them immediately after you arrived in Siena, hoping to be able to send them much sooner than this: do please save the box because it is not mine.

penato assai a riaversi da quella malattia che ebbe. Le £ 7 che ho appuntate di elemosina, le detti per amor della Madonna Santissima la mattina della Sua natività ad una persona che si trovava in gran necessità, con condizione che si facessi orazione particolare per V. S.

Se ella se ne andrà alla villa, come spero, in compagnia di Monsignore, potrà con maggior facilità andar tolerando la lontananza del suo caro tugurio; sì che, di grazia, procuri di star allegramente, e se gli par che il tempo sparisca, come in una sua mi scrisse non è molto, spariranno anco presto presto questi giorni o settimane che ella deve ancora trattenersi costì, a maggiore sarà la sua a nostra allegrezza quando ci rivedremo.

Gli raccomando il buon ricapito di queste lettere, che sono di monache nostre amiche, le quali, insieme con la Madre badessa, Suor Arcangela e Sr Luisa, la salutano affettuosamente; et io prego Nostro Signore che gli conceda il compimento di ogni suo giusto desiderio. Di S. Matteo in Arcetri, li 18 di 7mbre 1633.

Di V. S. Fig.^la Aff.^ma
Suor Maria Celeste

Mi ero scordata di dirgli che Suor Diamante desidererebbe di sapere se costì vi è della tela da pezzuole, della sorte che è questa mostra: se ve ne fussi, vorrebbe che V. S. gli facessi servizio di farne comprar una pezza et avvisar il prezzo, che subito ella sodisfarà. Il prezzo ordinario suol esser un giulio, 10 crazie, o più, secondo che è sottile; ma adesso in Firenze non ce n'è.

The list of expenses I enclose this time is much higher than the others; but it was not possible to curtail our spending. At least you will see, Sire, that Geppo does us honor with his good complexion, and has made a great effort to recover from that sickness he had. The 7 lire that I have earmarked as alms I gave for love of the Most Holy Madonna the morning of her birth to someone who was in dire need, on the condition that she say certain prayers for you, Sire.

September 8 is the feast day of the Blessed Virgin Mary.

If you go off to the villa, as I hope, in the company of Monsignore, you will more easily be able to tolerate the remoteness of your own dear little hovel, so please do try to be cheerful, and if it seems to you that the time evaporates, as you wrote in one of your letters not long ago, so too, and very soon, it will take with it these days or weeks in which you must continue to stay on where you are, and then our mutual delight will be all the greater when we see each other again.

I urge you to guarantee the safe delivery of these accompanying letters, for they come from nuns who are our friends, who, together with the Mother Abbess, Suor Arcangela, and Suor Luisa, send you their loving regards; and I pray Our Lord to grant you the fulfillment of your every just desire. From San Matteo, the 17th of September 1633.

Sire's Most Affectionate Daughter,

Suor Maria Celeste

I had forgotten to tell you that Suor Diamante would like to know if you can find her some material for handkerchiefs of the sort that I enclose herewith: if so, she would like you to

Amatiss.mo Sig.r Padre,

Dovevo veramente subito doppo il ritorno di Giuseppo, che seguì hieri fece otto giorni a un'hora di notte, darne ragguaglio a V. S., non parendo verisimile che in tutti questi giorni io non habbia potuto rubar tanto tempo che bastassi a scriver 4 versi. E pur è così la verità, perchè, oltre alle occupazioni del mio offizio, che di presente sono molte, Suor Luisa ha travagliato così fieramente con il suo solito mal di stomaco, che nè per lei nè per le assistenti c'è stato mai requie il giorno e la notte; et a me in particolare si conviene per debito il servirla senza intermissione alcuna. Adesso che per il suo miglioramento respiro alquanto, do sodisfazione anco a V. S., dicendole che Geppo e suo padre tornorno qui sani e salvi insieme con la muletta, la quale veramente ricevè torto a esser menata in così lungo viaggio, et io mi assicurai con la sicurtà che mi fecero quelli che più di me la praticano: basta, ella sta bene.

Hebbi gusto grandissimo nel sentire le nuove che mi portò il ragazzo del buon esser di V. S., dicendomi che ella haveva miglior cera che quando si partì di qua; il che io credo facilmente, perchè giudico che le comodità, le cortesie e delizie che ha godute, prima in casa il S.r Ambasciatore in Roma, e do her the service of buying a piece, and advising her of the cost so she can repay you right away: the usual price near here would be one *giulio*, 10 *crazie*, or more, depending on the fineness; but now in Florence there is none to be had.

Most Beloved Lord Father,

I simply had to give you news of Giuseppe's return, Sire, as immediately as possible upon his arrival, which occurred yesterday after eight days' absence at the first hour of the night, for it did not seem credible that in this many days I had not been able to steal sufficient time to write you even four lines. Yet still that is the truth, because, beyond the duties of my office, which at present are numerous, Suor Luisa has suffered so fiercely with her familiar stomach pain, that neither she nor those attending her found a moment's rest day or night. And I especially felt compelled by duty to wait on her without a single intermission. Now that her improvement allows me to breathe somewhat, I will also pay my debt to you, Sire, telling you that Geppo and his father came home hale and hearty together with the little mule, who really was dealt a great injustice being led off on such a long journey; and I needed my anxiety allayed by the reassurances of those who know her better than I do. But enough of that, she is fine.

I took the greatest delight in hearing the news the boy brought me of your well-being, Sire, as he told me you looked better than when you left here; which I can easily believe, because I judge that the comfort, the courtesy and charms di presente gode costì da quell'Ill.^{me} Monsr Arcivescovo, siano state potenti a mitigare, anzi annullare quasi del tutto, l'amarezza di quei disgusti che ha passati, e per conseguenza non ne habbia sentito nocumento alcuno. Et hora in particolare come non potrà V. S. non benedir questa carcere? e stimar felicissima questa ritenzione? mediante la quale se gli porge occasione di goder tanto frequentemente e con tanta familiarità la conversazione di prelato tanto insigne e signore tanto benigno? Il quale, non contento di esercitar nella persona di V. S. tutti quelli ossequii che si possono desiderar maggiori, per far un eccesso di cortesia e gentilezza, si è compiaciuto di favorir ancor noi poverelle con affettuose parole et amorevolissime dimostrazioni, per le quali non dubito che V. S. gl'habbia rese per nostra parte le dovute grazie: onde non replico altro, se non che havrei desiderio che V. S., facendole humilissima reverenza in nome nostro, l'assicuri che con l'orazioni procuriamo di renderci grate e tante grazie.

Quanto al suo ritorno, se seguirà conforme alla sua speranza a nostro desiderio, non seguirà se non in breve. In tanto gli dico che le botti per il vino rosso sono accomodate; e quella in particolare ove stette il vino guasto, è bisognato disfarla a ripulirla molto bene. Per il vino bianco il Sig.^{r} Rondinelli ne ha vedute 3 the sono bonissime; una fra l'altre ve n'è ove l'anno passato vi era il greco, del quale se ne sono cavati non so se 4 o 5 fiaschi assai forte (per quanto intendo), et ancora vi resta il fondo, acciò la botte non resti in secco: e dice il Sr Rondinelli the basta that you have enjoyed, first in the house of his lordship the Ambassador in Rome, and now at the home of that most illustrious Monsignor Archbishop, have been pleasantly powerful enough to mitigate almost all the bitterness of those distasteful events now past, and for this reason you have not felt any harm. And now in particular, how could you not bless this prison you inhabit, and deem your detention a most felicitous one? especially if it affords you the opportunity to enjoy even more frequently and with ever greater intimacy the conversation of such a renowned prelate and such a benevolent gentleman? And they, not content to exercise all the kind regards that one could most desire upon your person, Sire, take it upon themselves to also favor us poor nuns with affectionate words and the most loving demonstrations, for which I do not doubt you have rendered them due thanks on our behalf: wherefore I will not repeat them, except that I would like you, Sire, offering them the most humble reverence in our names, to assure them that with our prayers we will ever endeavor to render ourselves grateful for all these favors.

As for your homecoming, if all conforms to your hope and our desire, it will surely happen soon. Meanwhile I tell you that the casks for the red wine are all ready, even including the one that held the spoiled wine, though it had to be taken apart and cleaned with particular care: for the white wine Signor Rondinelli has seen that 3 casks are in extremely good condition, while there is one among the others that last year held the Greek wine, from which they drew I think 4 or 5 flasks' worth with a very strong taste, as I understand; and dar a tutte una lavata, avanti che vi si metta il vino, chè nel resto sono eccellentissime.

La Madre badessa la ringrazia infinitamente del zafferano, et io de gl'altri regali, cioè lino, lepre e pan di Spagna, il quale è veramente cosa esquisita.

Consegnai a Geppo la corona e i calcetti per la sua cugina.

Il Sig.r Giovanni Ronconi, il quale vien qui molto spesso per visitar 5 ammalate che haviamo tenute un pezzo, e tutte con la febbre, mi disse l'altro giorno che non credeva che io havessi mai fatte a V. S. sue raccomandazioni; et io gli risposi che pur le havevo fatte, e così ho in fantasia che sia stato al meno una volta. È ben vero che sono stata balorda in non rendergliele mai da parte di V. S., onde la prego a farmi grazia di supplire a questo mio mancamento con scrivergli due versi e mandarmeli, chè potrò io inviarglieli, già che ho ogni giorno occasione di tenerlo ragguagliato di queste ammalate; e certo che egli non c'è mai stato una volta, che non mi habbia domandato di V. S. e mostrato gran passione de i suoi travagli.

Haverei voluto poter indovinar il bisogno di V. S. quanto a i danari, per haverglieli potuti mandare; credo però che a quest' hora gli saranno pervenuti quelli che gli manda il Sig.r Alessandro, per quanto ho compreso da una lettera che V. S. gli scrive et egli mi ha mandata in cambio di quella che anco a me si perveniva questa settimana, che forse V. S. non mi ha mandata per vendicarsi che non ho scritto a lei: ma ha sentito la causa; et hora gli dico e Dio a do la buona notte, della since some wine still remains at the bottom, the cask has not had a chance to dry; Signor Rondinelli says it will be well to give them all a good cleaning before putting any wine inside, but they are otherwise excellent.

The Mother Abbess thanks you profusely for the saffron and I for the other gifts, namely the linen, the hare, and the Spanish bread, which is truly delicious.

I will have Geppo deliver the rosary and the slippers for your cousin.

Doctor Giovanni Ronconi, who comes by very often to visit five nuns who have been sick for some time now, all suffering from the fever, told me the other day that he did not believe I had ever given you his regards, Sire, and I answered him that indeed I had done so, and at least in my imagination this took place more than once. It is very true that I was delinquent in never conveying your regards, Sire, to him, wherefore I pray you to do me the favor of making good my error, by writing him two lines and sending them to me, so that I will be able to forward them to him, since I have occasion every day to give him a report of these feverish patients, and truly he has never once been here that he has not asked after you and shown great compassion for your troubles.

I would have liked to have been able to gauge your need, Sire, in terms of money, so as to be able to send you the right amount; I believe however that by now you have already received a sum sent by Signor Alessandro, as I understood from a letter you wrote to him, and which he sent me to stand quale è appunto passata la metà. Di S. Matteo in Arcetri, il p.mo di 8bre 1633.

Sua Fig.la Aff.ma

Suor M.a Celeste

Amatiss.mo Sig.r Padre,

Sabato scrissi a V. S., e domenica, per parte del Sig.r Gherardini, mi fu resa la sua, per la quale sentendo la speranza che ha del suo ritorno, tutta mi consolo, parendomi ogn'hora mill'anni che arrivi quel giorno tanto desiderato di rivederla; et il sentire che ella si ritrovi con buona salute, accresce e non diminuisce questo desiderio, di goder duplicato contento e sodisfazione, per vederla tornata in casa sua e di più con sanità.

Non vorrei già che dubitassi di me, che per tempo nessuno io sia per lasciar di raccomandarla con tutto il mio spirito a Dio benedetto, perchè questo mi è troppo a cuore e troppo mi preme la sua salute spirituale a corporale. E per dargliene qualche contrassegno, gli dico che ho procurato e ottenuto grazia di vedere la sua sentenza, la lettura della quale, se bene per una parte mi dette qualche travaglio, per l'altra hebbi caro di haverla veduta, per haver trovato in essa materia di poter giovar a V. S. in qualche pocolino, il che è con in for the one that was to have reached me this week, and that perhaps you did not send me as revenge for my not writing you; but now you have heard the reason: and here I bid you farewell and wish you a good night, of which precisely half has already passed. From San Matteo in Arcetri, the first of October 1633.

Your most affectionate daughter,

Suor M. Celeste

*Alessandro Bocchineri is Geri's and Sestilia's brother. (On September 24, following instructions from Geri, who had gone to Poppi to visit Vincenzio and Sestilia, Alessandro sent Galileo the sum of 50 **scudi** he had requested for paying tithes and taxes pertaining to his Florentine citizenship and real estate.)*

Most Beloved Lord Father,

Saturday I wrote to you, Sire, and Sunday, thanks to Signor Gherardini, your letter was delivered to me, through which, learning of the hope you hold out for your return, I am consoled, as every hour seems a thousand years to me while I await that promised day when I shall see you again; and hearing that you continue to enjoy your well-being only doubles my desire to experience the manifold happiness and satisfaction that will come from watching you return to your own home and moreover in good health.

Niccolò Gherardini, a young follower (and later biographer) of Galileo, is related to Suor Elisabetta.

I would surely not want you to doubt my devotion, for at no time do I ever leave off commending you with all my soul to blessed God, because you fill my heart, Sire, and nothing matters more to me than your spiritual and physical well-being. And to give you some tangible proof of this concern, I tell you that I succeeded in obtaining permission to view your sentence, the reading of which, though on the one hand it grieved me wretchedly, on the other hand it thrilled me to

Galileo's sentence was read aloud to all the mathematicians and philosophers in Florence on August 12, and Mario Guiducci obtained a copy of it.

l'addossarmi l'obligo che ha ella di recitar una volta la settimana li Sette Salmi; et è già un pezzo che cominciai a sodisfare, e lo fo con molto mio gusto, prima perchè mi persuado che l'orazione, accompagnata da quel titolo di obedire a S.ta Chiesa, sia assai efficace, e poi per levar a V. S. questo pensiero. Così havess'io potuto supplire nel resto, chè molto volentieri mi sarei eletta una carcere assai più stretta di questa in che mi trovo, per liberarne lei. Adesso siamo qui, e le tante grazie già ricevute ci danno speranza di riceverne dell'altre, pur che la nostra fede sia accompagnata dalle buone opere, chè, come V. S. sa meglio di me, *fides sine operibus mortua est.*

La mia cara Suor Luisa continua di star male, e mediante i dolori e tiramento che ha dalla banda destra, dalla spalla fino al fianco, non può quasi mai star in letto, ma se ne sta sopra una sedia giorno e notte. Il medico mi disse l'ultima volta che fu a visitarla, che dubitava che ella havessi una piaga in uno argnione; chè se questo fossi, il suo male saria incurabile. A me più d'ogn'altra cosa mi duole il vederla penare senza poterli dar alcuno aiuto, perchè i rimedii non gl'apportano giovamento.

Hieri s'imbottorno li 6 barili del vino dalle Rose, e ve n'è restato per riempier la botte. Il Sig.r Rondinelli fu presente, sì come anco alla vendemmia dell'orto, e mi disse che il mosto bolliva gagliardamente, sì che sperava che volessi riuscir buono, ma poco; non so già ancora, quanto per l'appunto. Questo è quello che per hora così in fretta posso dirgli. La have seen it and found in it a means of being able to do you good, Sire, in some very small way; that is by taking upon myself the obligation you have to recite one time each week the seven psalms, and I have already begun to fulfill this requirement and to do so with great zest, first because I believe that prayer accompanied by the claim of obedience to Holy Church is effective, and then, too, to relieve you of this care. Therefore had I been able to substitute myself in the rest of your punishment, most willingly would I elect a prison even straiter than this one in which I dwell, if by so doing I could set you at liberty. Now we have come this far, and the many favors we have already received give us hope of having still others bestowed on us, provided that our faith is accompanied by good works, for, as you know better than I, Sire, *fides sine operibus mortua est.*

As part of his penance, Galileo was ordered by the Holy Office to recite the seven penitential psalms (6, 32, 38, 51, 102, 130, and 143) once a week for three years.

"Faith without works is lifeless."

My dear Suor Luisa continues to fare badly, and because of the pains and spasm that afflict her right side, from the shoulder to the hip, she can hardly bear to stay in bed, but sits up on a chair day and night: the doctor told me the last time he came to visit her that he suspected she had an ulcer in her kidney, and that if this were her problem it would be incurable; the worst thing of all for me is to see her suffer without being able to help her at all, because my remedies bring her no relief.

Yesterday they put the funnels in the six barrels of rose wine, and all that remains now is to refill the cask. Signor Rondinelli was there, just as he also attended the harvesting saluto affettuosamente per parte delle solite, et il Signore la prosperi. Di S. Matteo in Arcetri, li 3 di 8bre 1633.

Di V.S. molto Ill.re Fig.la Aff.ma

Suor M.a Celeste

Amatiss.mo Sig.r Padre,

Il Sig.r Rondinelli, che rivedde le botticelle da vino bianco, mi disse che ve ne erano tre bonissime, come avvisai a V. S., et interrogato da me della loro tenuta, mi replico che questo non occorreva ch'io l'avvisassi, perchè V. S. poteva a un dipresso saperlo; mi disse bene esservene dell'altre, ma che non si assicurava a dirmi che fossero di tutta bontà. Questa settimana poi egli non è potuto venir qua su, onde nè anco si è potuto far nuova diligenza; ma ne ho fatta io una che non credo che le spiacerà, et è questa: the nella nostra volta sono 3 o 4 botti, una di 6, una di 5 e l'altre di 4 barili, le quali ogn'anno si sogliono empier di verdea; ma perchè quest'anno non se n'è fatta punta, le ho incaparrate per V. S., perchè son sicura che son buone, con autorità di mandarle nella sua cantina, acciò che quivi si possino empiere quando ella manderà il vino, e lasciarvelo fino che ella sia in persona a travasarlo a suo modo, o lasciarvelo tutto l'anno, se gli parrà. V. S. per tanto potrà rispondermi il suo pensiero. Il vino da San of the grapes, and told me that the must was fermenting vigorously so that he hoped it would turn out well, though there is not a lot of it; I do not yet know exactly how much. This is all that for now in great haste I am able to tell you. I send you loving regards on behalf of our usual friends, and pray the Lord to bless you.   From San Matteo in Arcetri, the 3rd of October 1633.

Sire's Most Affectionate Daughter,

Suor M. Celeste

Most Beloved Lord Father,

Signor Rondinelli, who inspected the kegs of white wine again, told me there were three extremely good ones, as I notified you, Sire, and then, when I questioned him about their capacity, he replied that I had no need to inform you about this, because you already knew roughly what that was: he assured me there were additional kegs, but that he did not feel he could promise them to be of the same quality: this week he has not been able to come up here, nor has it been possible for him, on that account, to make another new assessment; but I have made one myself which I do not think will displease you, and it is this, that in our cellar are 3 or 4 casks of various sizes, one of 6, one of 5 and the other of 4 barrels in capacity, which every year we fill with our white verdea wine, as is our custom, but because this year we did not make even one drop of it, I have reserved them for you, Sire, because I am certain they are sound, with the authority to deliver them to your wine cellar so they can be filled there when

Miniato al Todesco non è ancora comparso: di quello prestato se ne è riavuto in tanto un barile da questi contadini, e si è messo nella botte ove stette quel guasto, la qual botte si è fatta prima accomodare. Quello dell'orto non è ancora svinato. Al fabbro il S.r Rondinelli, pregato da me, ne passò una parola circa 3 barili che deve renderne, e ne riportò buone promesse.

La ricevuta delle 6 forme di cacio, non la tacqui nel mio linguaggio, che, per esser molto rozzo, V. S. non poteva intenderlo, poi che io hebbi intenzione di comprenderla, o per meglio dire ammetterla, nel ringraziamento che gli dicevo desiderare che ella facessi per nostra parte a Mons.r Arcivescovo, dal quale V. S. mi scrisse che veniva il regalo. Similmente l'uuova bufaline le veddi, ma sentendo che erano porzione di Geppo e di suo padre, glie le lasciai, e non replicai altro. Ero anco adunque in obligo di accusar la ricevuta del vino eccellentissimo che ne mandò Monsignore, del quale quasi tutte le monache assaggiorno; e Suor Giulia in particolare ha fatte con esso la sua parte di zuppe.

La ringrazio anco della lettera che mi mandò per il S.r Ronconi, la quale, doppo di haverla letta con molto mio gusto, fermai e presentai in propria mano hiermattina, e fu ricevuta molto cortesemente.

Ho caro di sentire il suo buono stato di sanità e quiete di mente, e che si trovi in occupazioni tanto proporzionate al gusto suo quanto è lo scrivere: ma, per l'amor di Dio, non siano materie che habbiano a correr la fortuna delle passate e già scritte!

you send the wine, and for the wine to be left in those casks until you can decant it yourself in your own way, or for the entire year, if that seems best: you can in any event let me hear your thoughts on all this. The wine from San Miniato has not yet been distributed: in return for the wine we gave away, meanwhile, we have recovered one barrel from the farmers here, and had it put into the cask which formerly held that spoiled wine; which cask was of course first set to rights; the wine from your vines has not yet been drawn from the fermenting vat: at my behest, Signor Rondinelli had a word with the blacksmith about the 3 barrels that he owes us, and brought back his solemn promise on that score.

It was not that I kept silent about the receipt of the 6 wheels of cheese, Sire, but rather that my language, for being very coarse, must have escaped your comprehension, since I had every intention of including you, or to say it better, acknowledging you, in the thanks that I said I wanted you to extend on our behalf to Monsignor Archbishop, from whom you wrote that the gift had come. I meant to do the same in regard to the buffalo eggs, but, assuming they were intended for Geppo and his father, I left the whole lot to them, and said no more about it. I should also have thanked you for the most excellent wine that Monsignore sent us, which almost every one of the nuns has tasted, and Suor Giulia made her portion into a soup.

I thank you, too, for the letter you sent me for Doctor Ronconi, which, after having read it myself with great pleasure, I sealed and delivered into his hands yesterday morning, where it was received most courteously.

Desidero di sapere se V. S. gode tuttavia la conversazione di Mons.re Arcivescovo, o pure se egli se n'è andato alle ville, come mi disse Geppo che haveva inteso che doveva seguire; il che mi persuado che a lei saria stata non piccola mortificazione.

Suor Luisa si trattiene in letto fra medici e medicine, ma i dolori sono alquanto mitigati, con l'aiuto del Signor Iddio; il quale a V. S. conceda la Sua santa grazia. Rendo le salute in nome di tutte, e le dico a Dio. Di S. Matt.o in Arcetri, li 8 di 8bre 1633.

Sua Fig.la Aff.ma

S.r Mar. Celeste

La Piera in questo punto mi ha detto che il vino dell'orto sarà un barile e 2 o 3 fiaschi, e che fa disegno di mescolarlo con quello che si è ricevuto, perchè da per sè è molto debole. Quello di S. Miniato si aspetta oggi, chè così ha detto il servitore del S.r Niccolò fino hierlaltro, et io adesso l'intendo.

I am delighted to hear of your good health and peace of mind, and that your pursuits are so well suited to your tastes, as your current writing seems to be, but for love of God may these new subjects not chance to meet the same luck as past ones, already written.

*Galileo is working on a new book (**Discourses and Mathematical Demonstrations Concerning Two New Sciences**), even though he may not be allowed to publish again.*

I want to know if you are still enjoying the conversation of Monsignor Archbishop, or if he has gone off to the villa, as Geppo told me he had heard would happen; an event that I feel certain would have caused you considerable mortification.

The Monsignor had invited Galileo along with him on this trip, but Roman authorities apparently refused him permission to go.

Suor Luisa remains in bed surrounded by physicians and physics, but the pains are somewhat mitigated with the help of the Lord God, whom I pray, Sire, to grant you His holy grace. I give you greetings from everyone here, and I commend you to God. From San Matteo in Arcetri, the 8th of October 1633.

Your Most Affectionate Daughter,

S. Mar. Celeste

La Piera has just this moment told me that the wine from your vines will amount to one barrel and 2 or 3 flasks, and that she plans to mix it with that from the local farmers, because by itself it is very weak: the San Miniato wine is expected today, or so the servant of Signor Niccolò said up till the day before yesterday, and now I believe him.

Niccolò Aggiunti sends the wine from nearby San Miniato, near Pisa, where he chairs the mathematics department.

Amatiss.mo Sig.r Padre,

Il vino da S. Miniato non è ancora comparso, et io lo scrissi 3 giorni sono al S.r Geri, il quale mi rispose che havrebbe procurato d'intender dal S.r Aggiunti la causa di questa dilazione. Non ho per ancora saputo altro, perchè questa settimana non ho havuta la comodità di mandar Geppo a Firenze, essendo egli stato, et è ancora, a S. Casciano da Mess.r Giulio Ninci, il quale già sono molti giorni che si ritrova ammalato, e perchè ha carestia di chi gli porga una pappa, mandò a ricercarmi, lui a Mess.r Alessandro, che per qualche giorno io gli concedessi l'assistenza del ragazzo, al che non ho saputo disdire.

Ho sentito il vino delle Rose, e mi par bonissimo: quando il S.r Cano to nico manderà a pigliar i danari, sodisfarò conforme allordine di V. S.

Il Sig.r Gherardini fu qui pochi giorni sono per visitar S.r Elisabetta sua parente, e fece chiamar ancor me per darmi nuove di V. S. Dimostra di esserle restato affezionato grandemente; e. mi disse che da poi in qua che ha parlato con lei è restato con l'animo quieto, dove che prima era tutto sospeso e irresoluto ne i suoi affari. Piaccia pur a Dio benedetto che il termine destinato al ritorno di V. S. non vadia più in lungo di quello che speriamo, acciò ella possa godere, oltre alla quiete della sua casa, la conversazione di questo giovane così compito.

Ma in tanto io godo infinitamente di sentire quanto Mons. Arcivescovo sia perseverante in amarla e favorirla. Nè dubito

Most Beloved Lord Father,

The wine from San Miniato has still not arrived, and so I wrote three days ago to Signor Geri, who responded that he would try to learn from Signor Aggiunti the cause of this delay. I have not heard anything more as yet, because this week I have missed the opportunity to send Geppo to Florence, as he was, and still is, at San Casciano with Master Giulio Ninci, who fell ill many days ago, and because there was no one to care for him, Master Alessandro sought me out to ask if I would grant them our boy's help for a while, which request I knew not how to deny.

This is Alessandro Ninci, cousin of the ill Giulio.

I have tasted the Rose wine. When the Canon sends someone to collect the money for the wine, I will carry out your orders, Sire.

Signor Gherardini was here recently to visit his relative, Suor Elisabetta, and had me called as well to give me news of you, Sire. He shows himself to be enormously fond of you; and he told me that ever since he spoke to you peace has entered his heart, which formerly had been ruled by uncertainty and anxiety over your trials. May it please Blessed God that the final decree regarding your return does not postpone it longer than we hope, so that you may enjoy, in addition the comfort of your own home, the conversation of this impressively accomplished young man.

But meanwhile I take endless pleasure in hearing how ardently Monsignor Archbishop perseveres in loving you and favoring you. Nor do I suspect in the slightest that you are punto che ella sia depennata, com'ella dice, *de libro viventium*, non solo nella maggior parte del mondo, ma nè anco nella medesima sua patria; anzi che mi par di sentire che se ella fossi stata qualche poco ombreggiata o cancellata, adesso ella sia restata ristaurata e rinovata, cosa che mi fa stupire, perchè so che, per un ordinario, *Nemo proféta accettus est in patria sua* (non so se per voler slatinare dirò qualche barbarismo), e pure V. S. è anco qua amata e stimata più che mai. Di tutto sia lodato il Signor Iddio, dal quale principalmente derivano queste grazie; le quali riputando io mie proprie, non ho altro desiderio che di esserne grata, acciò che S. D. M. resti servita di concederne dell'altre a V. S. et a noi ancora, e sopra a tutte la salute e beatitudine eterna.

Suor Luisa se ne sta in letto con un poca di febbre, ma i dolori sono assai mitigati, e si spera che sia per restarne libera del tutto con l'aiuto di buoni medicamenti, li quali, se non sono soavi al gusto come è il vino di costì, in simili occorrenze sono utili e necessarii.

Subito che veddi le 6 forme di cacio, ne destinai la metà per V. S., ma non glielo scrissi, perchè desideravo di riuscire più a fatti che a parole: e veramente che è cosa esquisita, et io ne mangio un poco più del dovere.

Mandai la lettera a Tordo per il nostro fattore, il quale intese dalla moglie che egli si ritrova all'ospedale a pigliar il legno, sì che non è meraviglia che non gl'habbia mai dato risposta.

Ho sempre havuto desiderio di sapere come siano fatte le torte sanese, che tanto si lodano; adesso che si avicina l'Ognisanti V. S. haverà comodità di farmele vedere, non dico gustare per crossed out, as you say, *de libro viventium*, certainly not throughout most of the world, and not even in your own country: on the contrary it seems to me from what I hear that while you may have been eclipsed or erased very briefly, now you are restored and renewed, which is a thing that stupefies me, because I am well aware that ordinarily: *Nemo proféta accettus est in patria sua* (I fear that my wanting to use the Latin phrase has perhaps made me utter some barbarism). And surely, Sire, here at the convent you are also beloved and esteemed more than ever; for all this may the Lord God be praised, as He is the principal source of these graces, which I consider my own reward, and thus I have no other desire but to show gratitude for them, so that His Divine Majesty may continue to concede other graces to you, Sire, and to us as well, but above all your health and eternal blessing.

Galileo's name has not been dropped from "the book of the living."

"No one is accepted [as] prophet in his own country."

Suor Luisa is confined to bed with a slight fever, yet the pains have abated appreciably, and we hope that she will be freed of them completely with the help of good medicaments, which, if they are not as sweet to the taste as the wine you are drinking, under these circumstances they are more useful and necessary.

The moment I saw the 6 wheels of cheese, I allocated half of them to you, Sire, but I did not write as much to you because I wanted this to be a matter of action more than words: and truly the taste is something scrumptious, and I am eating a little more than I should.

I sent the letter to Tordo via our steward, who learned from the man's wife that he is in the hospital taking the wood cure, thus it is no wonder you have not heard a response from him.

Tordo is a craftsman who has made telescope lenses for Galileo.

The purification treatment by wood-drawn water typically takes thirty or forty days.

non parer ghiotta. Ha anco obligo (perchè me l'ha promesso) di mandarmi del refe di ruggine, con il quale vorrei cominciar qualcoserella per il ceppo di Galileino, il quale amo perchè intendo dal Sig.^{r} Geri che, oltre al nome, ha anco dello spirito dell'avolo.

Suor Polissena hebbe risposta della lettera che per mezzo di V. S. mandò alla Sig.^{ra} sua nepote, et anco hebbe uno scudo, del quale ringraziandola nell'inclusa, prega V. S. del buon ricapito e la saluta, come fanno Madonna e l'altre solite.

Il Sig.^{r} Rondinelli già sono 15 giorni che non si lascia rivedere, perchè, per quanto intendo, egli affoga in un poco di vino che ha messo in due botticelle che versano e lo fanno tribolare.

Ho detto alla Piera che faccia vangare nell'orto, acciò vi si possino seminar o, per meglio dire, por le fave.

Adesso è comparso qui un lavoratore del Sig.^{r} Niccolò Cini, il quale mi scrive 4 versi nella medesima lettera che V. S. scrive a lui, avvisandomi la valuta del vino, che sono £ 19 la soma e £ 2 per vettura, in tutto £ 59: e tanto ne ho date, havendo ancora scritto a S. S.^{ria} due versi per ringraziarla.

Altro per hora non mi occorre, anzi pur mi sovviene che desidero di sapere se il Sr Ronconi gl'ha dato risposta: chè se non l'ha data, voglio rimproverarglielo la prima volta che lo veggo. Il Signor Iddio sia sempre seco. Di S. Matt.^{o} in Arcetri, li 15 di 8bre 1633.

Di V. S. molto Ill. Fig.^{la} Aff.^{ma}

Suor M.ª Celeste

I have always wanted to know how to make those Sienese cakes that everyone raves about; now that All Saints' Day is approaching, you will have the occasion, Sire, to let me see them, I do not say "taste" them so as not to sound gluttonous: you are further obliged (because of the promise you made me) to send me some of that strong reddish linen yarn which I would like to use to start preparing some little Christmas gift for Galileino, whom I adore because Signor Geri tells me that, beyond being the namesake, the boy also has the spirit of his grandfather.

Suor Polissena received an answer to the letter you helped direct to her niece, Sire, and she also got a *scudo*, for which she thanks you in the enclosed: she prays for your eternal blessing, and sends you her regards, as do Madonna and our usual friends.

Signor Rondinelli has not shown his face here for a fortnight, because, from what I hear, he is drowning in a little wine which he had put in two kegs that are turning bad and giving him great grief.

I told La Piera to do some digging in the garden, so that she would be able to sow, or, to be more precise, set the broad beans.

A worker just arrived from Signor Niccolò Cini, who writes me four lines right on the same letter you wrote to him, Sire, informing me of the value of this wine, which was 19 *lire* per mule load and 2 *lire* for the carrying, 59 *lire* in all, and I remitted that amount. I have also written a short note to His Honor to thank him.

Niccolò Cini of Florence produces an excellent rosé wine.

Amatiss.mo Sig.r Padre,

Mercoledì passato fu qui un fratello del Priore di S. Firenze a portarmi la lettera di V. S. insieme con l'invoglietto del refe ruggine, il qual refe, rispetto alla qualità del filo che è grossetto, par un poco caro; ma è ben vero che la tintura, per esser molto bella, fa che il prezzo di 6 crazie la matassa sia comportabile.

Suor Luisa se ne sta in letto con qualche poco di miglioramento, et oltre a lei haviamo qua parecchie altre ammalate; che se adesso ci fossi il sospetto della peste, saremmo spedite. Una di queste è Suor Caterina Angela Anselmi, che fu badessa avanti a questa presente, monaca veramente veneranda e prudente e, doppo [*sic*] Suor Luisa, la più cara e intrinseca amica che io havessi. Questa sta assai grave: hier mattina si comunicò per viatico, e, per quanto apparisce, può durar pochi giorni; e similmente Suor Maria Silvia Boscoli, giovane di 22 anni, e, perchè V. S. se la rammemori, quella che si diceva esser la pìu bella che fossi stata in Firenze da 300 anni in qua. Questa corre il sesto mese che sta in letto

Nothing else weighs on me at the moment to tell you; rather I recall something I want to ask you, which is that I really must know whether Doctor Ronconi ever wrote back to you, for if he has not, I want to scold him about that the very next time I see him. May the Lord God be with you always. From San Matteo in Arcetri, the 15th of October 1633.

Sire's Most Affectionate Daughter,

Suor M. Celeste

Most Beloved Lord Father,

Last Wednesday a brother of the Priory of San Firenze came to bring me a letter from you along with the little package of russet linen yarn, which, considering the rather thick quality of the thread, seems somewhat expensive; but indeed the color of the dye, being very beautiful, makes the price of 6 *crazie* per skein appear more tolerable.

Suor Luisa stays in bed with only the slightest improvement, and in addition to her, several of the others are also sick, so that if we now faced any suspicion of plague we would be lost. Among the sick is Suor Caterina Angela Anselmi who was formerly our Mother Abbess, a truly venerable and prudent nun, and, after Suor Luisa, the dearest and most intimate friend I have ever had: she is so gravely ill that yesterday morning she received the Extreme Unction, and it appears that she has only a few days to live; and the same must be said for Suor Maria Silvia Boscoli, a young woman of 22 years, and you may recall, Sire, how people once spoke of her as the most beautiful girl to grace the city of Florence for 300 con febbre continua, che adesso dicono i medici esser divenuta etica, et si è tanto consumata che non si riconosce; e con tutto ciò ha una vivacitá a fierezza, particolarmente nel parlare, che dà stupore, mentre che d'hora in hora si sta dubitando che quel poco spirito (che par ridotto tutto nella lingua) si dilegui et abbandoni il già consumato corpo. È poi tanto svogliata, che non si trova niente che gli gusti o, per dir meglio, che lo stomaco possa ricevere, eccetto un poca di minestra di brodo ove siano bolliti sparagi salvatichi secchi, dei quali in questa stagione se ne trovano alcuni pochi con gran difficultà: onde io andavo pensando se forse il brodo di starna, con quel poco di salvatico che ha, gli potesse gnstare; e già che costì ve ne sono in abbondanza, come V. S. mi scrive, potrebbe mandarmene qualcuna per lei e per S.r Luisa, chè quanto al pervenirmi ben condizionate non credo che ci fossi molta difficultà, già che la nostra S.r Maria Maddelena Squadrini hebbe a questi giorni alcuni tordi freschi e buoni, che gli furono mandati da un suo fratello, Priore del monasterio degl'Angeli, che è di Canonici Regolari, vicinissimo a Siena. Se V. S. potessi per mezzo nessuno far questo regalo, adesso che mi ha aguzzato l'appetito, mi sarebbe gratissimo.

Questa volta mi conviene esser il corvo con tante male nuove, dovendo dirle che il giorno di S. Francesco morì Goro, lavoratore de i Sertini; et ha lasciato una famigliuola assai sconcia, per quanto intesi dalla moglie, che fu qui hiermattina a pregarmi ch'io dovessi darne parte e V. S. a di ricordargli la promessa che V. S. fece al medesimo Goro et alla Antonia sua figliuola, cioè di donargli una gammurra nera quando ella si maritava. Adesso è alle strette, e domenica, che sarà domani, years: this marks the sixth month she has been lying in bed with a continuous fever that the doctors now say has turned to consumption, and she is so wasted as to be unrecognizable; yet with all that she retains a vivacity and energy especially in her speech that astounds us, while from hour to hour we doubt whether that faint spirit (which seems entirely confined to her tongue) will fade away and abandon the already exhausted body: then, too, she is so listless that we can find no nourishment to suit her taste, or to say it better, that her stomach can accept, except a little soup made from broth in which we have boiled some dried wild asparagus, and these are extremely difficult to find at this time of year, wherefore I was thinking that perhaps she could take some soup made from gray partridge, which has no gamy taste. And since these birds abound where you are, Sire, as you say in your letters, you might be able to send me one of them for her and for Suor Luisa, and I doubt you would encounter any difficulty having them reach me in good condition, since our Suor Maria Maddalena Squadrini recently received several fresh, good thrushes that were sent by a brother of hers who is Prior at the Monastery of the Angels, in part of the diocese very close to Siena. If, without too much trouble, Sire, you could help me make such a gift, now that the idea has whetted my appetite, I would be ever so grateful.

This time it devolves upon me to play the raven who bears bad tidings, as I must tell you that on the feast day of San Francesco, Goro, who worked for the Sertinis, died, and left a family in great distress, according to his wife who was here yesterday morning to beseech me that I must convey this news to you, Sire, and furthermore remind you of the promise

The feast day of San Francesco falls on October 4.

dice che si dirà in chiesa; e perchè ha consumati quei pochi danari che haveva, in medicamenti e nel mortorio, dice ritrovarsi in gran necessita, e desiderar di sapere se V. S. può farle la carità. Io gl'ho detto che gli farò sapere quanto V. S. mi risponderà.

Non saprei come darle dimostrazione dal contento che provo nel sentire che ella si va tuttavia conservando con sanità, se non col dirle che più godo dal suo bene che del mio proprio, non solamente perchè l'amo quanto me medesima, ma perchè vo considerando che se io mi trovassi oppressa da infirmità o pure fossi levata dal mondo, poco o nulla importerebbe, perchè a poco o nulla son buona, dove che nella persona di V. S. sarebbe tutto l'opposito per moltissime ragioni, ma in particolare (oltre che giova e può giovare a molti) perchè con il grande intelletto e sapere che gl'ha concesso il Signor Iddio può servirlo et onorarlo infinitamente più di quello che non posso io; sì che, con questa considerazione, io vengo ad allegrarmi e godere del suo bene che dal mio proprio.

Il. S.r Rondinelli si è lasciato rivedere, adesso che le sue botte si sono quietate. Rende le salute a V. S., e similmente il S.r Ronconi.

Assicuro V. S. che l'ozio non mi dà fastidio, ma più presto la fame, cagionata, credo io, non tanto dal molto esercizio che fo, quanto da freddezza di stomaco, che non ha il suo conto interamente del dormire il suo bisogno, perchè non ho tempo. Fo conto che l'oximele e le pillole papaline supplischino a questo difetto. In tanto gl'ho detto questo, per scusarmi di questa lettera che apparisce scritta molto a caso, you made to Goro himself and to Antonia his daughter, to give her a black woolen housedress when she got married: now they are in dire straits, and Sunday, which will be tomorrow, she will say her vows in Church; and because Goro's wife has spent what little money she had, first on medicaments and then for his funeral, she is hard pressed, and wants to know if you can do her this kindness: I promised that I would tell her your answer as soon as I heard from you, Sire.

I would not know how to make you realize the happiness I derive from learning that you continue conserving your health in spite of everything, except to say that I enjoy your good fortune more than my own, not only because I love you more than myself, but also because I can imagine that if I were oppressed by infirmity, or otherwise removed from the world it would matter little or nothing to anyone, since I am good for little or nothing, whereas in your case, Sire, the opposite holds true for a host of reasons, but especially (beyond the fact that you do so much good and are able to help so many others) because the great intellect and knowledge that the Lord God has given you enables you to serve Him and honor Him far more than I ever could, so that with this consideration I come round to cheer myself and take greater pleasure from your well-being than from mine.

Signor Rondinelli has allowed himself to be seen again now that his kegs have quieted down; he sends his greetings to you, Sire, and so does Doctor Ronconi.

I assure you that I am never vexed by boredom, Sire, but sooner by the hunger caused, I believe, if not by all the exercise I perform, then by the coldness of my stomach, which essendomi convenuto lasciare e ripigliar la penna più d'una volta avanti ch'io l'habbia condotta. E con questo gli dico a Dio. Di S. Matt.º in Arcetri, li 22 di 8bre 1633.

Sua Fig.la Aff.ma

Suor M.a Celeste

Conforme a che V. S. m'impone nell'altra sua, comparsami dopo che havevo scritto, scrivo alla S.ra Ambasciatrice. Non so se le tante occupazioni mi haveranno tanto cavato del seminato che io non habbia dato in nulla; V. S. vedrà e correggerà, e mi dica se gli manda anco il Crocifisso di avorio.

Spero pure che questa settimana V. S. haverà qualche resoluzione circa la sua spedizione, e sto ardendo di desiderio di esserne partecipe ancora io.

Amatiss.mo Sig.r Padre,

Ho tardato a scriver questa settimana, perchè desideravo pur di mandar gl'ortolani, de i quali finalmente non se ne trovano, e intendo che finirono quando cominciorno i tordi. Se pure io havessi saputo questo desiderio di V. S. alcune settimane in dietro, quando andavo pensando e ripensando a quello che gl'havessi potuto mandare che gli fossi grato! Padoes not get the full complement of sleep it requires, since I have no time. I rely on the oxymel and the papal pills to make up this deficit. I only tell you this to excuse myself for the haphazard appearance of my letter, as I was compelled to put down and then take up my pen again more than once before I could complete it, and on that note I commend you to God. From San Matteo in Arcetri, the 22nd of October 1633.

Your Most Affectionate Daughter,

Suor M. Celeste

The enclosed conforms to the wish you expressed in your previous letter, Sire, that after having written to you I should write also to Her Ladyship the Ambassadress. I suspect that my numerous activities have sapped my energy leaving me little to give her; you will be able to look it over and make corrections, and do let me know if you send her the ivory crucifix.

I still cling to the hope that this week you will have some resolution regarding your release, and I am burning with desire to share in that news.

Most Beloved Lord Father,

I delayed writing this week because I really wanted to send you the ortolans, but in the end none have been found, and I hear they fly away when the thrushes arrive. If only I had known this desire of yours, Sire, several weeks ago, when I was racking my brain trying to think of what I could possibly send you that might please you; but never mind! You have

These small birds are considered a delicacy at table.

zienza: ella è stata aventurata ne gl'ortolani, come fui io nelle starne, poi che feci fino smarrir l'astore.

Geppo tornò hieri da S. Casciano, e portò le due scatole, che V. S. mi ha mandate, ben condizionate: e già che da lei ne fui fatta assoluta padrona, mi sono prevalsa di questo titolo non mandandone altrimenti la metà alla Cognata, ma sì bene ne ho mandate 2 torte e due biricuocoli al Sig.r Geri, dicendoli che V. S. desiderava che ne partecipasse anco la sestilia; del restante ho havuto caro di farne parte al Sig.r Rondinelli, il quale si dimostra inverso di noi tanto amorevole e cordiale, et anco a molte amiche. Son cose veramente di gran bontà, ma anco di gran valore, chè per questo non sarei così pronta un'altra volta a far simil domanda, alla quale la liberalità di V. S. ha corrisposto quadruplicatamente; et io centuplicatamente ne la ringrazio.

Alla moglie di Goro ho fatto intendere il desiderio che V. S. ha di pareggiarsi con lei e farle la carità al suo ritorno: se poi essa tornerà a domandare, essequirò quanto V. S. ordina; et il simile farò a Tordo.

Il Ninci sta assai ragionevolmente di sanità, e sodisfattissimo dell'assistenza del nostro Geppo. Suor Luisa comincia a sollevarsi alquanto dal letto; Suor Caterina Angela si morì; la giovane si va trattenendo, ma in cattivo stato.

Il vino da S. Miniato non è venuto, credo io per esser stato il tempo molto piovoso, che per questo non si sono ancora poste le fave nell'orto, ma si porranno il primo giorno che sia bel tempo. Si è bon seminata lattuga e cavoli, et anco vi sono been unlucky in the ortolans, just as I was foiled by the gray partridges, because I lost them to the goshawk.

Geppo returned yesterday from San Casciano, and brought the two boxes that you sent me, both in good condition; and since you have made me absolute proprietress over them, I take full advantage of this title, not sending more than half the items to my sister-in-law, although I did give another two cakes and two apricots to Signor Geri, telling him that you intended these, too, to be shared with La Sestilia: of the remainder I simply had to offer a portion to Signor Rondinelli, who shows himself so caring and cordial toward the two of us, as well as to many of our friends: these are all truly generous gifts, but also very costly ones, so that I would not be quite so willing another time to make a similar demand, which your munificence, Sire, has met more than four times over, and for which I multiply my thanks a hundredfold.

I made Goro's wife aware of your wish, Sire, to settle with her and provide charity upon your return; if later she comes to ask again, I will carry out your orders, and I will do the same with Tordo.

Young Ninci has recovered his health reasonably well and expressed his great satisfaction with the assistance he received from our Geppo. Suor Luisa is beginning to rise fairly often from her bed; Suor Caterina Angela died; the young consumptive nun holds on, but in a bad state.

The wine from San Miniato has not come, probably detained by the heavy rains, the same reason the broad beans have not delle cipolle. I carciofi son belli; de i limoni ve ne sono comodamente, ma pochi aranci.

La muletta ha havuto un poca di scesa in un occhio, ma adesso sta bone; a similmente la Piera sua governatrice, la quale attende a filare et a pregar Iddio che V. S. torni presto: è ben vero che non credo che lo faccia tanto di cuore quanto lo fo io; se bene, mentre che sento che V. S. sta così bene, non so che mi dire, se non che il Signore corrisponde alla gran fede che ella ha nelle mie povere orazioni, o per meglio dire in una orazione che fo continua con il cuore, perchè con la voce non ho tempo. Non gli mando pillole, perchè il desiderio mi fa sperare che V. S. deva in breve venir da per sè a pigliarle: starò a sentire la resoluzione che ella haverà questa settimana. La commedia, venendo da lei, non può esser se non bella; fino a qui non ho potuto legger altro che il primo atto. Non mi manca materia da dire, ma sì bene il tempo; e per questo finisco, pregando Nostro Signore e la Madonna Santissima che siano sempre in sua compagnia, e la saluto caramente in nome delle solite. Di S. Matteo, l'ultimo di 8bre 1633.

Sua Fig.la Aff.ma

Suor M.a Celeste

been set in the garden, but they will be put in on the first day the weather turns fair; the lettuce and cabbage seeds have been sown, and there are also some onions; the artichokes are beautiful; of lemons we have an ample supply, though only a few oranges.

The little mule had some small discharge from one eye, but she is well now, as is La Piera her governess, who tends to the spinning and her praying to God that you come home soon, Sire: true as that is I cannnot believe she puts her heart into her praying as much as I do. Although, while I hear that you feel so well, Sire, I know not what to tell myself, if not that the Lord reciprocates according to the great faith you place in my poor prayers, or, to speak more precisely, in one single prayer that I utter continuously with my heart, because I do not have time to speak it aloud with my voice. I send you no pills because desire makes me hope that you must soon arrive here to claim them in person: I am all eagerness to hear the resolution that will reach you this week. The comedy, coming from you, can be nothing if not wonderful; but as yet we have not been able to read past the first act. I do not lack for matters to discuss with you, but I do lack the time; and for this reason I close here, praying Our Lord and the Most Holy Madonna to be always in your company, and I greet you lovingly in the name of our usual friends. From San Matteo, the last of October of 1633.

This play of unknown title may have been written by Galileo, or simply selected by him for performance at the convent—perhaps for the planned visit of the ambassadress.

Your Most Affectionate Daughter,

Suor M. Celeste

Amatiss.^{mo} Sig.^{r} Padre,

Se V. S. potessi penetrar l'animo et il desiderio mio come penetra i cieli, son sicura che non si lamenterebbe di me, come fa nell'ultima sua; perchè vedrebbe e si accerterebbe che io vorrei, se fossi possibile, ogni giorno ricever sue lettere et ogni giorno mandarne a lei, stimando questa la maggior sodisfazione ch'io possa dare e ricever da lei, fino che piacerà a Dio che ci possiamo goder di presenza. Credo non dimeno che da quelle poche ch'io gli scrivo così acciarpate, V. S. possa comprendere che sono scritte con molta strettezza di tempo, il quale sabato passato mi mancò affatto per poter mandarle il tributo debito; il che (sia detto con sua pace) ho caro che seguissi, perchè in quelle sue lamentazioni scorgo un eccesso di affetto dal quale son mosse, e me ne glorio. Supplii non dimeno la vigilia di Ogni Santi, mandando la lettera al Sig.^{r} Geri, la quale perchè credo che gli sarà pervenuta, non replico altro quanto a i quesiti ch'ella mi fa in questa ultima, se non quanto all'haver ricevuto il plico per Mess.^{r} Ipolito, il quale V. S. non mi ha mandato altrimenti, e quanto a Geppo, dicendole che egli, doppo che mi portò le scatole, non è tornato a S. Casciano, perchè il Ninci non haveva più bisogno di lui; tornerà ad ogni modo a rivederlo un giorno di questa prossima settimana.

La buona fortuna ha corrisposto al mio buon desiderio, facendomi trovar gl'ortolani che V. S. desiderava; et in questo punto consegnerò la scatola, dentrovi della farina, al ragazzo, dandoli commesione che vadia a pigliarli al serbatoio ch'è in Boboli, da un uccellatore del G. Duca che si chiama il Berna o il Bernino, dal quale gl'ho per grazia a una lira il paio; ma,

Most Illustrious Lord Father,

If only you were able to fathom my soul and its longing the way you penetrate the Heavens, Sire, I feel certain you would not complain of me, as you did in your last letter; because you would see and assure yourself how much I should want, if only it were possible, to receive your letters every day and also to send you one every day, esteeming this the greatest satisfaction that I could give to and take from you, until it pleases God that we may once again delight in each other's presence. I believe nonetheless that from those few lines I wrote you so hurriedly, Sire, you could gather that they were written in the most limited time available, as I had none at all last Saturday when I could render you your proper due; and I do have every good intention (if you will grant me this) of following through with that tribute, because in these lamentations of yours I descry an excess of affection that motivates them, and I glory in it. I did try nevertheless to make good during the vigil of All Saints' Day by sending you a letter via Signor Geri, and because I believe that one has already reached you, I will not reply extensively to the questions you pose in this last one, except to say I have received the packet for Master Ippolito, which you had not sent me previously: and as for Geppo, to tell you that, after he brought me the boxes, he did not return to San Casciano, because Il Ninci no longer needed him: he will go back there in any case to see him again one day this coming week.

Ippolito Francini is the real name of Tordo the lensmaker.

Good fortune has attended my ardent wish, enabling me to find the ortolans that you wanted, Sire, and I am just about to consign the box, with flour inside it, to the boy, commisper quanto mi dice il medesimo Geppo che hieri fu a vederli, sono bellissimi, et a'pollaiuoli intendo che vagliano fino in due giulii: il S.r Rondinelli poi per sua grazia ne favorirà di accomodargli nella scatola, perchè il ragazzo non havrebbe tempo di portarli qui e poi riportarli un'altra volta in giù, ma li consegnerà ad un tratto al Sig.r Geri. V. S. se li goda allegramente, e mi dica poi se saranno stati a sua sodisfazione. Saranno 20, com'ella desiderava.

Son chiamata all'infermeria, onde non posso dir altro se non che la saluto di cuore insieme con le solite raccomandate et in particolare di Suor Luisa, la quale sta assai meglio, Dio lodato. Il quale a V. S. conceda vera consolatione. Di S. Matt.o in Arcetri, li 5 di 9mbre 1633.

Sua Fig.la Aff.ma

Suor M.a Celeste

Amatiss.mo Sig.r Padre,

Guccio oste, qua nostro vicino, viene in coteste bande per suoi negozii, et io con questa occasione scrivo a V. S. questi pochi versi, dicendole che se nell'ultima ch'io gli scrissi mi lodavo della, fortuna che mi fece trovar gl'ortolani, i quali all'hora mi pareva di haver in pugno, adesso me ne lamento, sioning him to go and get them at the game preserve, which is in the Boboli Gardens, from a birdkeeper of the Grand Duke named Berna or Bernino, from whom I bought them as a favor at one *lira* the pair, but judging by what Geppo tells me after having seen them yesterday, they are quite beautiful and to buy them from the poulterer would cost as much as two *giuli*: Signor Rondinelli will then graciously do us the favor of packing them in the box, because the boy would not have time to carry them all the way up here and then back down again once more, but will deliver them straight away to Signor Geri. May you enjoy them happily, Sire, and then tell me whether they were to your liking: there will be 20 as you wished.

The Boboli Gardens lie immediately behind the Pitti Palace, home of the grand duke.

I am called to the infirmary, wherefore I cannot say another word except that I send you my love together with the usual regards from the others, and especially Suor Luisa who fares considerably better, God be praised, and may He grant you, Sire, every true consolation. From San Matteo, the 5th of November 1633.

Your Most Affectionate Daughter,
Suor M. Celeste

Most Beloved Lord Father,

Guccio the innkeeper, our neighbor here, comes to your vicinity to tend to business matters, and I seize the occasion to write you these few lines, Sire, telling you that if in my last letter I lauded the luck that made me find the ortolans, which I seemed at that moment to have in my grasp; now I lament perchè non volse che fossero il numero ch'io desideravo, sì come a quest'hora V. S. haverà veduto, et anco inteso dal Sig.^{r} Geri. La causa fu, perchè fra quelli che haveva il Berna non ve ne furono de i buoni altro che quegl'undici; e poi che Geppo haveva fatto l'errore di pigliar questi pochi, doppo haver io fatto cercar de gl'altri qui in paese et in Firenze, mi risolvei a mandarli, inanimita dal guardaroba qui del Poggio Imperiale, il quale disse che erano gran presente di questo tempo che non se ne trovano. Basta, V. S. accetterà se non altro la mia buona volontà.

Mess.^{r} Ipolito mandò per li 4 scudi, e glieli mandai subito.

Il vino da S. Miniato non comparisce. L'orto non si può ancora lavorare, chè è troppo molle. Il ragazzo è andato oggi a riveder il Ninci.

Suor Luisa sta meglio, ma non bene affatto: saluta caramente V. S., et il simile fanno Sr Arcangela, Madonna, Sr Cammilla et il suo babbo, il quale è un pezzo che non si è lasciato vedere mediante il cattivo tempo, ma scrive spesso. Nostro Signore la conservi. Di S. Matt.^{o}, li 7 di 9mbre 1633.

Sua Fig.^{la} Aff.^{ma}

Suor M.ª Celeste

that same luck for it did not land me the number I had wanted, as by now you will have seen for yourself, Sire, and also heard from Signor Geri: the reason was because among those that Il Berna had none were of good quality except for that group of eleven that we sent; and since Geppo had made the blunder of accepting these few, after I had searched for other sources around the countryside and in Florence, I resolved to send them to you, encouraged by the gamekeeper at the villa of the Poggio Imperiale, who said to consider them as grand gifts at this time of year now that they are so rare; enough: if nothing else, Sire, you will accept my good will.

The Poggio Imperiale, another of the seventeen Medici palaces, stands in Arcetri, not far from the convent.

Master Ippolito asked for the 4 *scudi*, and I sent them to him right away.

The wine from San Miniato has still not arrived. The garden cannot be worked, because it is too wet. The boy went today to look in on Il Ninci again.

Suor Luisa is better, but not entirely well; she greets you lovingly, Sire, and so do Suor Arcangela, Madonna, Suor Cammilla and her papa, who has not let himself be seen around here for quite some time on account of the bad weather, but writes often. May Our Lord preserve you. From San Matteo, the 7th of November 1633.

Your Most Affectionate Daughter,
Suor M. Celeste

Amatiss.mo Sig.r Padre,

Con l'occasione che mi si porge della venuta costì del lavoratore di Mess.r Santi Bandi, scrivo di nuovo a V. S., dicendole in prima che mi maraviglio ch'ella in quest'ultima non tratti di haver havute lettere di Roma nè risoluzione circa il suo ritorno, il quale pur si sperava quest'Ogni Santi, per quanta mi disse il Sig.r Gherardini. Desidero che V. S. mi dica come veramente passa questo negozio, per quietar l'animo, et anco sopra a che materia sta scrivendo di presente, se però è cosa che io possa intenderla: e non habbia sospetto ch'io cicali.

Tordo ha havuti li 4 d., come gli scrissi giovedì passato, e li SS.ri Bini mi hanno mandato a domandare per Domenico lavoratore i danari del fitto della casa. Ho risposto che si darà sodisfazione subito che V. S. ne sarà consapevole e me ne darà l'ordine.

Nell'orto non si è potuto lavorare altro che una mezza giornata fino a qui, mediante il tempo che va tanto contrario, il quale credo che sia buona causa che V. S. travagli tanto con le sue doglie.

Le due lib. di lino che mandò per Geppo mi paiano dei medesimo di quello che vale 20 crazie, il quale riesce buono, ma secondo il prezzo credo che potrebbe esser migliore. Quella lib. sola di 4 giuli è finissimo, e non è caro.

Mess.r Giulio Ninci sta bene affatto, per quanto intendo da Geppo, e c'ha mandate dell'amorevolezze: e particolarmente Mess.r Alessandro suo cugino mi mandò un cedro, del quale ne ho fatti questi 10 morselletti che gli mando, che per esser

Most Beloved Lord Father,

Taking advantage of the opportunity to write to you again, Sire, via this worker for Sir Santi Bindi who is setting out in your direction, I must tell you first how astounded I was that you made no mention in your most recent letter of having received any word from Rome, nor any resolution regarding your return, which we had so hoped to have before All Saints' Day, from what Signor Gherardini led me to believe. I want you to tell me truly how this business is progressing, so as to quiet my mind, and also please tell me what subject you are writing about at present: provided it is something that I could understand, and you have no fear that I might gossip.

Tordo has received the 4 *scudi,* as I wrote to you last Thursday, and the Bini's have sent their worker Domenico to collect the rent for the house: I replied that their request will be satisfied the moment you are made aware of it, Sire, and you give me your orders.

No one has been able to work in the garden more than half a day in all this time, because the weather has been so hostile, which I think explains why you feel thus afflicted, Sire, by your pains.

The two pounds of linen that you sent with Geppo seemed the same quality as the previous batch at 20 *crazie,* which turned out very well, but considering the cost I believe this lot could be better; the single pound at 4 *giuli* is extremely fine and not overpriced.

Master Giulio Ninci feels altogether well, from what Geppo tells me, and has sent us some very thoughtful gifts: and un poco aromatici saranno buoni, se non per il gusto, per lo stomaco. V. S. potrà assaggiarli e, se gli giudica a proposito, presentarli a Monsr Illmo insieme con la rosa. Il pinocchiato con quei due pezzi di cotognato gl'ho havuti dalla mia Sr Ortensia, alla quale in contraccambio mandai una di quelle torte che mi mandò V. S.

Non mando pillole, perchè non ho havuto tempo a riformarle, oltre che non sento che gli bisognino.

Al ritorno del latore di questa, sarà conveniente ch'io gl'usi amorevolezza, havendolo richiesto: havrò caro che V. S. mi avvisi quel che potrò dargli, per sodisfarlo e non soprapagarlo; già egli viene costì principalmente per servizio suo proprio.

Finisco con far le solite raccomandazioni, e dal Signor Iddio gli prego vero contento. Di S. Matt.^{o} in Arcetri, li 12 di 9mbre 1633.

Sua Fig.^{la} Aff.^{ma}
Suor M.ª Celeste

La pioggia continua non ha concesso a Giovanni (chè così si chiama il latore di questa) che egli possa partire questa mattina chè è domenica, et a me in tanto lascia campo per cicalar un altro poco, e dirgli come poco fa mi sono cavata un dente mascellare grande grande, che era gusto e mi dava gran fastidio; ma peggio è che ne ho de gl'altri, che fra poco faranno il simile.

Dal Sig.^{r} Rondinelli intendo che i due figliolini di Vincenzio Landucci di presente hanno buon governo da una donna che

Master Alessandro his cousin gave me a citron, from which I have made these 10 sweets I am sending you, each of which, for being slightly aromatic will prove pleasing, if not to the taste, then to the stomach. You will be able to sample them, Sire, and, if you deem it fitting, present them to our Most Illustrious Monsignor together with the Rose. The pine nut cake with the two pieces of quince pear I received from my Lady Ortensia, and in exchange I gave her one of those Sienese cakes I requested of you, Sire.

I send you no pills because I have not had time to reformulate them, aside from the fact that I sense you have no need of them.

When the bearer of this letter returns I will be expected to reward him kindly for having carried out my request; I would value your advice, Sire, as to what I might give him to compensate him yet not overpay him: since he travels to that region principally to serve his own needs.

I end by giving you the usual greetings, and from the Lord God I pray for your true contentment. From San Matteo, the 12th of November 1633.

Your Most Affectionate Daughter,
Suor M. Celeste

The continuous rain has not allowed Giovanni (as the bearer of this letter is called) to leave this morning, which is Sunday, and this leaves me time to chat with you a little longer, and to tell you that recently I pulled a very large molar, which had rotted and was giving me great pain; but what is worse is that I have several others that soon will do the same.

egli ha tolto in casa a questo effetto da poco in qua. Lui è stato male di febbre, ma va migliorando.

Desidero di sapere come Vincenzio nostro scrive spesso a V. S.

Per rispondere a quel particolare che ella mi dice, che le occupazioni sono tanto salutifere, io veramente per tali le riconosco in me medesima; chè se bene talvolta mi paiano superflue e incomportabili, per esser io amica della quiete, con tutto ciò a mente salda veggo chiaramente, queste esser la mia salute, e che particolarmente nel tempo, che V. S. è stata lontana da noi, con gran provvidenza ha permesso Nostro Signore che io non habbia mai, si può dire, un'hora di quiete, il che mi ha impedito il soverchiamente afiliggermi: il che a me sarebbe stato nocivo, et a lei di disturbo e non di sollevamento. Benedetto sia il Signore, dal quale spero nuove grazie per l'avvenire, sì come tante ce ne ha concesse per il passato. In tanto V. S. proccuri di stare allegra e confidare in Lui, che è fedele, giusto e misericordioso; e con Esso la lascio.

From Signor Rondinelli I hear that the two children of Vincenzio Landucci, for the time being, are under the good care of a woman who took them into her own home a while ago to tend to them: Vincenzio himself was sick with fever, but is feeling better.

I have a wish to know how often our Vincenzio writes to you, Sire.

To respond to that personal detail you shared with me, that you find occupations so salubrious, truly I recognize them as having that same effect on myself as well: so that even though the activities occasionally seem superfluous and intolerable to me, on account of my being a friend of tranquility, I nevertheless see clearly how staying active is the foundation of my health, and particularly in the time that you have been far away from us, Sire, with great providence did the Lord arrange it so that I never had what you might call an hour of peace, thus preventing the oppression of your absence from distressing me. Such grief would have been harmful to me, and given you cause for worry instead of the relief I have been able to provide. Blessed be the Lord, from whom I anticipate new graces for the future, just as He has granted us so many in the past. Meanwhile, Sire, endeavor to be of good cheer and rely upon the One who is faithful, just, and merciful, and with Him I leave you.

Amatiss.^mo^ Sig.^r^ Padre,

Ho ricevuta la sua gratissima insieme con li 4 biricuocoli, quali ho consegnati alla Piera acciò li dispensi alle vicine. Mi son grandemente rallegrata di sentire che V. S. esca fuori della vittá a pigliar aria, perchè so quanto gli sia utile e dilettevole. Piaccia pur a Dio che ella possi venirsene presto a goder la sua casetta, per il fitto della quale ho mandato stamani a i padroni li d. 17 1/2, perchè facevano instanza di haverli, et a V. S. mando la nota delle spese fatte per la medesima casa: dicendole anco come il fabbro ha reso li 3 barili di vino che ci doveva; è di quello del Navicello, et è buono a bastanza per la servitù: sì che adesso si è riavuto tutto quello che si era dato, o per dir meglio prestato.

La verdea non è ancora in perfezione; ma quando sarà, procurerò di haverne della esquisita, e quest'huomo ci farà servizio di portarla. Volevo mandargli delle melarance dell'orto, ma dalla mostra the me ne ha portata la Piera ho veduto che non sono tanto fatte. Se la buona sorte faceva che V. S. trovassi almeno una starna o cosa simile, l'havrei havuto carissimo per amor di quella poverella giovane ammalata, la quale non appetisce ad altro che a qualche salvaggiume. Nel plenilunio passato stette tanto male, che se li dette l'Olio Santo; ma adesso è ritornata tanto che si crede che arriverà alla nuova luna. Discorre con una vivacità grande, e piglia il cibo con agevolezza, pur che siano cose gustose. Hiernotte stetti da lei tutta notte; e mentre gli davo da mangiare, mi disse: "Non credo già che quando si è in termine di morire si mangi come fo io; con tutto ciò non mi curo di tornare in dietro, ma sia

Most Beloved Lord Father,

I received your most welcome letter together with the four apricots, which I turned over to La Piera so that she could distribute them to the neighbors. I am greatly cheered to hear that you go outside the city to take the air, because I know how it sustains and delights you. May it please God that you can come home soon to enjoy your own little house, the rent for which I sent this morning to the landlords in the amount of 17 *scudi* and 1/2, because they were insisting on having it, and I enclose the list of expenses as well, telling you furthermore how the blacksmith has returned the 3 barrels of wine that he owed us: it is of the Navicello variety and good enough for the servants; thus now we have recovered all that was given, or rather loaned, to others.

The white verdea grapes have not yet reached their peak of perfection, but when they do I will try to acquire some excellent ones, and this man will do us the service of carrying them to you. I wanted to send you some of the oranges from the garden, but from the sample La Piera brought me I see they are not quite ready. If good luck had enabled you to find even one gray partridge or something similar, I would have been thrilled to have it for love of that poor sick young girl, who craves nothing but wild game: at the last full moon she was so ill that she was annointed with holy oil, but now she has made such a comeback that we believe she will live to see the new moon. She speaks with great vivacity, and gulps her food readily, provided we give her tasty things. Last night I stayed with her all through the night, and while I fed her, she said:

pur fatta la volontà di Dio." Il quale io prego che a V. S. conceda la Sua santa grazia; e la saluto in nome delle solite. Di S. Matteo in Arcetri, li 18 di 9mbre 1633.

Sua Fig.la Aff.ma

Suor M.a Celeste

Amatiss.mo Sig.r Padre,

Sabato sera mi fu resa l'ultima di V. S. insieme con una della Sig.ra Ambasciatrice di Roma, piena di affettuosi ringraziamenti del cristallo a di condoglienza mediante la privazione che per ancora V. S. ha di potersene venire a casa sua; e veramente che ella dimostra di esser quella gentilissima Signora che V. S. più volte mi ha dipinta. Non mando la lettera, perchè sto in forse se devo riscrivergli; ma prima aspetterò di sentire che risposta habbia V. S. di Roma.

Non lascio di far diligenza per trovar le pere che V. S. desidera, e credo io che farò qualcosa. Ma perche intendo che quest'anno le frutte non durano, non so se sarà meglio che, quando io le habbia, le mandi, e non aspetti il suo ritorno, che potrebbe indugiar qualche settimana a seguire, o almeno il desiderio me ne fa temere.

Il Sig.r Geri c' ha fatto paste di tutte le frutte dell'orto, delle quali ve ne sono state poche e poco buone, per quanto ho inteso da Geppo che andava a corle; e particolarmente delle melagrane la maggior parte è stata la nostra, ma, come gli dico, stentate e poche.

"I cannot believe that when one stands on the verge of death it is possible to eat the way I do, yet for all that I have no desire to turn back; only to see God's will be done." I pray Him to grant you His holy grace, Sire, and I greet you on behalf of all our friends. From San Matteo in Arcetri, the 18th of November 1633.

Your Most Affectionate Daughter,

Suor M. Celeste

Most Beloved Lord Father,

Saturday evening brought me your latest letter, Sire, together with one from Her Ladyship the Ambassadress in Rome, full of loving thanks for the crystal, and condolences upon the deprivation you still endure, Sire, by being barred from returning to your own home. It is surely true that she shows herself to be that same most gracious lady, as you have so often depicted her. I am not sending you her letter because I am uncertain as to whether I must write back to her, but first I will wait to hear what response you may have had from Rome.

I have not failed to conduct a thorough search for the pears you wish, Sire, and I believe I will find something. But because I hear that this year the fruits do not last long, I wonder if it might be better, once I have them, to send them to you right away and not wait for your return, which could be delayed for several more weeks, or so my desire leads me to fear.

Signor Geri shared with us all the fruits from his garden, which were small in number and poor in quality, according to

Domenica prossima cominciamo l'Avvento, onde se V. S. ci manderà i biricuocoli, ci saranno grati per far colazione la sera; ma basteranno di quelli più dozzinali, come quelli che mandò alle vicine, le quali dice la Piera che insieme con lei ringraziano V. S. e se le raccomandano: et il simile facciamo noi tutte, pregando Nostro Signore che la feliciti. Di S. Matt.^{o} in Arcetri, li 23 di 9mbre 1633.

Di V. S. molto Ill.^{e} Fig.^{la} Aff.^{ma}

Suor Mar. Celeste

V. S. volti carta.

Mercoledì sera vicino alle 24 hore, doppo che havevo scritto la prima faccia, comparve qui Giovanni e mi recò le lettere di V. S. al Sig.^{r} Geri. Non fu possibile il mandarle prima che la mattina seguente, come feci di buon'hora. Hebbi anco il paniere, entrovi 12 tordi; gl'altri 4, che havrebbero compito il numero che V. S. mi scrive, bisogna che qualche graziosa gattina se gli sia tolti per assaggiarli avanti a noi, perchè non vi erano, et il panno che li copriva haveva una gran buca. Manco male che le starne e le acceggie erano nel fondo: delle quali una, e due tordi, donai all'ammalata e che ne fece grande allegrezza, e ringrazia V. S.; un'altra, e medesimamente 2 tordi, ho mandato al Sig.^{r} Rondinelli; et il restante ci siamo godute insieme con le amiche: et ho havuto gran gusto di scompartir il tutto fra molte persone, perchè cose buscate con tanta diligenza e fatica è stato bene che siano partecipate da parecchi. E perchè i tordi arrivorno assai stracchi, è bisognato cuocerli in guazzetto, et io tutto il giorno sono stata lor dietro; sì che per una volta mi sono data alla gola da vero.

what I hear from Geppo who went to gather them; and he took almost all of the pomegranates for us; though, as I tell you, they are stunted and scant.

Next Sunday we mark the beginning of Advent, wherefore if you will send us the apricots we will be so grateful to have them for the evening meal, but the very plainest ones will suffice us, like those you sent to the neighbors, who join La Piera, she tells me, in thanking you for them and wishing you well; and all of us here do the same while praying Our Lord to bless you. From San Matteo, the 23rd of November 1633.

Sire's Most Affectionate Daughter,

Suor Mar. Celeste

Please turn the page, Sire.

Wednesday at twilight around the twenty-fourth hour, after I had written the other side of this paper, Giovanni appeared here and handed me your letters. It was not possible to send Signor Geri his until the following morning, which I did at a very early hour. Of course I also received the panier containing the 12 thrushes: the additional 4, which would have completed the number you state in your letter, Sire, must have been liberated by some charming little kitten who thought of tasting them ahead of us, because they were not there, and the cloth cover had a large hole in it. How fortunate that the gray partridges and the woodcocks were at the bottom, one of which and two thrushes I gave to the sick girl, to her great joy, and she thanks you, Sire. I sent another gift, also in the form of two thrushes, to Signor Rondinelli, and the remainder we enjoyed together with our friends. I have taken the greatest pleasure in distributing all this among various people,

La nuova che V. S. mi dà della venuta di quelle Signore, mi è stata tanto grata, che, doppo quella del ritorno di V. S., sto per dire che non potrei haver la migliore; perchè, essendo io tanto affezzionata a quella, con la quale haviamo tanto obligo, desidero sommamente di conoscerla di vista. È ben vero che alquanto mi disturba il sentire che esse mi habbino in tanto buon concetto, essendo sicura che non riuscirò in voce quale mi dimostro per lettera; e V. S. sa che nel cicalare, o, per dir meglio, nel discorrere, io non sono da nulla. Ma non mi curo per questo di scapitar qualche poco appresso di persone tanto benigne, che mi compatiranno, pur che io contragga servitù con la mia cara Signora, Andrò in tanto pensando a qualche regalo, da povera monaca.

Havrò caro che V. S. vegga di farmi haver i cedrati, perchè io non saprei dove gli buscare; e mi sovviene che il S.r Aggiunti gliene mandò parecchi bellissimi lanno passato, sì che V. S. potrà tentare anco adesso: et io poi mi metterò a bottega a far i morselletti, con mio grandissimo gusto d'impiegarmi in questo poco per servizio di Mons.r Ill.mo, e mi pregio grandemente di sentire che questi siano anteposti da Sua Sig.ria a tutte le altre confetture. Saluto di nuovo V. S. e gli prego felicità.

because prizes sought after with such diligence and difficulty deserve to be shared by several, and as the thrushes arrived a little the worse for wear, it was necessary to cook them in a stew, and I stood over them all day, and for once I truly surrendered myself to gluttony.

The news you gave me of the coming of that great Lord and Lady, Sire, was most welcome, as, after word of your own return, I can tell you that I could not possibly receive better tidings; because being so fond of that Lady, and considering how we are obliged to her, I want above all else to meet her in person. Indeed it disturbs me somewhat to hear what a high opinion they both have of me, as I feel certain I will not succeed in expressing with my voice what I have shown of myself by letter. And you well know, Sire, that when it comes to chitchat, or rather I should say discussion, I am good for nothing; but I cannot let these concerns deprive me of a moment's nearness to persons so kind as to indulge me thusly, provided that I can be of service to my dear Lady. Meanwhile I will set about thinking of what gift a poor nun might offer her.

The ambassador and his wife are expected.

I will be so happy if you can see about getting me some citrons, Sire, because I would not know where to find them, and I recall that Signor Aggiunti sent you several very beautiful ones last year, so that you may be able to try asking him again now, and then I will set myself to work and turn them into candied morsels, extremely delighted to employ myself in this small service for our most illustrious Monsignor, now that I have the grand honor of hearing how these are preferred by His Lordship over all the other confections. I greet you once more, Sire, and pray for your happiness.

Amatiss.mo Sig.r Padre,

Giovedì passato scrissi a V. S. lungamente, et hora scrivo di nuovo, solo per dirgli che hieri venne 10 barili di vino da S. Miniato al Todesco. Intendo dalla Piera che ci fu a vederlo imbottare il servitore del Sig.r Aggiunti, et anco che lo pagò, ma ella non sa dirmi quanto per appunto. Se ne è piena una botte interamente, e credo che sia di 6 barili: l'altra di 5 1/2 perchè non resti così scema, ho detto che si finisca di empiere con di quello che bevano di presente, che è ragionevole; ma prima, che ne cavino parecchi fiaschi avanti che sia mescolato, per riempier l'altra di 6 barili; et anco noi ne piglieremo qualcuno, perchè è vino leggieri e mi par buono per l'estate per V. S.: a me piace anco di questo tempo. La botte che non è mescolata si contrassegnerà per lasciarla stare, e l'altra potrà servire per la servitù.

Questo per hora m'occorre dirli. Finisco con le solite raccomandazioni, e prego Nostro Signore che la conservi. Di S. Matteo in Arcetri, li 26 di 9mbre 1633.

Di V. S. molto Ill.re Fig.la Aff.ma
Suor Mar. Celeste

Amatiss.mo Sig.r Padre,

Ho ancor io conosciuta la dapocaggine del mio ambasciatore Giovanni; ma il desiderio che havevo di mandar a veder V. S. è stato causa che non ho guardato a nulla, tanto più che il favore di potermi servir di lui l'ho ricevuto dalle Madri

Most Beloved Lord Father,

Last Thursday I wrote to you at length, Sire, and now I write again only to tell you that yesterday there came 10 barrels of wine from San Miniato at Todesco. I hear from La Piera that Signor Aggiunti's servant arrived to pour it into the casks; and also that she paid him, though she cannot seem to tell me exactly how much: one cask is completely filled, and I believe it is the one that holds 6 barrels: as for the other of 5 1/2, in order that it not remain half-empty, I told them to finish filling it with the wine they are drinking now, which is reasonably good, but first to draw off several flasks, before the mixing, to top off the cask of 6 barrels. And we will take some, too, because it is light wine, and seems to me to be perhaps a good summer wine for you, Sire; I like the lighter wine at this time of year as well: the cask that is not mixed will be distinguished by being left alone, and the other will take care of the servants.

This for now is all I need to tell you: I close with the usual loving greetings, and pray Our Lord to keep you. From San Matteo, the 26th of November 1633.

Sire's Most Affectionate Daughter,

Suor Mar. Celeste

Most Beloved Lord Father,

I have long known the ineptitude of my ambassador Giovanni; but the desire I had to send for a sight of you, Sire, was the reason I paid no heed to any impediment; all the more so since the Squarcialupi widows granted me the favor of being

Squarcialupe, le quali adesso son tutte mie. E tanto basti.

Tordo mandò hieri per li 4 d., e gl'hebbe.

La Madre Archilea manda il mottetto. È ben vero che in contraccambio desidererebbe qualche sinfonia o qualche ricercare per l'organo; il quale, gli ricorda che ne gl'alti non serve, perchè gli manca non so che registro, sì che le sonate, per farvi sopra, vorrebbono più presto andar ne i bassi.

Mi giova di sperare, et anco creder fermamente, che il Sr Ambasciatore, quando partirà di Roma, sia per portare a V. S. la nuova della sua spedizione, et anco di condurla qua in sua compagnia. Io non credo di viver tanto ch'io giunga a quell'hora. Piaccia pur al Signore di farci questa grazia, se è per il meglio. Con che a V. S. mi raccomando con tutto l'affetto, insieme con le solite. Di S. Matteo in Arcetri, li 3 di Xmbre 1633.

Sua Fig.^{la} Aff.^{ma}

Suor M.ª Celeste

Amatiss.^{mo} Sig.^{r} Padre,

Il Sig.^{r} Francesco Lupi, cognato della nostra Suor M.ª Vincenzia, passando di costì per andarsene a Roma sua patria, si è offerto di portar a V. S. lettere o altro ch'io volessi mandare; onde io, accettando la cortesia, gli mando una scatola, dentrovi 13 morselletti, chè tanti e non più ne sono riuallowed to employ him for these services; and that is enough said.

Tordo sent yesterday for the 4 *scudi* and had them right away.

Mother Achillea herewith returns the motet. What she would really like in exchange are a few symphonies or ricercar compositions for the organ; you may remember that ours does not function in the high registers, because one or another stop is missing, so that any sonatas to be played upon it would have to be willing to descend very quickly into the low notes.

It does me good to hope, and also to believe firmly, that his Lordship the Ambassador, when he departs from Rome, will be bringing you the news of your dispatch, and also word that he personally will conduct you here in his company. I do not believe that I will live to see that day. May it please the Lord to grant me this grace, if it be for the best; with that thought I greet you with all my love, Sire, and the regards of our usual friends. From San Matteo in Arcetri, the 3rd of December 1633.

On this same day, Ambassador Niccolini wrote to Galileo to say that after five months of negotiations, the pope had finally consented to send him home.

Your Most Affectionate Daughter,
Suor M. Celeste

Most Beloved Lord Father,

Signor Francesco Lupi, the brother-in-law of our Suor Maria Vincenzia, passing through Siena en route to his home in Rome, offered to carry this letter to you, Sire, or anything else I wished to send; wherefore I, accepting the courtesy, offer you this box containing 13 citron candy morsels, for just these sciti delli 6 cedrati che mi mandò il S.r Rinuccini, perchè furno piccoli e tutti da una banda magagnati: di bontà credo che saranno eccellenti, ma quanto alla vista potrebbon esser pi belli, perchè, mediante il tempo tanto umido, mi è bisognato asciugarli al fuoco. Mando anco una rosa di zucchero, acciò che V. S. vegga se gli piacessero alcuni fiori di questa sorte per adornare il bacino che faremo in occasione di quelle nozze che V. S. sa, ma fiori più gentili e piccoli assai più di questa.

Hebbi da maestro Agostino la scatola con li 6 biricuocoli, e la ringrazio insieme con quelle che ne hanno partecipati, che sono le solite amiche.

Intendo che in Firenze è voce comune che V. S. sarà qua presto; ma fino che non lintendo da lei medesima, non credo altro se non che gl'amici suoi cari dichino quel tanto che l'affetto e il desiderio gli detta. Io intanto godo grandemente sentendo che V. S. habbia così buona cera quanto mi disse maestro Agostino, che mi affermò non haverla mai pi veduta con la migliore. Tutto si può riconoscere, doppo l'aiuto di Dio benedetto, da quella dolcissima conversazione ch'ella continuamente gode di quell' Ill.mo Mons.r Arcivescovo, e dal non si strapazzare nè disordinare, come ella fa qualche volta quando è in casa sua. Il Signor Iddio sia sempre ringraziato, il quale sia quello che la conservi in Sua grazia. Di S. Matteo in Arcetri, li 9 di Xmbre 1633.

Sua Fig.la Aff.ma

Suor M.a Celeste

many and not one more turned out well from the 6 citrons that Signor Rinuccini sent me, as all of the fruits were small and blemished on one side: their taste I believe will prove excellent, but as for their appearance they could be a bit more beautiful, and would be except that the extremely damp weather obliged me to dry them by the fire. Here, too, is a rose of sugar so that you may see if you would like to have several flowers of this sort to adorn the upside-down cake that we will make for that wedding celebration, Sire, but with flowers much smaller and more delicate than this one.

I received from Master Agostino the box containing the 6 apricots, and I thank you together with those nuns who shared them, who are our usual friends.

I understand that in Florence everyone is saying you will soon be here; but until I have this from your lips, all I will believe is that your dear friends are allowing their affections and desires to give themselves voice. Meanwhile I greatly enjoy hearing that you have such a vibrant complexion, as Master Agostino tells me and further affirms he has never seen you with better color. Everyone can recognize how you have benefited, after the help of blessed God, from the extremely sweet conversation you continue to enjoy with that most illustrious Monsignor Archbishop, as well as from not being careless of your health nor going to extremes as you sometimes do in your own home. Everlasting thanks be offered to the Lord God, for it is He who keeps you in His grace. From San Matteo in Arcetri, the 9th of December 1633.

Your Most Affectionate Daughter,
Suor M. Celeste

Amatiss.mo Sig.r Padre,

Appunto quando mi comparve la nuova della spedizione di V. S., havevo [. . . . . . .]no la penna per scriver alla Sig.ra Ambasciatrice per raccomandarle questo neg[. . . . .] vedendo andar in lungo, temevo che non fossi spedito anco qu[. . . . .], sì che l'allegrezza è stata tanto maggiore quanto più inaspettata; [. . . . .] sole a rallegrarci, ma tutte queste monache, per lor grazia, danno segni [. . . . .] allegrezza, sì come molto hanno compatito a i nostri travagli. La stiamo [. . . . .] con gran desiderio, e ci rallegriamo di veder il tempo tanto tranquillo.

Il Sig.r G[. . .] partiva stamani con la Corte, et io a buon'hora l'ho fatto avvisato del quando V. S. torna qua, chè quanto alla spedizione egli la sapeva, e me n'haveva dato parte hiersera. Gl'ho anco detto la causa per la quale V. S. non gl'ha scritto, e lamentatami perchè egli non potrà ritrovarsi qua all'arrivo di V. S. per compimento delle nostre allegrezze, essendo veramente persona molto compita e di garbo.

Serbo la canovetta della verdea, che il S.r Francesco non potè portare per haver la lettiga troppo carica. V. S. potrà mandarla nella lettiga che sarà di ritorno. I morselletti già gl'havevo consegnati. Le botte per il vino bianco sono all'ordine.

Altro non posso dire per carestia di tempo, se non che a lei ci raccomandiamo affettuosamente. Di S. Matteo, li 10 di Xmbre 1633.

Sua Fig.la Aff.ma

Suor M.a Celeste

Most Beloved Lord Father,

Only a moment before the news of your dispatch reached me, Sire, I had taken my pen in hand to write to Her Ladyship the Ambassadress to beg her once more to intercede in this affair; for having watched it wear on so long, I feared that it might not be resolved even by the end of this year, and thus my sudden joy was as great as it was unexpected: nor are your daughters alone in our rejoicing, but all these nuns, by their grace, give signs of true happiness, just as so many of them have sympathized with me in my suffering. We are awaiting your arrival with great longing, and we cheer ourselves to see how the weather has cleared for your journey.

Signor Geri was leaving this morning with the Court, and I made sure to have him notified before daybreak of your return, Sire; seeing as he had already learned something of the decision, and came here last evening to tell me what he knew. I also explained to him the reason you have not written to him, Sire, and I bemoaned the fact that he will not be here when you arrive to share in our celebration, since he is truly a perfect gentleman, honest and loyal.

I set aside the container of verdea wine, which Signor Francesco could not bring along because his litter was too overloaded. You will be able to send it to the Archbishop later, when the litter makes a return trip: the citron candy morsels I have already consigned to him. The casks for the white wine are all in order.

Galileo returned within days, but the happiness of his homecoming was short-lived. Suor Maria Celeste fell sick three months later and died in the convent the night of April 2 at the age of thirty-three.

More I cannot say for the dearth of time, except that all of us send you our loving regards. From San Matteo, the 10th of December 1633.

Your Most Affectionate Daughter,
Suor M. Celeste

The Sisters of San Matteo

(a partial list)

Suor Achillea

Suor Arcangela Galilei

Suor Barbara

Suor Brigida

Suor Cammilla

Suor Caterina Angiola Anselmi

Suor Chiara Landucci

Suor Clarice Burci

Suor Diamante

Suor Giulia Corso

Suor Elisabetta (Lisabetta)Gherardini

Suor Isabella

Suor Laura Gaetani

Suor Luisa

Suor Maria Celeste Galilei

Suor Maria Grazia Del Pace

Suor Maria Maddalena Squadrini

Suor Maria Silvia Boscoli

Suor Maria Teodora Ninci

Suor Maria Vincenzia

Suor Maria Virginia Castrucci

Suor Oretta

Suor Ortensa del Nente

Suor Polissena Vinta

Suor Prudenza

Suor Violante Rondinelli

Suor Virginia Canigiani

Florentine Weights, Measures, & Currency

WEIGHT

libbra =12 *oncie* = .75 pound =.3 kilogram (plural is *libbre*)

LINEAR MEASURE

braccio = about 23 inches (plural is *braccia*)

DRY MEASURE

staio = 1 bushel

moggio = 24 bushels

LIQUID MEASURE

fiasco = 4 pints

barile = 20 *fiaschi* = 10 gallons

CURRENCY

scudo = 7 *lire*

piastra = 22.42 grams of silver = about 5 *lire*

lira (silver coin; plural is *lire*) = 10 *quattrini* = 12 *crazie* = 20 *soldi* (Four lire could feed one person for a week.)

giulio (silver coin) = slightly more than half a *lira* = 13 *soldi*

quattrino = .1 *lira* = 2 *soldi*

The text of this book is set in Bodoni,
designed by Giovanni Battista Bodoni in 1798.
Born in 1740 in Northern Italy, Bodoni's letterforms
are known for their contrast of light and shade.

The paper in this volume is Q Liberty Antique
manufactured by P. H. Glatfelter Company,
in Spring Grove, Pennsylvania.

Page design and composition by
Maura Fadden Rosenthal of
Mspace, Katonah, New York.

The text of this book was printed and bound by
Quebecor World, Fairfield, Pennsylvania.